UNIVERSITÉ CATHOLIQUE DE LOUVAIN
INSTITUT SUPÉRIEUR D'ARCHÉOLOGIE ET D'HISTOIRE DE L'ART

AURIFEX 5

édité par

Tony Hackens

This project was supported by a grant from the National Endowment for the Arts in Washington, D.C., Brown University, anonymous European contributions and the Museum of Art, Rhode Island School of Design

Imprimé sur les presses de l'Imprimerie Orientaliste
à Winksele, Belgique.

Dépôt légal 1983/1900/02

PUBLICATIONS D'HISTOIRE DE L'ART ET D'ARCHÉOLOGIE
DE L'UNIVERSITÉ CATHOLIQUE DE LOUVAIN — XXXVI

AURIFEX 5

GOLD JEWELRY

Craft, Style and Meaning from Mycenae to Constantinopolis

An exhibition organized by the art history graduate students of Brown University and the archaeology students of the Catholic University at Louvain-la-Neuve, held at the Museum of Art, Rhode Island School of Design from February 24, 1983- April 3, 1983

EDITED BY

Tony HACKENS and Rolf WINKES

LOUVAIN-LA-NEUVE
INSTITUT SUPÉRIEUR D'ARCHÉOLOGIE ET D'HISTOIRE DE L'ART — COLLÈGE ÉRASME
1983

CONTENTS

ACKNOWLEDGMENTS

Many individuals, foundations and institutions have provided us with assistance in our work and have willingly shared their expertise and their collections during the preparation of this exhibition. Special thanks are due to our lenders, so many providing us with the opportunity to present unpublished material.

Professor Tony Hackens, editor of this series, has generously supported our efforts by providing funding and criticism invaluable to this publication. Scholarly suggestions were provided by Professor R. Ross Holloway, Director, Center for Old World Archaeology and Art, Brown University. We also wish to thank Professor Guy Demortier, Facultés Notre-Dame de la Paix, Namur, for his contribution to this catalogue. Our special thanks to Professor Kermit S. Champa, Chairman, Brown University Art Department, for his continued enthusiasm and encouragement during this project. Mrs. Nancy Versaci, Director, Bell Gallery, Brown University and Dr. Florence Friedman, Associate Curator of Antiquities, Museum of Art, Rhode Island School of Design as well as Pat Loiko, Registrar of the Museum, have assisted with the mounting of the exhibition.

We are especially grateful to Professor Rolf Winkes, Project Director, for having suggested this cooperative effort. Without his scholarly assistance and conviction, this exhibition would not have been realized.

The Authors

PREFACE

The graduate program for archaeology in the Catholic University of Louvain and the graduate program for art history in Brown University have a long tradition of student training resulting in publication. Up to this time, however, the collaboration between the faculty of the two universities has not united students of the two institutions. The present catalogue which accompanies an international exhibition is, for both, an initial attempt not only to merge different programs, but also to overcome the language difference and to bridge the Atlantic Ocean. Furthermore, we are gratified that the exhibition is held at a major American museum and thank Dr. Franklin Robinson, Director of the Museum of Art, Rhode Island School of Design, for this opportunity. We are also grateful for the support we have received from the numerous sources mentioned in the appropriate entries of the catalogue. Special thanks go to Mrs. B. Googins who typed the manuscript and whose assistance went far beyond the call of duty. For final proofreading in Louvain-la-Neuve the volontary assistant team to the editions (Georges Bernard, Philippe Colyn, Bernard and Carine Derouau, Ghislaine Moucharte) has been an invaluable help to the editors and authors. But it is not merely the subject which makes such a project exciting: above all, it is the educational and organizational challenge of this united effort by students which has stimulated and rewarded our work.

Tony HACKENS
Université Catholique de Louvain,
Louvain-la-Neuve.

Rolf WINKES
Brown University,
Providence.

AUTHORS

Graduate Students of the *Department of Art*, Brown University, Providence have provided most of the catalogue entries and the essays:

Marie Jeannine Aquilino
Margaret Barry
Audrey R. Gup
Boyd T. Hill
William E. Mierse
Morag Murray
Ivette M. Richard
Richard W. Sadow
Ellen S. Spencer

Students of the *Graduate Seminar in Greek archaeology at the Institut d'Archéologie et d'Histoire de l'Art*, Université Catholique, Louvain-la-Neuve, have written a few catalogue entries and the texts for the technological section.

Sabine Cornelis
François de Callataÿ
Frédérique De Cuyper
Myriam Destrée
André Dumont
Christiane Larock
Francine Lecomte
Anne Catherine Lemaigre
Bernadette Schuiten
Agnès Stoffel

Dimitri Tzavellas, M.A., Université de Liège, and Professor G. Demortier, Laboratoire d'Analyse par Réactions Nucléaires (LARN), Facultés universitaires Notre-Dame, Namur, also have contributed to the second section of this book.

Drawings: Mrs Mary Winkes, unless otherwise stated.

LENDERS TO THE EXHIBITION

Anonymous European Loans
Bowdoin College Museum of Art, Brunswick, Maine
Dumbarton Oaks Collection, Washington, D.C.
Field Museum of Natural History, Chicago, Illinois
Fogg Art Museum, Harvard University, Cambridge, Massachusetts
Mr. and Mrs. Artemis Joukowsky
Museum of Art, Rhode Island School of Design, Providence, Rhode Island
The Museum of Fine Arts, Houston, Texas
The St. Louis Art Museum, St. Louis, Missouri
Smith College Museum of Art, Northampton, Massachusetts
The Toledo Museum of Art, Toledo, Ohio
Virginia Museum of Fine Arts, Richmond, Virginia
Walters Art Gallery, Baltimore, Maryland
Williams College Museum of Art, Williamstown, Massachusetts

PHOTO CREDITS:

Unless otherwise noted, all photographs are by Brooke Hammerle, Department of Art, Brown University. Macroscopic photography was done by Robert Stanton, Department of Engineering, Brown University, in collaboration with Brooke Hammerle. We are grateful to Professors R. Asaro and J. Gurland of the Department of Engineering for permission to use their equipment and generous support of the project.

Entry

2, 8, 23, 28, 39, 41	Courtesy of the Walters Art Gallery
3, 15, 33	Courtesy of the Virginia Museum of Fine Arts
5	Courtesy of the Toledo Museum of Art
6, 11, 14, 16-22, 24, 29, 30, 31, 34, 35	Courtesy T. Hackens
27	Courtesy of the Fogg Art Museum, Harvard University
32	Courtesy of the Bowdoin College Museum of Art
37, 42, 43	Courtesy of the Dumbarton Oaks Collection
40	Courtesy of the Saint Louis Art Museum

Color plates

by Brooke Hammerle and for entries nos. 4, 9 by J. Piron, Institute of Archaeology, Louvain-la-Neuve.

Illustrations in the text, first part (catalogue)

Fig. 1, 2 Foto-Hirmer, Munich; 3, 4 After Charles Seltman; 5 Walters Art Gallery, Baltimore; 6 After M. Cristofani; 7, 9 After Marshall; 8 After Becatti; 10, 12 After Higgins; 11 Courtesy, Musée National de Carthage; 13 After H. Tait and C. Gere; 14 Courtesy, Princeton University, Department of Art and Archaeology; 15 Courtesy, Museum of Fine Arts, Boston; 16 Yale University Art Gallery; 17 Museum of Art, Rhode Island School of Design; 18 Virginia Museum.

Illustration credits of the second part are mentioned under the figures.

ABBREVIATIONS

Unless otherwise cited, all English translations of Classical sources are from *The Loeb Classical Library Series*.

AJA	*American Journal of Archaeology.*
AnatSt	*Anatolian Studies.*
ArchCl	*Archeologia Classica.*
AthMitt	*Mitteilungen des Deutschen Archäologischen Instituts, Athenische Abteilung.*
BCH	*Bulletin de correspondance hellénique.*
Marshall, *BMCJ*	MARSHALL, F.H., *Catalogue of the Jewellery, Greek, Etruscan, and Roman, in the Departments of Antiquities, British Museum*, London, 1911.
BMMA	*Bulletin of the Metropolitan Museum of Art.*
BSA	*The Annual of the British School of Athens.*
BullRISD	*Bulletin of the Museum of Art, Rhode Island School of Design.*
CahArch	*Cahiers archéologiques.*
JHS	*Journal of Hellenic Studies.*
JNES	*Journal of Near Eastern Studies.*
JRS	*Journal of Roman Studies.*
MAAR	*Memoirs of the American Academy in Rome.*
MelRome	*Mélanges d'archéologie et d'histoire de l'École francaise de Rome.*
RA	*Revue archéologique.*
RBibl	*Revue biblique.*
RömMitt	*Mitteilungen des Deutschen archäologischen Instituts, Römische Abteilung.*
SMEA	*Studi Micenei ed Egeo-Anatolici.*
StEtr	*Studi Etruschi.*
Walters, 1979	*Walters Art Gallery, Jewelry: Ancient to Modern*, A. Garside, ed., New York, 1979.

BIBLIOGRAPHY

ALEXANDER, C., *Jewelry. The Art of the Goldsmith in Classical Times as Illustrated in the Museum Collection*, The Metropolitan Museum of Art, New York, 1928.

AMANDRY, P., *Collection Hélène Stathatos*, vol. 1, *Bijoux Antiques*, Strasbourg, 1953.

AMANDRY, P., *Collection Hélène Stathatos*, vol. 3, *Objets antiques et byzantins*, Strasbourg, 1963.

BAUR, P. V. C. and ROSTOVTZEFF, M., eds., *The Excavations at Dura-Europos*, Second Season, New Haven, 1931, p. 78-82.

BAUR, P. V. C. and ROSTOVTZEFF, M., eds., *The Excavations at Dura-Europos*, Fourth Season, New Haven, 1933, p. 254-256.

BECATTI, G., *Oreficerie antiche dalle minoiche alle barbariche*, Rome, 1955.

BENEDETTI, C., *La Tomba Vetuloniese del 'Littore'-II*, in *StEtr*, 28, 1960, p. 449-477.

BIELEFELD, E., *Schmuck*, in *Archaeologia Homerica*, Göttingen, 1968.

BLAKEMORE, K., *The Book of Gold*, New York, 1971.

BLEGEN, C. W. and RAWSON, M., *The Palace of Nestor at Pylos in Western Messenia*, I, *The Buildings and their Contents*, Princeton, 1966.

BLEGEN, E. P., *Jewellery and Ornaments*, in C. W. BLEGEN, *Prosymna. The Helladic Settlement Preceding the Argive Heraeum*, Cambridge, 1937, p. 264-327.

BOARDMAN, J., *Engraved Gems. The Ionides Collection*, London, 1964.

BOARDMAN, J., *Archaic Greek Gems*, Evanston, 1968.

BOARDMAN, J., *Intaglios and Rings, Greek, Etruscan and Eastern, from a Private Collection*, London, 1975.

BOARDMAN, J. and SCARISBRICK, D., *The Ralph Harari Collection of Finger Rings*, London, 1977.

BOATSWAIN, T. and KNOWLES, L., eds., *The Byzantine World, A.D. 330-1453*, exh. cat., Chichester, W. Sussex, U. K., Chichester District Museum, 1978.

BÖHME, A., *Frauenschmuck der römischen Kaiserzeit*, in *Antike Welt*, 9, 1978, p. 3-16.

BORDI, S. and PICCARDI, G., *Sull'oreficeria granulata etrusca*, in *StEtr*, 24, 1956, p. 353-363.

BOYD, S. and VIKAN, G., *Questions of Authenticity Among the Arts of Byzantium: Catalogue of an exhibition held at Dumbarton Oaks, January 7-May 11, 1981*, Washington, D.C., 1981.

BREGLIA, L., *Catalogo delle Oreficerie del Museo Nazionale di Napoli*, Rome, 1941.

British Museum, Trustees of., *Jewellery Through 7000 Years*, London, 1976.

BROWN, K. R., *The Mosaics of San Vitale: Evidence for the Attribution of Some Early Byzantine Jewelry to Court Workshops*, in *Gesta*, 18, 1979, p. 57-62.

CAMPOREALE, G., *La Tomba del Duce*, Florence, 1967.

CAMPOREALE, G., *I commerci di Vetulonia in età orientalizzante*, Florence, 1969.

CANBY, J. V., BUITRON, D. and OLIVER, A., *Ancient Jewelry in Baltimore*, in *Archaeology*, 32, 1979, p. 53-56.

CARDUCCI, C., *Gold and Silver Treasures of Ancient Italy*, Greenwich, Conn., 1963.

EL CHEHADEH, J., *Untersuchungen zum antiken Schmuck in Syrien*, Ph.D. diss., . Berlin, 1972.

COCHE DE LA FERTÉ, É., *Les bijoux antiques*, Paris, 1956.

COCHE DE LA FERTÉ, É., *Collection Hélène Stathatos*, vol. 2, *Les objets byzantins et post-byzantins*, Limoges, 1957.

CURTIS, C. D., *The Bernardini Tomb*, in *MAAR*, 3, 1919, p. 9-90.

CURTIS, C. D., *The Barberini Tomb*, in *MAAR*, 5, 1925, p. 9-52.

DALTON, O. M., *Byzantine Art and Archaeology*, Oxford, 1911.

DALTON, O. M., *Catalogue of Early Christian Antiquities and Objects from the Christian East in the British Museum*, London, 1901.

DALTON, O. M., *Catalogue of the Finger Rings, Early Christian, Byzantine*, London, 1912.

DALTON, O. M., *The Treasure of the Oxus, with Other Examples of Early Oriental Metalwork*, London, 1964.

DAVIDSON, P., *The Bastis Gold*, in *The Brooklyn Museum Annual*, 8, 1966-1967, p. 90-99.

DAVIS, E. N., *The Vapheio Cups and Aegean Gold and Silver Ware*, New York, 1972.

DENNISON, W., *A Gold Treasure of the Late Roman Period*, New York, 1918.

DUSENBERY, E. B., *A Samothracian Necropolis*, in *Archaeology*, 12, 1959, p. 163-170.

EVANS, A., *The Shaft Graves and the Beehive Tombs of Mycenae*, London, 1929.

EVANS, J., *A History of Jewellery, 1100-1870*, Boston, 1970.

FALCHI, I., *Vetulonia e la sua necropoli antichissima*, Florence, 1891.

FORBES, R. J. *Studies in Ancient Technology*, vols. 7 and 8, Leiden, 1963, 1964.

FORMIGLI, E., *L'antica tecnica dei bracciali a filigrana*, in *StEtr*, 44, 1976, p. 203-210.

FURTWÄNGLER, A., *Die antiken Gemmen*, Leipzig and Berlin, 1900.

Galerie Koller Zurich, *Collection d'orfèvrerie antique, Moyen-Orient, Antiquité Classique, Époque Byzantine, 15 Novembre 1982*, Zurich, 1982.

GECHER, M., *Die Anfänge des Niedergermanischen Limes* (mit Beiträgen von G. Binias), in *Bonner Jahrbücher*, 179, 1979, p. 1-129.

GECHER, M., *Die Fibeln des Kastells Niederbieber*, in *Bonner Jahrbücher*, 180, 1980, p. 589-610.

GREIFENHAGEN, A., *Schmuckarbeiten in Edelmetall*, 2 vols., Berlin, 1970-1975..

GUZZO, P. G., *Le fibule in Etruria dal VI al I secolo*, Florence, 1972.

HACKENS, T., *Catalogue of the Classical Collection: Classical Jewelry*, Museum of Art, Rhode Island School of Design, Providence, 1976.

HACKENS, T., *Un bandeau funéraire en or de style protoattique*, in *Études sur l'orfèvrerie antique, Studies in Ancient Jewelry (Aurifex, 1)*, T. Hackens, ed., Louvain-la-Neuve, 1980, p. 1-12.

HACKENS, T. and LÉVY, E., *Trésor hellénistique trouvé à Délos en 1964*, in *BCH*, 89, 1965, p. 535-566.

HADACZEK, K., *Der Ohrschmuck der Griechen und Etrusker*, Vienna, 1903.

HANFMANN, G.M.A., *Ancient Art in American Private Collections, The Fogg Art Museum*, Cambridge, Mass., 1955.

HAVELOCK, C., *Hellenistic Art*, New York, 1981.

HENKEL, F., *Die römischen Fingerringe der Rheinlande und der benachbarten Gebiete*, Berlin, 1913.

HERBERT, K., *Ancient Art in Bowdoin College, a Descriptive Catalogue of the Warren and Other Collections*, Cambridge, Mass., 1964.

HIGGINS, R., *The Aegina Treasure: an Archaeological Mystery*, London, 1979.

HIGGINS, R.A., *Greek and Roman Jewellery*, 2nd ed., Berkeley, 1980.

HOFFMANN, H. and DAVIDSON, P., *Greek Gold. Jewelry from the Age of Alexander*, Mainz, 1966.

HOFFMANN, H. and VON CLAER, V., *Antiker Gold- und Silberschmuck, Museum für Kunst und Gewerbe Hamburg*, Mainz, 1968.

HOLLOWAY, R.R. and NABERS, N., *Le canthare d'argent de Roscigno (Monte Pruno, Salerne)*, in *Études sur l'orfèvrerie antique, Studies in Ancient Jewelry (Aurifex, 1)*, T. Hackens, ed., Louvain-la-Neuve, 1980, p. 64-79.

HOOD, S., *The Arts in Prehistoric Greece*, Norwich, 1978, p. 187-208.

IKER, R., *À propos des 'supports de flacons' italiotes*, in *Études sur l'orfèvrerie antique, Studies in Ancient Jewelry (Aurifex, 1)*, T. Hackens, ed., Louvain-la-Neuve, 1980, p. 30-63.

IMMERWAHR, S.A., *The Athenian Agora, 13, The Neolithic and Bronze Ages*, Princeton, 1971.

JACOBSTHAL, P., *Greek Pins and their Connections with Europe and Asia*, Oxford, 1956.

KANTOROWICZ, E., *On the Golden Marriage Belt and the Marriage Rings of the Dumbarton Oaks Collection*, in *Dumbarton Oaks Papers*, 14, 1960, p. 3-16.

KARO, G., *Le Oreficerie di Vetulonia — Parte Prima*, in *Studi e Materiali di Archeologia e Numismatica*, 1, 1899, p. 235-283.

KARO, G., *Le Oreficerie di Vetulonia — Parte Seconda*, in *Studi e Materiali di Archeologia e Numismatica*, 2, 1902, p. 97-147.

KARO, G., *Die Schachtgräber von Mykenai*, Munich, 1930.

KENT, J.P.C., *Excursus on the "Comes Sacrarum Largitionum"*, in E. CRUIKSHANK-DODD, *Byzantine Silver Stamps*, Washington, D.C., 1961, p. 35-45.

KENT, J.P.C. and PAINTER, K.S., eds., *Wealth of the Roman World, AD 300-700*, London, 1977.

KOLKÓWNA, S., *Remarques sur les sources archéologiques antiques relatives à la production d'orfèvrerie sur les rivages septentrionaux et occidentaux de la Mer Noire*, in *Études sur l'orfèvrerie antique, Studies in Ancient Jewelry (Aurifex, 1)*, T. Hackens, ed., Louvain-la-Neuve, 1980, p. 106-154.

KRUG, A., *Antike Gemmen im Römisch-Germanischen Museum Köln*, Frankfurt am Main, 1981.

KURTZ, D.C. and BOARDMAN, J., *Greek Burial Customs*, London, 1971, p. 49-67, 200-217.

KURUNIOTIS, K., *Goldschmuck aus Eretria*, in *AthMitt*, 38, 1913, p. 289-328.

LAFFINEUR, R., *L'orfèvrerie rhodienne orientalisante* (*École Française d'Athènes, Travaux et Mémoires des anciens membres étrangers...* XXI), Paris, 1978, p. 159-197.

LAFFINEUR, R., *L'orfèvrerie rhodienne orientalisante*, in *Études sur l'orfèvrerie antique, Studies in Ancient Jewelry* (*Aurifex*, 1), T. Hackens, ed., Louvain-la-Neuve, 1980, p. 13-29.

LAFFINEUR, R., *Collection Paul Canellopoulos (XV)*, BCH, 104, 1980, p. 345-457.

LEPAGE, C., *Les bracelets de luxe romains et byzantins du IIe au VIe siècle. Étude de la forme et de la structure*, in *CahArch*, 21, 1971, p. 1-23.

MACKAY, D., *The Jewellery of Palmyra and its Significance*, in *Iraq*, 11, 1949, p. 160-187.

MACMULLEN, R., *The Emperor's Largesses*, in *Latomus*, 21, 1962, p. 159-166.

MANTSEVICH, A., *Sur l'origine des objets de toreutique dans les tumuli de l'époque scythe (d'après les matériaux de l'Ermitage)*, in *Études sur l'orfèvrerie antique, Studies in Ancient Jewelry* (*Aurifex*, 1), T. Hackens, ed., Louvain-la-Neuve, 1980, p. 80-105.

MARSHALL, F.H., *Catalogue of the Finger Rings, Greek, Etruscan, and Roman, in the Departments of Antiquities, British Museum*, Oxford, 1907.

MARSHALL, F.H., *Catalogue of the Jewellery of the British Museum*, London, 1911.

MARYON, H., *Metalwork and Enamelling: A Practical Treatise on Gold and Silversmiths' Work and Their Allied Crafts*, 5th rev. ed., New York, 1971.

MATZ, F., *The Art of Crete and Early Greece*, Baden-Baden, 1962.

MAXWELL-HYSLOP, K.R., *Western Asiatic Jewellery, c. 3000-612 B.C.*, London, 1971.

MCCARTHY, J.R., *Rings Through the Ages*, New York, 1945.

MILLER, S.G., *Two Groups of Thessalian Gold* (*University of California Publications in Classical Studies*, vol. 18), Berkeley, 1979.

MONTELIUS, O., *La Civilisation Primitive en Italie depuis l'introduction des métaux. Première Partie. Fibules et Italie septentrionale*, Stockholm, 1895.

MONTELIUS, O., *La Civilisation Primitive en Italie depuis l'introduction des métaux. Deuxième Partie. Italie Centrale*, Stockholm, 1910.

MUSCARELLA, O.W., *Fibulae Represented on Sculpture*, in *JNES*, 26, 2, 1967, p. 82-86.

MYERS, J.L., *Handbook of the Cesnola Collection of Antiquities from Cyprus*, New York, 1914.

NEUMANN, G., *Ein frühhellenistisches Golddiadem aus Kreta*, in *AthMitt*, 80, 1965.

OHLY, D., *Griechische Goldbleche des 8. Jahrhunderts v. Chr.*, Berlin, 1953.

OLIVER, A., Jr., *Greek, Roman and Etruscan Jewelry*, in *BMMA*, 24, 9, 1966, p. 269-284.

PARETI, L., *La Tomba Regolini-Galassi*, Vatican City, 1947.

PERSSON, A., *The Royal Tombs at Dendra Near Midea*, Lund, 1931.

PFEILER, B., *Römischer Goldschmuck des ersten und zweiten Jhds n. Chr. nach datierten Funden*, Mainz, 1970.

PFEILER-LIPPITZ, B., *Späthellenistische Goldschmiedearbeiten*, in *Antike Kunst*, 15, 1972, p. 107-119.

QUILLARD, B., *Bijoux carthaginois*, 1, *Les colliers (Aurifex*, 2), Louvain-la-Neuve, 1979.

RICHTER, G. M. A., *Catalogue of Engraved Gems of the Classical Style*, The Metropolitan Museum of Art, New York, 1930.

RICHTER, G. M. A., *Handbook of the Etruscan Collection*, The Metropolitan Museum of Art, New York, 1940.

RICHTER, G. M. A., *The Metropolitan Museum of Art. Handbook of the Greek Collection*, Cambridge, Mass., 1953.

RICHTER, G. M. A., *Catalogue of Greek and Roman Antiquities in the Dumbarton Oaks Collection*, Cambridge, Mass., 1956.

RICHTER, G. M. A., *A Handbook of Greek Art*, New York, 1959, p. 262-272.

RICHTER, G. M. A., *The Engraved Gems of the Greeks, Etruscans and Romans*, 2 vols., London, 1968-1971.

ROSS, M. C., *Byzantine Goldsmith-work*, in *Byzantine Art: An European Art. Ninth Exhibition Held under the Auspices of the Council of Europe*, Athens, 1964, p. 358-390.

ROSS, M. C., *Catalogue of the Byzantine and Early Mediaeval Antiquities in the Dumbarton Oaks Collection*, vol. 2, *Jewelry, Enamels and Art of the Migration Period*, Washington, D.C., 1965.

ROSS, M. C., *Luxuries of the Eastern Empire*, in *Arts in Virginia*, 8, 1967-68, p. 56-65.

ROSS, M. C., *Jewels of Byzantium*, in *Arts in Virginia*, 9, 1968, p. 12-31.

ROSS, M. C., *Objects from Daily Life*, in *Age of Sprituality: Late Antique and Early Christian Art, Third to Seventh Century*, K. Weitzmann, ed., New York, 1979, p. 297-301.

RUDOLPH, W. and E., *Ancient Jewelry from the Collection of Burton Y. Berry*, Bloomington, Indiana, 1973.

RUXER, M. S., *Historia naszyjnika greckiego* [History of the Greek necklace], I, Poznań, 1938.

RUXER, M. S. and KUBCZAK, J., *Naszyjnik Grecki w Okresach Hellenistycznym i Rzymskim* [Greek Necklace of the Hellenistic and Roman Ages], Warsaw, 1972.

SCHLUNK, H., *Kunst der Spätantike im Mittelmeerraum: spätantike und byzantinische Kleinkunst aus Berliner Besitz*, Berlin, 1939.

SCHWEITZER, B., *Greek Geometric Art*, trans. Peter and Cornelia Usborne, London, 1971, p. 186-195, 201-212.

SEGALL, B., *Katalog der Goldschmiedearbeiten, Museum Benaki, Athen*, Athens, 1938.

SEGALL, B., *Zur griechischen Goldschmiede-Kunst des 4. Jahrhunderts v. Chr.*, Wiesbaden, 1966.

SIVIERO, R., *Jewelry and Amber of Italy*, New York, 1959.

STRØM, I., *Problems Concerning the Origin and Early Development of the Etruscan Orientalizing Style*, Odense, 1971.

STRONG, D.E., *Greek and roman gold and silver plate (Methuen's handbook of archaeology)*, London, 1966.

SUNDWALL, J., *Die älteren italischen Fibeln*, Berlin, 1943.

TALOCCHINI, A., *Le oreficerie ed il vasetto configurato del Circolo dei Leoncini d'Argento di Vetulonia*, in *StEtr*, 31, 1963, p. 67-89.

VERMEULE, C., *Numismatics in Antiquity*, in *Revue suisse de numismatique*, 54, 1975, p. 5-32.

VERMEULE, E., *Greece in the Bronze Age*, Chicago, 1964.

VIKAN, G., *Byzantine Pilgrimage Art*, exh. cat., Dumbarton Oaks, Washington, D.C., 1982.

WACE, A.J.B., *Mycenae, an Archaeological History and Guide*, Princeton, 1949.

WACE, A.J.B., et al., *Excavations at Mycenae 1939-1955*, Elizabeth French, ed., (*BSA Supplementary*, 12), Oxford, 1979.

Walters Art Gallery, *Early Christian and Byzantine Art*, Baltimore, 1947.

WALTERS, H.B., *Catalogue of the Engraved Gems and Cameos, Greek, Etruscan and Roman, in the British Museum*, London, 1926.

WENEDIKOW, I. and MARASOW, I., *Gold der Thraker, archäologische Schätze aus Bulgarien*, Mainz, 1979.

YOUNGER, J.G., *The Lapidary's Worshop at Knossos*, in *BSA*, 74, 1979, p. 258-268.

ZAHN, R., *Ausstellung von Schmuckarbeiten aus Edelmetall aus den Staatlichen Museen zu Berlin*, Berlin, 1932.

ZOUHDI, B., *Les influences réciproques entre l'Orient et l'Occident, d'après les bijoux du Musée National de Damas*, in *Annales Archéologiques Arabes Syriennes*, 21, 1971, p. 95-103.

HISTORICAL INTRODUCTIONS
AND
CATALOGUE

THE MYCENAEAN WORLD

Jewelry is part of the archaeological record on the Greek mainland in the early Bronze Age. The first pieces are simple and consist of diadems, gold ring pendants and single rings for the ears and hair [1]. A major change in the quality and variety of jewelry appears to occur in the latter part of the middle Helladic and the beginning of the late Helladic periods, a time known to us almost exclusively from the two grave circles at Mycenae, A and B, each of which contained royal shaft graves. Vermeule has stressed the differences in the type of burial represented by these graves which, together with their contents, show the impact of foreign influences on the local Helladic culture [2].

Circle B, the older of the two, is the less splendid but nonetheless, the graves contain jewelry among the goods. One woman was buried with a diadem of three gold leaves with repoussé decoration joined together with a bronze backing. Over her left shoulder was found a gold band, probably intended to hold her hair in place. Silver circles behind each ear seem to represent the remains of earrings. Another woman was found with a large repoussé gold rosette attached with a pin to the remains of her garment. She also had a gold band with repoussé decoration and a bracelet of heavy wire doubled to make two straps. The top strap was coiled into a series of spirals which were secured to the lower band. One grave occupant had an electrum armlet and two gold ornaments, perhaps clothing decoration, near his pelvis. Dickinson notes that during the middle Helladic period such jewelry accompanied female burials [3]. There were traces of the gold decoration of the hem of a man's robe in another burial. A mask of electrum beaten to represent a face is the only such object from Circle B. There were necklaces of semi-precious stones and gold, and one carved seal with the profile of a bearded man.

The display of jewelry in the shaft graves of Circle A reaches regal magnificence. Two of the graves contained numerous small gold plaques impressed with images of marine animals, flowers and spiral patterns. They were probably attached to garments. Women had diadems placed on the forehead with pins to secure the crown into the deceased's hair [4]. These diadems are often made of several pieces of thin gold, sometimes with copper tubing for added strength. Usually they bear a

[1] S. Hood, *The Arts in Prehistoric Greece*, Norwich, 1978, p. 192.
[2] E. Vermeule, *Greece in the Bronze Age*, Chicago, 1964, p. 90, 108; Idem, *Art of the Shaft Graves*, Norman, Okl., 1973; O. T. P. K. Dickinson, *The Origins of Mycenaean Civilisation*, Göteborg, 1977, p. 51-57.
[3] G. Mylonas, *Mycenae: a Guide to the Ruins and its History*, Athens, 1981, fig. 46. For the complete contents of the circle B graves, see G. Mylonas, *Ancient Mycenae, the Capital of Agamemnon*, London, 1957, p. 97-105; Id., Ὁ ταφικὸς κύκλος Bτῶν Μυληνῶν, Athens, 1972; Dickinson, *op. cit.*, p. 40-46. On p. 43, Dickinson states that the arm band is gold and the garment ornaments are electrum.
[4] Mylonas, *Ancient Mycenae*, p. 107.

repoussé decoration. Some men were buried with masks of thin gold which include the famous bearded countenance taken by Schliemann to reproduce the features of Agamemnon. The man buried in Grave V had a necklace composed of ten pairs of beads intended to represent eagles. Also found were necklaces of semi-precious stones, faience and gold, besides some simple twisted wire bracelets and armlets.

The early Helladic jewelry appears to have been manufactured locally, but already in the beginning of the second millenium B.C. there are noticeable outside influences. A silver pin with a double spiral head from Zygouries is similar to an example from the Cyclades [5]. Some of the diadems show dot repoussé decoration like that on pieces from Crete. Simple wire earrings appear to have Cretan parallels [6]. A pin from Thyreatis is comparable to pins from Troy [7].

The Shaft Grave contents appear to be a mixture of local and Minoan jewelry. Their sources are debated. A. Evans maintained that the bulk of the material was Minoan manufacture. He could see a resemblance between the Shaft Grave jewelry and that which had been discovered in the tombs on Crete dating from early Minoan II and III. The two signet rings from Shaft Grave IV were examples of a ring style invented on Crete [8]. He stated that several spiral bracelets probably originated around Troy [9]. Tsountas had the amber found in one of the Shaft Graves tested and determined that the Baltic Sea was the place of origin [10]. G. Karo and Evans saw a Minoan quality in the ornament on many of the jewelry pieces. However, Karo also thought the decoration on the pommels and some of the swords to originate in Celtic art [11]. S. Hood has considered the quality of the Shaft Grave jewelry too poor to be Minoan workmanship. He states that the pieces came from local workshops staffed with less skilled craftsmen [12]. F. Matz regards the jewelry from the Shaft Graves to be based on Minoan models that the Mycenaean artisans have transformed. The change is most apparent on the repoussé plaques. The vegetal and marine motifs are Minoan, but the rigidity and regularity to which they are subjected are not Minoan treatments, but rather the Mycenaean aesthetic preferences [13].

The contents of the Shaft Graves reveal that the period was one of transition on the mainland when local tastes and styles appear to have been developing often under the influence of Minoan artistic ideas. Some of the items such as the metal or gem set bezel signet rings are Minoan inventions which became popular on the mainland [14]. The most impressive ones from the Shaft Graves are the two gold rings

---

[5] HOOD, *op. cit.*, p. 192.

[6] E. BIELEFELD, *Schmuck*, in *Archaeologia Homerica*, Göttingen, 1968, p. C 36-37.

[7] HOOD, *op. cit.*, p. 192.

[8] A. EVANS, *The Shaft Graves and Beehive Tombs of Mycenae*, London, 1927, p. 30.

[9] *Ibid.*, p. 47-48.

[10] C. TSOUNTAS, *The Mycenaean Age*, New York, 1897, p. 180. For more recent studies see, C. W. BECK, C. G. SOUTHARD and A. B. ADAMS, *Analysis and provenience of Minoan and Mycenaean Amber, IV, Mycenae*, in *Greek, Roman and Byzantine Studies*, 13, 1971, p. 359-385.

[11] G. KARO, *Die Schachtgräber von Mykenai*, Munich, 1930, p. 289, 346.

[12] HOOD, *op. cit.*, p. 197.

[13] F. MATZ, *The Art of Crete and Early Greece*, Baden-Baden, 1962, p. 169.

[14] K. BRANIGAN, *Early Aegean Seals and Signets*, in *SMEA*, 17, 1976, p. 157-167.

from Grave IV, but there are also bronze and silver examples from other graves. Two gold cups with repoussé decorations come from a slightly later tomb at Vapheio. In addition to the cups, the tomb contained several objects imported from Crete [15]. Though the two cups have a similarity of scenes, the capture of bulls, there is enough difference in the style to lead to the conclusion that two different hands were involved. Some scholars maintain that both cups were the work of Minoan goldsmiths [16]; others favor the notion that one of the cups was made by a Mycenaean craftsman [17].

Egyptian items found in Shaft Graves I and II were faience vases of an XVIIIth dynasty type, and Grave V yielded an ostrich egg shaped rhyton [18]. Other objects have Egyptian stylistic qualities. Bielefeld has seen a similarity in the decoration of two diadems with the crown of an Egyptian princess [19]. The repoussé rosette pattern on some diadems is known from Middle Kingdom headdresses [20]. A. Persson has pointed out that the handle of the octopus cup from the Tholos Tomb at Midea has a handle decorated by a fluted column with a double flower-shaped capital; the closest parallels are Egyptian [21]; however these features, like the nilotic scene on one of the daggers from Shaft Grave V, may be Egyptian in origin but probably were transmitted to the mainland via Crete [22].

During the Shaft Grave era, the local middle Helladic centers became part of a larger cultural unit which would come to politically, artistically and culturally dominate the mainland and much of the Aegean until the twelfth century B.C. [23], generally referred to as Mycenaean. Now we encounter much more information about jewelry. Aside from finds, there are representations of figures wearing jewelry, and there exist descriptions of jewelry, especially in the Odyssey [24].

Homer's epics were given their form four hundred years after the disappearance of the Mycenaean world. Often elements from Homer's age are juxtaposed with items from the past. There are mainly two terms for jewelry [25]: ἄγαλμα and

---

[15] E. DAVIS, *The Vapheio Cups and Aegean Gold and Silver Ware*, New York, 1977, p. 1. IDEM, *The Vapheio Cups: One Minoan and One Mycenaean*, in *Art Bulletin*, 56, 1974, p. 472-487; J. HURWIT, *The Dendra Octopus Cup and the Problem of Style in the Fifteenth Century Aegean*, in *AJA*, 83, 1979, p. 413-426.

[16] VERMEULE, *op. cit.*, p. 129; MATZ, *op. cit.*, p. 127.

[17] HOOD, *op. cit.*, p. 167; DAVIS, 1977, *op. cit.*, p. 8-9.

[18] J.D.S. PENDLEBURY, *Aegyptiaca, a Catalogue of Egyptian Objects in the Aegean Area*, Cambridge, 1930, p. 53-58, no. 89-90; see BIELEFELD, *op. cit.*, p. C 20; KARO, *op. cit.*, no. 828.

[19] BIELEFELD, *op. cit.*, p. C 14.

[20] *Ibid.*, p. C 15.

[21] A. PERSSON, *The Royal Tombs at Dendra near Midea*, Lund, 1931, p. 45.

[22] J.T. HOOKER, *Mycenaean Greece*, London, 1976, p. 52; MATZ, *op. cit.*, p. 180.

[23] On the end of the Mycenaean civilization, V.R. DESBOROUGH, *History and Archaeology in the Last Century of the Mycenaean Age*, in *Atti e Memorie del I° Congresso Internazionale di Micenologia*, 3, Rome, 1968, p. 1073-1093.

[24] Homer as a reliable source of information about the Mycenaean world is still a debated issue. For a recent survey of scholarly opinion see N.I. BARBU, *Mycènes et le problème homérique*, in *SMEA*, 6, 1968, p. 33-38; Barbu indicates that there is a general willingness to trust Homer on selected points. See J.L. MYERS, *Homeric Art*, in *BSA*, 45, 1950, p. 229-260.

[25] The following discussion is taken from BIELEFELD, *op. cit.*, p. C 1-9.

κόσμος. Homer also uses ἄγαλμα to refer to other precious possessions such as horses and their bridles (*Iliad*, 4.144). The term describes the valuable objects Aigisthos offers the gods (*Odyssey*, 3.273), one of the gifts given to Penelope (*Odyssey*, 18.299) and the present of a man's fibula (*Odyssey*, 19.257). Specific types of jewelry are also named. Earrings occur twice; both times called ἕρματα (*Iliad*, 14.182; *Odyssey*, 18.297). Earrings are also called τρίγληνα which is literally three-eyed, but appears to have been a reference to mulberry clusters. The dark mulberry fruit may have been an allusion to the dark stones inlaid into the earring drops [26]. Jewelry for the neck is indicated by one of two words: ἴσθμιον or ὅρμος. The former seems to be confined to necklaces and it is used to denote one of the suitors' gifts (*Odyssey*, 18.299) which is further defined by ἄγαλμα. Ὅρμος is a broader term for neck ornament and is used to describe a neck chain of amber and gold (*Odyssey*, 15.459), a necklace of amber and gold (*Odyssey*, 18.295) and one of the types of ornaments that Hephaistos made when he worked for Thetis and Eurynome (*Iliad*, 18.400). Περόναι indicates the twelve fibulae that serve as clasps on a garment (*Odyssey*, 18.292). Hera pins her robe across her breast with a ἕνεται (*Iliad*, 14.180). There are two types of girdles. Women wear ζώνη, though it is not clear whether these are made of fabric or metal or both materials (*Iliad*, 14.181; *Odyssey*, 5.231; 10.544; 11.245). The girdles can also have a decorative fringe θύσανοι (Iliad, 14.181). Men's girdles are more like armored belts. Agamemnon is protected by his Ζωστήρ from Iphidamas' sword thrust (*Iliad*, 11.236).

Two pieces of jewelry receive great attention. The headdress that falls from Andromache's head is described by several words (*Iliad*, 22.468) [27]. Χρυσάμπυκες may refer to a textile or gold band. Κεκρύφαλος seems to have an Anatolian origin and may have been used originally to refer to horse trappings. Κρήδεμνον is probably a veil and στεφάνη designates a wreath or garland reserved for deities or heroines. The description of Odysseus' fibula (*Odyssey*, 19.225) is the most lavish and detailed observation of a jewelry item in either epic. Both the attaching mechanism and the scene on the fibula are explained. The information is complete enough to allow some scholars to suggest that the fibula represents a type used in Homer's day [28].

In Homer, men do not usually wear jewelry. There are only Odysseus' fibula and the gold and silver rings in Euphorbos' hair. Bielefeld suggests that Euphorbos is wearing an eastern hair style [29]. The only Mycenaean representation of a man with jewelry is the warrior on an ivory plaque from Delos who wears armlets. Bielefeld assumes the armlets to be an indication of social rank [30]. Sometimes the belts of Homeric heroes are decorated with silver (*Iliad*, 18.598). The greaves are tied with silver fastenings (*Iliad*, 11.18).

[26] *Ibid.*, C 4.
[27] *Ibid.*, C 2-3.
[28] MYERS, *op. cit.*, p. 242-243.
[29] BIELEFELD, *op. cit.*, p. C 9.
[30] Minoan frescoes from the era preceding the Mycenaean domination show men wearing armlets, HOOD, *op. cit.*, p. 202. BIELEFELD, *op. cit.*, p. 31-32.

The women shown on the ivory triad from Mycenae wear several necklace strands that form collars. The ladies painted on the wall of the fifteenth century palace at Thebes wear Minoan type garbs with flounced skirts and open bodices, and necklaces and bracelets made up of alternating black and red oblong beads[31]. Similar processions are known from the palace decorations at Tiryns and Pylos dated in the thirteenth century. The Tiryns fragments show women with head bands studded with pearls[32]. Those bits of fresco that preserve the arms and wrists indicate that the figures have bracelets of the same alternating red and black bead type[33]. A quite different female figure, the "White Goddess" from Pylos is dressed in an elaborate crown which is preserved for three bands[34]. A lady from a fresco at Mycenae has a head band with pendant spirals, and on her neck are three necklace strands, one of alternating red and yellow beads and the other two with a series of triangular pendants also in red and yellow. On each wrist she wears three bracelets, the first a single bent wire, the other two of yellow and red beads which must have been intended to match the necklace.

The painters of the procession frescoes seem to have portrayed older dress styles. Figures from other wall paintings at Tiryns and on painted pottery do not wear the flounced skirt[35]. It is also possible that alterations had taken place in jewelry designs which are not reflected in the painted representations.

Late Helladic jewelry did change. The evidence comes from the burials. In the last part of the middle Helladic and the beginning of the late Helladic eras, agate, rock crystal, amethyst, amber and other semi-precious stones were strung for necklaces[36]. By late Helladic II glass and faience beads were regularly used instead of the semi-precious stones[37]. Glass jewelry is even found in rich burials[38]. Faience and glass beads can be moulded into patterns. If the glass is blue, it is a cheap imitation of lapis lazuli, and both glass and faience beads are often gilded to suggest gold[39]. During this same period the use of shell for jewelry increases[40]. Small gold beads are manufactured during the late Helladic era; granulation becomes sometimes a popular means of decorating beads and other gold surfaces[41]. A variety of mass produced, stamped out beads, usually of gold, are employed for necklaces. The designs are stylized floral and marine motifs and include rosettes,

---

[31] H. REUSCH, *Die zeichnerische Rekonstruktion des Frauenfrieses im Böotischen Theben*, Berlin, 1956.

[32] G. RODENWALDT, *Tiryns*, 2, *Die Fresken des Palastes*, Athens, 1912, no. 92.

[33] *Ibid.*, no. 104.

[34] M. LANG, *The Palace of Nestor*, 2, *The Frescoes*, Princeton, 1969, p. 51-55.

[35] See the chariot fresco at Tiryns, RODENWALDT, *op. cit.*, p. 108; also REUSCH, *op. cit.*, p. 58. Vermeule and Karageorghis have recently pointed out that on Crete and the mainland and Cyprus, the long robe had replaced the flounced skirt, cf. The Warrior Vase female figure, V. KARAGEORGHIS and E. VERMEULE, *Mycenaean Pictorial Vase Painting*, Cambridge, Mass., 1982, p. 91.

[36] PERSSON, *op. cit.*, p. 36, no. 14. For an amber necklace in Shaft Grave omikron, MYLONAS, *Ancient Mycenae, op. cit.*, p. 104.

[37] R. HIGGINS, *Greek and Roman Jewellery*, 2nd ed., Berkeley, 1980, p. 72-73.

[38] PERSSON, *op. cit.*, p. 103-104.

[39] *Ibid.*, p. 103, no. 21.

[40] BIELEFELD, *op. cit.*, p. C 26.

[41] *Ibid.*; see also HIGGINS, *op. cit.*, p. 72-73; PERSSON, *op. cit.*, p. 58.

lilies, lotus blossoms, figure-eight shields and nautilus and argonaut shells[42]. Several different analogous pairs of beads or a series of repeated beads can comprise a necklace.

Diadems are rare after the Shaft Grave era. Bielefeld considers the pieces of cobalt blue glass found around the skull of a female from the Tholos Tomb at Midea to be from a diadem. The gold rosettes and gold and glass beads which lay about the heads of the occupants of chamber tomb 10 at Mycenae might also come from headdresses[43].

Certain jewelry disappears entirely in the late Helladic period. Earrings are found only on the islands[44]. Higgins notes that in several late Helladic mainland burials hair spirals are found, and not earrings. Arm bands are uncommon. Bielefeld thinks that a carved carnelian gem found near the wrist of a woman is the remnant of one of the few examples of a late Helladic bracelet[45].

Signet rings continue to be manufactured. Both gemstones and metal bezels are carved with intaglio designs. The metals used from the middle Helladic throughout the late Helladic centuries are gold, silver, bronze, copper and iron. An interesting development is demonstrated by four rings from the princely burial at Midea. The rings are each composed of four metals — iron, copper, lead and silver — arranged in thin layers[46]. The discovery of enameled jewelry at Pylos shows that the technique was being used[47].

With the shift of political, economic and cultural dominance from Crete to the mainland after the mid-fifteenth century, new centers of jewelry production emerged and different sources of inspiration influenced designs. Archaeological evidence suggests local palace workshops. From Mycenae have come steatite moulds used to make faience and glass ornaments[48]. The find of a bronzesmith's tools in his grave at Mycenae is proof of the existence of specialized craft personnel in the palace structure[49]. Pylos also has evidence for a jewelry or fine crafts workshop in the northeastern building[50]. Stone moulds over which a sheet of gold could have been beaten to form an impressed design were discovered in a lapidary's workshop at Knossos which probably dates from the Mycenaean era at the palace[51].

The existence of specialized craft personnel in the palace hierarchies is further

---

[42] HIGGINS, *op. cit.*, p. 76-82; BIELEFELD, *op. cit.*, p. C 28-30, fig. 2. For examples, PERSSON, *op. cit.*, p. 55.

[43] BIELEFELD, *op. cit.*, p. C 15-16; PERSSON, *op. cit.*, p. 36, no. 13, also p. 64. Persson thinks the glass beads were part of the decoration for a helmet.

[44] HIGGINS, *op. cit.*, p. 72, 74. BIELEFELD, *op. cit.*, p. C 36.

[45] BIELEFELD, *op. cit.*, p. C 32.

[46] PERSSON, *op. cit.*, p. 33, no. 4.

[47] C. W. BLEGEN and M. RAWSON, *The Palace of Nestor*, 1, *The Buildings and their Contents*, Princeton, 1966, p. 75-88.

[48] A. J. B. WACE, *Mycenae, an Archaeological History and Guide*, Princeton, 1949, p. 110.

[49] A. J. B. WACE et al., *Excavations at Mycenae, 1939-1955*, E. French, ed., Oxford, 1979, p. 292-296.

[50] BLEGEN and RAWSON, *op. cit.*, p. 323-325.

[51] J. G. YOUNGER, *The Lapidary's Workshop at Knossos*, in *BSA*, 74, 1979, p. 258-268.

evidenced by the appearance on the Pylos Linear B archive tablets of a term which may translate as goldsmith, "ku-ru-so-wo-ko" (PY An 207. 10. N. p), provided that Linear B is read as a Greek based orthographic system[52]. Another tablet suggests the social position held by craftsmen, for bronzesmiths are referred to as slaves (PY Jn 605)[53], and the same may have been true for goldsmiths.

E. P. Blegen argued for the local production of the late Helladic jewelry from the tombs at Prosymna in western Greece. She pointed out that these were commoners' burials and therefore not likely to contain imported goods. Yet, the jewelry types were all similar to pieces known from Mycenae[54].

Higgins has suggested that the floral and marine patterns for the stampedout beads are borrowed from decoration of the palace-style painted pottery[55]. Furumark suspects that it was the other way around and that the potters were getting their ideas from the jewelry[56]. The other possible source for these designs may have been the fresco borders. Floral patterns, spirals and figure-eight shields all serve as border decorations, and all these occur as stamped bead varieties[57].

Rodenwaldt pointed out that the rosettes on stems and certain of the spirals on the fresco borders from the wall paintings of the earlier palace at Tiryns may be remotely related to Egyptian models, though changed with Minoan influences[58] from as early as the middle Minoan period. The lily motif which is one of the stamped designs may be Egyptian in origin[59]. We know that at least one Egyptian jewelry manufacturing technique was being practiced on Mycenaean Cyprus; the substitution for lapis lazuli of a paste made of blue glass colored with copper oxides and cobalt which was used in cloisonné enamels[60].

Yet Mycenaean overseas involvement was not limited to Egypt. They had colonies on the coast of Asia Minor[61] and some of their gold may have been coming from Anatolia[62]. The ivory which was such a popular item for carving may

---

[52] L. R. PALMER, *The Interpretation of Mycenaean Greek Texts*, 2nd ed., Oxford, 1969, p. 136, 229.

[53] *Ibid.*, p. 140. The eighth century levels at Gordion show archaeological evidence that the labor force was confined in the citadel; K. DE VRIES, *Greeks and Phrygians in the Early Iron Age*, in *From Athens to Gordion: The Papers of a Memorial Symposium for Rodney Young*, K. DeVries, ed. (*The University Museum Papers*, 1), Philadelphia, 1980, p. 41.

[54] E. P. BLEGEN, *Jewellery and Ornaments*, in C. W. BLEGEN, *Prosymna. The Helladic Settlement Preceding the Argive Heraeum*, Cambridge, 1937, p. 264-327.

[55] R. HIGGINS, *Jewellery from Classical Lands*, London, 1969, p. 14-15.

[56] A. FURUMARK, *Mycenaean Pottery*, I, *Analysis and Classification*, Stockholm, 1972, p. 150, 160, 183.

[57] Furumark does not think that this was the case for the pottery painters; *ibid.*, p. 450-451, 462-463.

[58] RODENWALDT, *op. cit.*, p. 50.

[59] BIELEFELD, *op. cit.*, p. 29.

[60] R. HALLEUX, *Lapis-lazuli, azurite ou pâte de verre; À propos de* Kuwano *et* Kumanowoko *dans les tablettes mycéniennes*, in *SMEA*, 9, 1969, p. 48-66, esp. 52; see also, HIGGINS, *op. cit.*, p. 23.

[61] C. MEE, *Aegean Trade and Settlement in Anatolia in the Second Millennium, B.C.*, in *AnatSt*, 28, 1978, p. 121-155. For linguistic evidence, see J. HARMATTA, *Ahhiyawa: Names-Mycenaean Names*, in *Atti e Memorie del 1° Congresso Internazionale di Micenologia*, Rome, 1968, p. 401-409, esp. 402.

[62] P. DE JESUS, *Metal Resources in Ancient Anatolia*, in *AnatSt*, 28, 1978, p. 97-102.

be Syrian[63]. The discovery at the palace in Thebes of several Near Eastern cylinder seals which can be dated to the late fourteenth century B.C.[64] is illustrative for the expansion of Mycenaean trade during these centuries.

Jewelry and gold and silver possessions served a variety of functions in a pre-monetary society. The suitors in the *Odyssey* try to purchase Penelope by displays of wealthy gifts (18.300-305). Gold, certainly in massive show, was a sign of power and prestige. When Homer wants to create an image of vast wealth and power as in his description of the palace of Alkinoos, he makes numerous references to riches (*Odyssey*, Book 7). The doors are of gold and lapis lazuli, posts and lintels are of silver and two great silver hounds stand guard. Odysseus sits in the seat of honor, a chair studded with silver (a chair which may in reality reflect the furnishings of Homer's own time)[65], and he washes his hands in a silver bowl with water poured from a golden pitcher. Our bowls (cat. nos. 3 and 4) may not be too unlike the kind Homer had in mind. At Menelaos' palace Helen sits spinning her wool on a gold distaff, and she keeps her materials in a basket of silver rimmed in gold (*Odyssey*, 4.130-131). The inventory lists from the palace at Pylos include many items which correspond to Homer's descriptions. We know that gold formed tribute (Jn 438) and must have been in the palace in the storage areas. Other lists of property tell of gold bowls (Tn 996), some inlaid with metal (Ta 642), and there is mention of furniture with precious ornament (Ta 642, T 713, Ta 714)[66].

Jewelry as an element in the ritual of gift exchange is alluded to in the poems, and it was important in the Homeric era[67]. In the epics most of the treasure is in the form of goblets or other utilitarian objects made of gold, silver, bronze or iron. These are Homer's recurring silver bowls and gold pitchers. Treasure thus could be displayed as evidence of wealth, and it could be given away when such an action was considered valuable[68]. Gifts are presented when Agamemnon tries to reconcile himself with Achilles (*Iliad*, 9.121-156). Riches are given in tribute to a ruler, a practice which may be reflected in the Pylos tribute lists. Precious items are dedicated to the gods, an action also recorded on the Pylos tablets. The social ritual of formal gift exchange is preserved in sections of the *Odyssey* such as when Telemakhos leaves Menelaos' palace. Menelaos gives him a costly bowl, and before Telemakhos leaves, Helen prepares for him a robe which she herself has made. This garment is given him for his future bride (15.105-106, 124-125); a woman's gift to another woman. We might assume that jewelry passed from one seat of power to

---

[63] VERMEULE, *op. cit.*, p. 218; WACE, *op. cit.*, p. 108.

[64] C. HOPKINS, *The Second Late Helladic Period*, in *SMEA*, 12, 1970, p. 58-67, esp. 65.

[65] K. KARAGEORGHIS, *Homeric Furniture from Cyprus*, in *Atti e Memorie del 1° Congresso Internazionale di Micenologia*, Rome, 1968, p. 216-221.

[66] J. CHADWICK, *Documents in Mycenaean Greek*, 2nd. ed., Cambridge, 1973, p. 358, no. 258; p. 338, no. 238; p. 339, no. 237.

[67] DE VRIES, *op. cit.*, p. 41 suggests that some of the wealth accumulated in the form of textiles and metal vases in the eighth century Phrygian burials at Gordion might be the result of the practice of gift giving.

[68] M. I. FINLEY, *The World of Odysseus*, New York, 1965, p. 58-59, 129-130.

another in just this manner. A man's true worth was to some extent determined by his ability to give away expensive objects.

Mylonas has noted that some of the gold ornaments in the Shaft Graves are made of such thin foil as to have been impratical as real jewelry [69]. These must have been funerary jewelry, something to adorn the body of the dead, to make a suitable shroud for the powerful. Bielefeld has suggested that in some instances necklaces were the insignia of priestly rank since both men and women wear them [70]. The great gold masks of the Shaft Graves may have been intended to close the eyes of the deceased [71]. Some Mycenaean burials have yielded lead wires which must have been used to hold the corpse's mouth closed [72].

Whether jewelry played any role in the various religious rites is not clear. Pylos tablet TN 316 lists offerings to one of the divinities which include gold and gold vessels along with men and women to serve the god [73]. Another of the Pylos tablets preserves the title "Priestess in charge of the sacred gold" (Ac 303) [74]. The small cases that the various ladies carry in the procession frescoes could have represented jewelry cases, and the scenes might portray actual rituals.

Jewelry and gold vessels were important elements in the palace society of the Mycenaean world. The court ladies adorned themselves with jewelry and in so doing boasted of the wealth of their lords. The gold vessels which must have been on display from time to time served to underscore the lord's riches, and when he chose to give something valuable away, he emphasized the abundance of his treasury. In a society without coinage, gold, silver, bronze plate, and probably also jewelry provided portable, liquid assets. The powerful could take their wealth to their tombs, so even in death no one had to relinquish the signs of his position or importance.

William E. MIERSE

---

[69] MYLONAS, *Ancient Mycenae*, p. 170.
[70] BIELEFELD, *op. cit.*, p. C 16.
[71] M. ANDRONIKOS, *Totenkult*, in *Archaeologia Homerica*, Göttingen, 1968, p. W 41.
[72] *Ibid.*
[73] CHADWICK, *op. cit.*, p. 286, no. 172.
[74] PALMER, *op. cit.*, p. 127, no. 30.

1
Necklace of gold and lapis lazuli

Probably Mesopotamian mid-second millenium B.C.; bought in Beirut.

L. 97 cm; cylinders: average length, 0.9 cm; thickness, 0.5 cm; biconical beads: largest, length, 1.8 cm; thickness, 0.8 cm; smallest, length, 1.2 cm; thickness, 0.6 cm; quadruple spiral spacer bars: largest, length, 1.4 cm; width, 1.5 cm; thickness, 0.2 cm; smallest, length, 0.7 cm; width, 1.0 cm; thickness, 0.2 cm.

Loan from Mr. and Mrs. Artemis Joukowsky.

Sixty-eight lapis lazuli beads, alternating with twenty-five gold spacer bars, with quadruple spiral attachments, form this necklace. The beads and the spacer bars are strung onto thin pieces of gold wire that each terminate in loops at either end. The larger pieces of wire are joined together by small, intermediate gold wire hoops. The necklace is a single strand and terminates at either end in half of a hook-and-eye clasp. The present arrangement is modern. The gold spacers and the lapis lazuli lozenges came from two different sources in Beirut, and were strung together. The lapis lazuli beads are in excellent condition; none appears to be broken. The gold spacer bars include some modern imitations: the two ends and tenth bar on the eye side of the clasp. Some of the wire spirals are loose. Solder is visible on nine of the gold spacer bars and several of the coiled gold wire beads that separate the lapis lazuli stones. The solder is probably due to later repairs.

Three types of lapis lazuli beads are used. As the two ends nearest the clasp, the beads are small cylinders. The next stone beads are two analogous groupings of a cylinder sandwiched between two smaller beads. Each group is strung onto a single piece of wire. Two small beads of coiled gold wire are inserted on either side of the larger central bead in order to prevent the stones from rubbing one another. Beginning with the third arrangement of lapis lazuli beads

on either side of the clasp, the larger central member of the group becomes a roughened biconical-shaped stone. The two flanking beads can be either rounded or cylindrical. The beads of gold wire are placed on both sides of the big stone. This pattern is repeated for the remaining lapis lazuli beads. The grouping is arranged into a larger plan of gradation in a symmetrical manner of increasing size moving from the two sides of the clasp toward a central point at the necklace's front. The biconical beads are not cut with great precision. Several have uneven sides, and all are flat, though some have a slight ridge on one surface.

Every group of lapis lazuli beads and the two single cylinders at the end are separated from each other by gold spacer bars. These spacer bars consist of a hollow tube through which a wire runs. On either side of the tube are double spirals of wire. These are bent around the tubes and held in a fixed position. The two sets of spirals face each other and form a unit of four spirals, two on the top and two on the bottom of the spacer bar. The two ends of the clasp are formed by two of these spacer bars, through which the wires, forming the hook and eye, run. The apex of the necklace, the largest bead in the chain, is also one of these spacer bars. As with the lapis lazuli beads, the gold spacer bars are arranged on either side of the necklace so that they increase in size from the clasp to the middle.

The necklace contains three distinct elements: the alternating gold and lapis lazuli arrangement (the result of the modern restoration), the biconically-shaped lapis lazuli beads and the gold spacer bars with quadruple spirals. We may assume that the present arrangements of elements does reflect to some degree ancient styles. The lapis lazuli beads and the gold spacer bars, though not originally part of this necklace, do probably come from necklaces or headdresses, since the beads and bars follow the same pattern of gradual increase in size. If we disregard the present light appearance of the necklace, which is due to the added space between elements caused by the stringing of the beads onto individual wires, joined together by secondary connectors, then we find the earliest parallels for the necklace arrangement in the jewelry from the Early Dynastic tombs at Ur. In these graves were discovered necklaces with the same mixture of gold and lapis lazuli, but without the extra links between beads. From the contemporary site of Mari, comes a bracelet with pieces of gold and lapis lazuli [1].

Biconical lapis lazuli beads are found on both headdresses and necklaces from the Sumerian Early Dynastic tombs [2]. Late second millenium jewelry from Ashur also contains biconical beads, and they occur elsewhere in the Levant [3].

Wires bent to create double-facing spirals were also discovered in the Early Dynastic graves at Ur. These are isolated forms and probably were used as pendants [4]. Quadruple spirals occur on a pendant from the same tomb; the spirals are made of tightly coiled wire which pushes out and resembles a pinecone (British Museum WAA121425). There is also a toggle pin on which the quadruple spiral pattern is an intaglio (British Museum WAA121372). We find the earliest parallels to our quadruple spiral spacer bars in silver beads from Brak which date to the late third millenium B.C. However, these are made of a single piece of silver, the ends of which are drawn out to form a spiral [5]. Mallowan has studied these early forms of quadruple spiral beads and concluded that the ultimate source might be Hissar, a site in the central plain of Iran. The examples from Ur might represent slightly more refined forms, and the first fully developed spiral beads are those from Brak and Troy II-III [6]. Slightly later in date are nineteen gold quadruple spiral beads from Grave 20 at Ashur which date to the late third or early second millenium B.C. [7]. Our closest parallel may be the gold quadruple spiral beads from Mari which Parrot dates to the period of the Assyrian garrison, ca. 1300 B.C. [8]. The Mari beads have spirals of bent wire attached to the central gold bar, and in this way reflect the same construction as our examples.

Though the elements of our particular necklace come from Lebanon and are probably of Mesopotamian origin, the necklace is not out of place in the Mycenaean portion of the catalogue. There are four quadruple spiral beads from Grave III of the Shaft Graves at Mycenae which Karo identified as earrings [9]. The spirals are formed from separate pieces of wire attached to the ends of the tubes. Evans suggested that these were items worn by foreign princesses in Mycenae and reflected northeastern, Trojan rather than native style [10].

WEM

[1] For Ur finds, British Museum, 1976, nos. 12e, f, g, h. For Mari bracelet, A. PARROT, *Le Trésor d'Ur*, Paris, 1968, no. 17.

[2] MAXWELL-HYSLOP, p. 8-9.

[3] W. ANDRAE, *Gruft 45*, in A. HALLER, *Die Gräber und Grüfte von Assur*, Berlin, 1954, pl. 28. MAXWELL-HYSLOP, p. 29-30, p. 97, fig. 72, p. 126e.

[4] See jewelry as restrung in British Museum, 1976, no. 12g (WAA121425).

[5] MAXWELL-HYSLOP, p. 31, fig. 22a.

[6] M. E. I. MALLOWAN, *Excavations at Brak and Chagar Bazar*, in *Iraq*, 9, 1947, p. 171-176.

[7] A. HALLER, p. 10.

[8] A. PARROT, *Les Fouilles de Mari. Troisième Campagne (Hiver 1935-36)*, in *Syria*, 18, 1937, p. 82-83.

[9] KARO, 1930, nos. 54-55.

[10] MALLOWAN, p. 176; A. EVANS, *The Shaft Graves and Bee-hive Tombs of Mycenae and their Interrelation*, London, 1929, p. 47, fig. 37.

2
Signet ring

Mycenaean, provenance unknown, Late
  Helladic, ca. 1450-1400 B.C.
L. of bezel 0.026 cm; diam. 0.026 cm.
The Walters Art Gallery, Baltimore.
  Acc. no. 57.1006.
Formerly collection of Arthur Sambon,
  Paris.
Bibliography:
WALTERS, 1979, p. 74, no. 233.

According to Dr Buitron, the ring is composed of two parts: a gold bezel of two sheets
of gold seamed together and a hollow gold
hoop which is treated with repoussé to form a
ridge on the exterior. The hoop is flat on the
interior and is set perpendicularly to the
bezel. The oval bezel is on line with the finger.

The scene presented on the bezel depicts
two dueling warriors. The figures stand with
their torsos turned to the front and the lower
halves of their bodies in profile. Rows of
rouletting along the bottom and the top serve
to indicate the ground line and the horizon.
The warrior on the right has bent his right
knee behind the shield as if having fallen
down. He holds his shield out in front to
protect himself and has his sword drawn
ready to thrust. From the opposite side the
opponent strides with his spear held aloft in
his left hand. Both figures are dressed in kilts,
greaves and helmets. They both carry round
grip shields.

The closest stylistic parallels are a signet
ring and seal from Grave IV of the Circle A
of the Shaft Graves [1]. There is a similar
rendering of the figures' details with single
cuts representing the arms, the heads, the legs
and so forth. Several intaglios from mainland
Mycenaean contexts demonstrate the same
concern with locating figures in space by the
use of either a ground line or the suggestion
of a landscape [2].

The figures' stance is paralleled by the
hunters on the Lion Hunt dagger from
Shaft Grave IV who have frontal torsos
and profile legs, and by the fighting men
portrayed on a crater from Mycenae. The
convention was being used even as late as
the thirteenth century. The procession of
warriors of the "Warrior Vase" has some
figures with torsos to the front and lower
bodies in profile.

Fighting warriors are a common mainland
motif in Mycenaean art. Battle scenes appear in other media, particularly fresco
paintings [3]. If T. L. Webster is correct in
assigning an earlier date to the great figure-
eight body shields and a later date to these
round grip shields, our ring comes after the
period of the Shaft Graves [4].

Sakellariou has studied the battle scenes
represented on silver plate and stone rhyta.
She suggests that they do not represent
reality, but rather are part of the epic and
heroic tradition. The scenes are lacking
in naturalism and reality because of their
strong sense of equilibrium and their balanced compositions (figures arranged around
a central point). As on this ring, they portray
not a real world but a world of heroes [5].

WEM

3
Bowl

[1] KARO, 1933, no. 240, 241. A. SAKELLARIOU, *Die Minoischen und Mykenischen Siegel des Nationalmuseums in Athen (Corpus der Minoischen und Mykenischen Siegel,* 1), Berlin, 1964, no. 16.
[2] N. PLATON, I. PINI, G. SALIES, *Iraklion Archäologisches Museum,* 2, *Die Siegel der Altpalastzeit,* Berlin, 1977, no. 16, 19, 20, 57, 68.
[3] J. HURWIT, *The Dendra Octopus Cup and the Problem of Style in the Fifteenth Century Aegean,* in *AJA,* 83, 1979, p. 413-426. M. LANG, *The Palace of Nestor,* 2, *The Frescoes,* Princeton, 1969.
[4] T. L. WEBSTER, *From Mycenae to Homer,* New York, 1958, p. 100; J. T. HOOKER, *Mycenaean Greece,* London, 1976, p. 89.
[5] A. SAKELLARIOU, *Un cratère d'argent avec scène de bataille provenant de la IVe tombe de l'acropole de Mycènes,* in *Antike Kunst,* 17, 1974, p. 18. *Eadem, La scène du 'siège' sur le rhyton d'argent de Mycènes d'après une nouvelle reconstitution,* in *RA,* 2, 1975, p. 195-208.

Mycenaean, said to be from Syria, between Tripoli and Homs, Late Helladic.
Diam. ca. 18.5 cm.
Virginia Museum of Fine Arts, Purchase, The Glasgow Fund.
Acc. no. 67.30.
Formerly collection of the Comte M. X. du Puytison, Paris.
Bibliography:
J. BROWN, *Ancient Art in the Virginia Museum,* Richmond, 1973, no. 73.
A. PARROT, *Acquisitions et inédits du Musée du Louvre,* in *Syria,* 41, 1964, p. 249, fig. 31.

The shallow bowl is raised from a single sheet of gold plate. The lip and the walls are undecorated. The bottom is decorated with a repoussé pattern hammered so that the relief is on the inside. There is no base and the bottom is slightly rounded.

The decoration consists of a twelve-petalled rosette set into a circle in the middle of the bowl and defined by a raised border. The rosette medallion is surrounded by a maeander pattern that runs from one side of the bowl to the other in eight rows. Both the rosette and the line that forms the maeander are given some finer linear detailing.

The shallow bowl shape is not known on the mainland prior to the late Helladic period. Early Bronze Age silver bowls have been found in the Cyclades[1]. The Shaft Graves yielded many cups with concave sides, some with repoussé decoration of spirals[2]. Persson discovered shallow gold bowls among the contents of the late Helladic royal tombs at Midea. Some of these he thought dated to the fifteenth century B.C., though the burials were later[3]. These cups have a more globular shape than our two bowls. They also rest on raised bosses and have handles. E. Davis has pointed out that during the late Helladic period, bowls were more common on the mainland than on Crete[4].

Repoussé decoration on the late Helladic cups is common. One of the Midea pieces carries a pattern of an interlocking ivy leaf

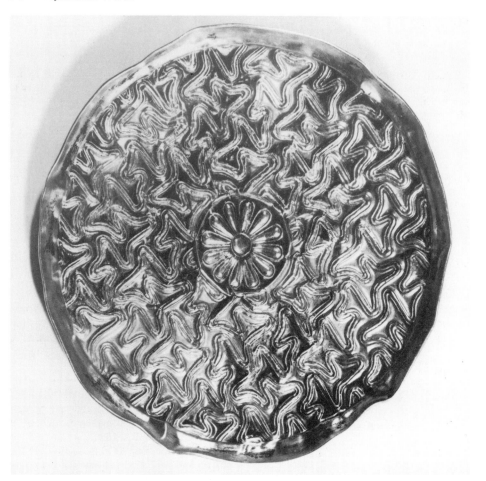

3

chain around its middle. The octopus cup is so-called because of the decoration of four octopuses that float over its entire surface except for the lip and the raised boss. Both these cups were worked from the inside so that the relief is on the exterior.

In addition to the somewhat unusual shape of the Virginia bowl, the pattern of a maeander is not common on Mycenaean pieces. This bowl a curvilinear maeander. One of the grave stele from Shaft Grave Circle A has a similar curved pattern decorating the sides[5]. It is also found on some of the gold repoussé discs garments[6]. The pattern was used to decorate export objects; Frankfort identified an ivory found in Syria at Atchana as Mycenaean because it had this curvilinear decoration[7]. However, in none of these examples is the pattern employed as a maeander.

This bowl and its companion (cat. no. 4), probably belong to a series of twelve bowls all of which have repoussé decorations on the bottom, and each one of which is a variation of one of these two bowls[8]. The bowls are given some individuality through the variation of the rosette and background combinations. Not every bowl in the series has a rosette. Several dishes have swastika background patterns instead of the curvilinear maeander. Always, the bowl shape remains constant. The closest parallel to the Virginia bowl is a dish in Beirut.

The bowls come from the same workshop. They were probably all made by being hammered over a mould. Parrot has argued that their presence in Syria is due to the fact that they were in a royal burial[9]. Aegean gold and silver plate was hoarded by foreigners in some instances[10]. Parrot suggests

4

that this group of bowls comes from a Syrian workshop, but the craftsmen were inspired and influenced by Mycenaean objects [11].

It is still important to note that the bowls lack close parallels for their shape and decoration. The Metropolitan Museum of Art, which owns a similar dish that must be part of the series, considers it to be the product of Phoenician craftsmen [12].

WEM

[1] E. DAVIS, nos. 3, 4, 5.

[2] G. KARO, 1933, no. 868.

[3] A. PERSSON, p. 44, 67.

[4] E. DAVIS, *The Vapheio Cups: One Minoan and One Mycenaean?*, in *Art Bulletin*, 1974, p. 483, n. 64.

[5] H. SCHLIEMANN, *Mycenae; A Narrative of Researches and Discoveries at Mycenae and Tiryns*, New York, 1880, fig. 142, p. 91.

[6] KARO, p. 270-271.

[7] H. KANTOR, p. 101.

[8] Two in the Louvre (AO21115, AO21379), one in the Metropolitan Museum of Art, New York (60-17), one in Seattle (CS6.18), two in Beirut and several in private collections, Parrot, p. 249. One bowl in the series went 1982 on auction in Zürich, Galerie Koller, no. 4.

[9] PARROT, p. 249.

[10] H. SEYRIG, *Note sur le trésor de Tôd*, in *Syria*, 1954, p. 218-224.

[11] PARROT, p. 249.

[12] *BMMA*, 19, no. 2, 1960, p. 38.

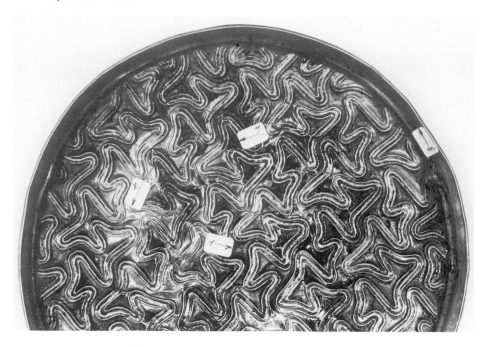

4
Bowl

Mycenaean, said to be from Syria, Late Helladic.
Diam. 17.8 cm; thickness 0.2 cm.
Anonymous European Loan.
Formerly collection of the Comte M.X. du Puytison, Paris.

The surface of the bottom of this bowl is entirely covered with an intricate motif of sinuosities similar to those of no. 3. These repeat themselves while they are alternately disposed to the right and to the left, so that the expanding figure of one sequence is corresponding to the recessing figure of the neighboring sequence (see drawing, p. 37). The curves never touch each other. The curves themselves are made of three grooves embossed into the main curve, worked from outside toward inside. At regular intervals, one may observe small interruptions in the curves which may mark places where the partial mould for the repoussé was readjusted to continue the design (see drawing, p. 39).

This bowl is one of the series originally described by Parrot in 1964. The comparison of the objects themselves (no. 3 and 4) shows that they are made from the same moulds, thus coming from the same workshop.

The ornament is well-known on objects and stelae of the mycenaean shaft graves discovered by Schliemann, as was realized by the scholars who commented the bowls (Parrot, Hankey, Buchholz quoted in the note which follows). These parallels may indicate that the bowls are of a rather early date in mycenaean times.

AD

EDITORIAL NOTE TO 3 AND 4

Although the editors have selected two objects from the well known series of Levantine shallow bowls in gold, they are quite aware that such bowls are the focus of a long lasting authenticity dispute. Parrot first published the find of the bowls two of which, he thought, had been cut into pieces by clandestine finders. Those are now in the

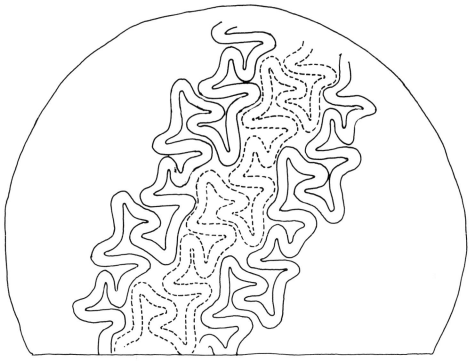

Bowl no. 4. Structural analysis of the decoration (A. Dumont, redrawn by A. van Noorbeek).

museum in Beirut. Parrot listed twelve bowls which are now partly *on exhibit* in various museums, notably the Louvre, the Metropolitan Museum of Art, the Virginia Museum of Fine Arts and the Art Museum in Seattle. Several of these are known to have passed through a famous French private collection in Europe and possibly in the United States. Recently such a bowl in gold was offered for sale at an auction in Zurich.

V. Hankey and H. G. Buchholz have gone so far as to suggest that none of the bowls are authentic. In the interest of truth and fairness, we here reproduce both scholars' statements in full.

V. Hankey, *Mycenean pottery in the Middle East*, in *Annual of the British School at Athens*, 62, 1967, p. 116f.:

Two gold bowls in Beirut Museum (Plate 26 a, b, d, e) are said to have come from a site in Lebanon between Tripoli and Homs (footnote: Syria XLI (1964) 240). This treasure-trove falls outside the category of pottery, but since it is published as Mycenaean (and Mycenaean objects other than pottery are

practically unknown in the Middle East) some comment may be allowed. Parrot asks "s'agit-il d'une œuvre phénicienne mais avec une inspiration mycénienne? L'influence de Mycènes s'est exercée sur la côte phénicienne, sans doute par l'intermédiaire des Crétois". He suggests a date of fourteenth to thirteenth century for the bowls, but does not give any reasons for this conclusion. The bowls are very shallow and have no base ("assiettes, sans grande profondeur"), D. from 0.16 to 0.197, and were obviously intended for ostentation rather than mere use (perhaps they are solar discs). Eleven of the twelve listed by Parrot are worked in the repoussé technique, finished off with a chasing tool, in apparently higher relief than work on the gold cups from Peristeriá (*ILN, Archaeological Section* 2238 of 4.12.65). There are four elements of decoration (*a*) an all-over meander; (*b*) an all-over continuous swastika pattern with a central dot to each swastika; (*c*) a central rosette of six, eight, or twelve petals; (*d*) a central ring of running spiral pattern. The bowls have either (*a*) or (*b*) all over, or a combination of (*a*) or (*b*) with (*c*)

and/or (*d*). The meander and swastika patterns are reminiscent of Early Minoan or Early Helladic sealings, but a later parallel could be found for them on stelai from Grave Circle A at Mycenae (Shaft-Graves II and IV), or in the stele and jug from Grave Circle B, Shaft-Grave *Gamma*. In Asia parallels could also be found in Hittite sealings, and at Troy I. There is, too, a resemblance between the spirals on these pieces and the fragmentary silver cup found in the tomb of Abi Shemou at Byblos. The rosettes are of a recognizable type found at many Mycenaean sites in gold leaf, but by no means an exclusively Mycenaean motif. The shape is much shallower than the gold bowl with a hunting scene from Ras Shamra. The work therefore combines Asiatic and Aegean features, but so far as I know there are no examples of Mycenaean repoussé gold-work combining these elements and the shape. Parrot does not doubt the authenticity of these remarkable works, and if they are genuine they are indeed a rare addition to the list of finds vaguely described as of Aegean inspiration, and seem to be earlier than 1400 B.C. Dealers' provenances, however, are notoriously unreliable especially when they concern gold, and these pieces, being separated from the circumstances of their finding, can add little to the list of contacts along the Phoenician coast.

No Late Bronze remains are known at Tripoli, south of the Akkar plain, but a few Late Bronze finds from tombs south of the city are in private collections in Lebanon. No Mycenaean pottery is among this material.

H. G. Buchholz, *Ägäische Kunst gefälscht*, in *Acta praehistorica et archaeologica* 1, 1970, p. 127: "The exquisitely refined gold of the 'Minoan' gold-ivory goddess in Boston (analysis no. 6) and two richly decorated 'Mycenaean' gold bowls done in repousse, which belong to the Louvre (analysis nos. 8, 9) belong to a much later state in the history of gold, for which reason I ask to be forgiven, that I introduce, again, the 'authenticité indiscutable'.

Buchholz presents then on the same page among his lists the following analysis:

6. Golden snake, the attribute of the 'Minoan' gold-ivory goddess in Boston Inv. no. 14.863 contains mainly gold, traces of silver, a medium amount of copper, and traces of bismuth and iron; not present is

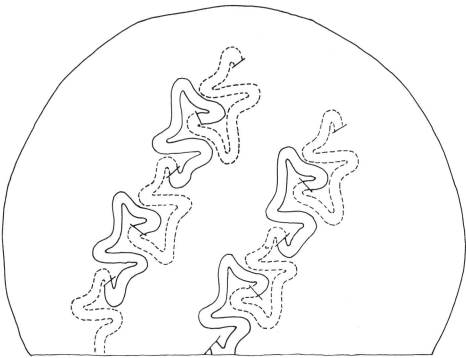

Bowl no. 4, hypothesis for the method of manufacturing (A. Dumont, redrawn by A. van Noorbeek).

iridium; see Vermeule/Young in *Bull Fine Arts Boston* 57, p. 20. The analysis is mostly identical with the analysis made in Boston in order to check a gold bowl from Olympia.

8. "Mycenean" gold bowl from Syria in the Louvre, Inv. no. AO 21115 contains mainly gold, traces of silver, copper, tin, lead, nickel, cobalt, calcium, magnesium and silicon. Cf. Parrot, in *Syria* 41, 1964, 240 ff., fig. 21, pl. 15 and also V. Hankey, in *AnnBSA* 67, 1967, 116 f., pl. 26 a, b (with cautious scepticism). Lebanon is mentioned as the place of the find, while the bowl in Seattle, Art Museum (gift of Mr. and Mrs. Reed) is said to have been found in the neighborhood of Homs: M. B. Rogers, in *Archaeology*, 17, 1964, 269 with figure.

9. Same kind of bowl in the Louvre Inv. no. AO 21379 contains mainly gold, traces of silver, copper, tin lead, calcium, magnesium and silicon. Cf. Parrot p. 242 f., fig. 22, pl. 16, p. 249, a list of altogether twelve examples from Syria, mostly in private collections. To be added is a gold bowl strangely decorated with spirals, formerly in the collection of

Giamalakis; see L. von Matt, *Das antike Kreta*, 1967, p. 171" [1].

In 1974 H. G. Buchholz resumed the argument citing his and Hankey's earlier publications in the following words (*Archäologischer Anzeiger*, 89, 1974, p. 434 f.):

"In addition V. Hankey has discussed two flat bowls in the National Museum in Beirut, done in repousse and decorated with ornaments, the infinite rapport and in the center rosettes and spirals. It is self-evident that these ornaments derive largely from Aegean motifs. Hankey mentioned a combination of Near Eastern and Cretan-Mycenaean traits and arrived at a date which was considerably before 1400 B.C. 'if they are genuine'? One wonders about the old age in view of the meagerness of Aegean imports into Syria during the 16th and 15th centuries B.C., to be added is Lebanon as the site where they were said to be found 'between Tripolis and Homs', an information that goes back to the art dealers, who talked about a clandestine dig. Evidently from the same dealers' sources came two additional such bowls made in gold, which are now in the Louvre; these were published by Parrot as undoubtedly authentic. This must be a strange, hidden find place, from which beside the examples mentioned come ten more, which ended up mostly in private collections and for which there are no stylistic comparisons nor parallels as far as such a concentration of a find in the Aegean culture nor the Near East goes! The piece in Seattle is said to be found 'near Homs', i.e. not found in the Lebanon! (M.B. Rogers, *Archaeology*, 17, 1964, 269 with fig.). The last word has yet to be said as far as the authenticity of these pieces goes. To the contrary: the high degree of purity of the gold has no parallel in the second millennium B.C., it is indicative for refining methods as they were known only much later" [2].

This argumentation evokes several provisional thoughts. First, it is well known that the 16th and 15th centuries have not yet been subjected to as much archaeological investigation as the subsequent periods. Without supporting evidence from numerous other finds and sites, an exceptional find complex may strike the observer as isolated, hence implausible, and, finally, suspect. Secondly, relations between the Aegean and the area stretching from the Levant down to Egypt are well documented at least as far back as the Middle Minoan period. Imports from the Aegean are attested in coastal regions and also the interior. Naturally, the older the period, the scarcer are the finds in this particular case. Thirdly, as to the sizable number of objects in this find, which appears to startle Prof. Buchholz, it is rather astonishing that the Treasure of Tod, the Royal Tombs of Byblos and many Aegean finds bear testimony to the concentration of wealth in just a few institutions or families. The Pylos tablets indicate that concentrations of precious metal objects were the norm (see the article by W. Mierse in this catalogue) such as the recently discovered Hebla tablets. Even in Classical Athens it was well known that gold and silver plates were stored in temples. Archaeological finds of such concentration are naturally exceptional, but are hardly suspect for that reason alone. 4. The fragmentary state of the bowls now in Beirut is

matched by chiseled marks on the rims of some as if they had been destined for cutting into pieces as well. Furthermore, there are traces of reshaping on the rims as duly noted in the Koller auction catalogue. All this evidence does not indicate a uniformly invented group of forgeries, although one could theoretically imagine that some of the pieces were produced by imitation, when the clandestine finders discovered that the first fragmentary items encountered a vivid interest in the Beirut museum, especially among French archaeologists. From archaeological circles the tale could have spread to the commercial circles, as happens so often. Looking at the facts and the probabilities, one sees no necessity for an overall acceptation or damnation. 5. With respect to the purity of the gold, the analysis for the pieces in the Louvre is not given in terms of percentages and Parrot (*Syria* 41, 1964, 241 [2]) interpreted the same report in another way. Very few gold objects from this period have been analysed and a mere handful of analyses have been published. Due to the kindness of Prof. G. Demortier we can present here the analysis of the bowl offered for sale at the Koller auction and a recent analysis of cat. no. 4.

The technique used for such analyses is described by Prof. Demortier in this volume p. 215 ss.

Bowl no. 4
Relative concentrations in percentages

Cu	Ag	Au	Impact no.
0.05	17.35	82.6	1
0.1	17.85	82.05	2
0.05	16.2	83.75	3
0.05	17.95	82.0	4
0.15	18.0	81.85	5

Bowl in Zurich sale

0.0	13.8	86.2	487
0.2	17.6	82.2	488

These results don't seem to be "indicative for refining methods as they were known much later".

Furthermore, we are providing a report by Dr. R. Mauterer, the Secretary for the

Austrian Society for Archaeometry, on the reddish polishing substance left on the surface of the bowls, at least in many spots[3].

In our view there is no doubt that such questions of authenticity have to be raised and possibly settled with the aid of circumstantial evidence, the more so, because several institutions of international reputation have considered these objects as important examples illustrating the Mycenean presence in the Levant. Despite the scepticism quoted above, Prof. Amiet selected one of the bowls in the Louvre for illustration in his most representative book on the Ancient Near East (*L'art ancien de l'Orient*, coll. Mazenod, Paris 1977, no. 510). Prof. Buchholz wrote in 1974: "Über die Echtheit dieser Objekte ist das letzte Wort nicht gesprochen", which amounts to our conclusion: *Adhuc sub iudice lis est*.

Tony HACKENS and Rolf WINKES

[1] "Die fein geläuterten Goldsorten von der 'minoischen' Gold-Elfenbein-Göttin in Boston (Analysen-Num. 6, cf. supra Pag. 115) und von zwei, mit reichem Dekor in Treibtechnik versehenen 'mykenischen' Goldschalen des Louvre (Analysen-Num. 8, 9) entsprechen einem viel späteren Befund in der Geschichte des Goldes, weshalb man mir verzeihen möge, wenn ich ihre 'authenticité indiscutable' nun doch erneut zur Diskussion stelle".

"6. Goldene Schlange, Attribut der 'minoischen' Gold-Elfenbein-Göttin, Boston, Inv. Num. 14.863. Gold: Hauptmenge, Silber: Spuren, Kupfer: mittlere Menge, Zink: Spuren, Eisen: Spuren, cf. Nota 80 (Nota 80: Iridium: Spuren; cf. Vermeule/ W. J. Younng, in: Bull. Mus. Fine Arts Boston 57 Num. 307 (1959) 4 ss.; ferner R. J. Forbes, Bergbau, Steinbruchtätigkeit und Hüttenwesen (1967) 19, Nota 100 (= F. Matz/H. G. Buchholz (Ed.) Archaeologia Homerica — Die Denkmäler und das frühgriechische Epos, Lieferung K).

8. 'Mykenische' Goldschale aus Syrien, Louvre, Inv. Nr. AO 21115. Gold: Hauptmenge, Silber: Spuren, Kupfer: Spuren, Blei: Spuren, Kobalt: Spuren, cf. Nota 81 (Nota 81: Cf. Nota 26. — Iridium: nicht vorhanden; Vermeule/Young[80], Pag. 20, Analyse fast identisch mit der zur Kontrolle an einer griechischen Goldschale aus Olympia in Boston vorgenommenen Analyse).

9. Ditto, Inv. Num. AO 21379. Gold: Hauptmenge, Silber: Spuren, Kupfer: Spuren, Blei: Spuren, cf. Nota 84 (Nota 84: Ausserdem in Spuren enthalten: Kalzium, Magnesium, Silizium;

Parrot[83], Pag. 242s., Fig. 22, Tab. 16; Pag. 249: Liste von insgesamt 12 Exemplaren aus Syrien, überwiegend in Privatbesitz. Hinzu tritt eine merkwürdig spiralverzierte Goldschale der ehemaligen Sammlung Giamalakis: Matt[32], Pag. 171, Fig. supra)".

[2] "Außerdem hat V. Hankey zwei flache Goldschalen im Nationalmuseum von Beirut (Notes 116f. Taf. 26a, b) besprochen, die in Treibtechnik über mit Ornamenten 'unendlichen Rapports', im Zentrum mit Rosetten und Laufspiralen verziert sind. Daß diese Ornamente größtenteils dem ägäischen Motivschatz entlehnt sind, liegt auf der Hand. V. Hankey sprach von einer Kombination asiatischer mit kretisch-mykenischen Zügen und gelangte zu einer Datierung wesentlich vor 1400 v. Chr., "if they are genuine"! Das hohe Alter gibt zu denken, wenn man die Geringfügigkeit der ägäischen Importe nach Syrien während des 16. und 15. Jhs. v. Chr. berücksichtigt, dazu die Fundangabe "Libanon, zwischen Tripolis und Homs", welche auf Kunsthändler zurückgeht, die von einer Raubgrabung sprachen. Offenbar aus gleicher Händlerquelle gelangten zwei solcher Goldteller in den Louvre (AO 21115 und AO 21379); sie wurden von A. Parrot als unzweifelhaft echt publiziert (Syria 41, 1964, 240 ff. Taf. 15, 16). Welch eigenartiger, geheimer Fundplatz müßte das sein, von welchem außer den genannten Stücken noch zehn weitere stammen, die größtenteils in Privatsammlungen gelangten (Liste bei A. Parrot a.O. 249) und für die es weder dem Stil und der angeblichen Fundkonzentration nach Vergleiche im ägäischen Kulturkreis oder im Nahen Osten gibt! Das Stück in Seattle, Art Museum, gilt als "bei Homs gefunden", also nicht im Libanon! (M. B. Rogers, Archaeology 17, 1964, 269 mit Abb.).

Über die Echtheit dieser Objekte ist das letzte Wort nicht gesprochen. Im Gegenteil: die bemerkenswert große Reinheit des verwendeten Goldes findet keine Parallele im 2. Jt. v. Chr.; vielmehr bekundet sie Läuterungsverfahren, welche erst bedeutend später aufkamen (H.-G. Buchholz, APA 1, 1970, 126 f. mit Liste und Literaturangaben von Goldanalysen)".

[3] Letter dated Jan. 23rd 1983: "Der auf den Schalen aufsitzende rote Belag bestand im wesentlichen aus Polierrot (Synonyme: Pariser Rot, Englisch Rot, Rouge, Englisch-rot, Pompejanisch Rot, Venezianisch Rot), chemisch im wesentlichen Roteisenerz, d.h. Fe_3O_4 mit Fe_2O_3. Diese — leicht zugänglichen — Stoffe wurden seit dem Altertum für Polierzwecke — besonders bei harten Werkstoffen — verwendet. Irgend welche weiteren Folgerungen aus der An- oder Abwesenheit dieses Stoffes zu ziehen erscheint mir daher nicht zweckmässig".

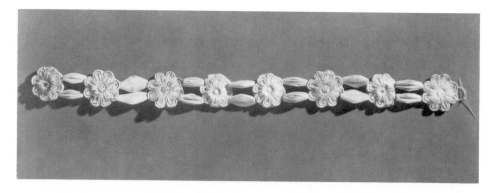

5

Necklace of glass paste and faience

Mycenaean, provenance unknown, Late
Helladic III.
L. 28 cm.
The Toledo Museum of Art, Gift of
Edward Drummond Libbey.
Acc. no. 53.139.
Bibliography:
*A Land Called Crete: An Exhibition
Organized by the Smith College Mu-
seum of Art*, October 6 - November 9,
1967, Northampton, Mass., 1967,
no. 55.
R. M. RIEFSTAHL, *Ancient and Near
Eastern Glass*, in *Museum News, The
Toledo Museum of Art*, N.S. 4, no. 2,
1961, p. 29.

This necklace is composed of eight blue
glass paste rosettes with double linking
faience bands. The rosettes are pressed out
of a mould and are all identical: each with
eight petals and incised details for the petals
and the central point. Two strings would
have passed through the two faience bands
securing the rosettes along the top and
bottom. The necklace shows some signs of
weathering but is otherwise in fine condition.

The rosette as a decorative motif appears
early in Mycenaean art. Applied and repoussé rosettes decorate goblets from the Shaft
Graves [1]. Rodenwaldt catalogued a rosette
atop a stalk as one of the fresco border
patterns from the older palace at Tiryns.
The source for the rosette he thought might

ultimately be Egypt, but he maintained that it
had come by way of the Minoans who had
altered the Egyptian form [2].

We find mould-made or pressed and
stamped rosettes on jewelry from the beginning of the late Helladic I and II periods at
Prosymna [3]. A necklace of eighteen large
gold rosettes was found in the Tholos Tomb
at Midea [4]. Gold rosette ornaments for
clothing came from the so-called Tomb of
Clytemnestra and probably date to about
1300 B.C. [5]. There are ivory combs from the
late Helladic III period that are decorated
with a rosette [6].

Faience was both locally produced and
imported from Egypt and the Levant at this
time [7]. Steatite moulds for casting faience
have been uncovered at Mycenae [8]. The
faience from the Shaft Graves probably came
from Knossos [9].

The glass and faience necklace form
appears to have become popular during the
late Helladic era. Pressed and moulded gold
ornaments began to be replaced by paste and
faience versions. Sometimes the copies were
gilded to represent gold, or the paste was
blue, as in our example, to suggest lapis
lazuli. A close parallel to our piece is one in
the Metropolitan Museum of Art, New York
which is terracotta with gilt [10]. Becatti has
pointed out that during the late Helladic era,
imitation became standard practice [11].

WEM

[1] G. Karo, 1933, no. 122, 351.
[2] G. Rodenwaldt, *Tiryns*, 2, *Die Fresken des Palastes*, Athens, 1912, p. 33-34.
[3] C. W. Blegen, p. 297.
[4] A. Persson, p. 40, no. 2.
[5] A. J. B. Wace, *Mycenae, an Archaeological History and Guide*, Princeton, 1949, p. 18, 36.
[6] Blegen, p. 282.
[7] *Ibid.*, p. 306-307.
[8] Wace, p. 110.
[9] A. J. B. Wace et al., *Excavations at Mycenae 1939-1955*, E. French, ed., (*BSA, Suppl. vol.*, 12), Oxford, 1979, p. 111-112.
[10] C. Alexander, *Some Late Helladic Gilt Terracottas*, in *BMMA*, 34, 1939, p. 216, fig. 2.
[11] Becatti, p. 29.

6
Pair of earrings

Mycenaean, perhaps from Cyprus, Late Helladic III C.
Heads: L. 1.8 cm, max. w. 1.5 cm; L. 1.7 cm, max. w. 1.5 cm; Hoops: diam. 1.6 cm.
Anonymous European loan.

The pair of gold earrings consists of a gold hoop with overlapping ends and a pendant. The bull's head pendants are raised from thin sheets of gold beaten over a mould to create the embossed details. A separate sheets form the backside and is seamed to the front. The pendants are hollow.

Except for some bent edges, a tear in the gold foil, and a hole in the forehead of one animal, the earrings are in excellent condition.

The two heads are analogous but not identical. They appear to be almost mirror images. The modeling defines certain facial features, and both sides of the head are embossed with similar details. Eyes and eye sockets are clearly rendered. The ears are treated sculpturally. The forehead, snout and muzzle are covered with repoussé patterning of crisscrossed recessed lines and raised areas. To set off the muzzle, it has been patterned with horizontal striping and the nostrils are indicated by slight indentations of the gold skin. The crisscrossing does not extend to the cheeks. A curved incised line running between the ears separates the forehead clearly. The horns are not represented, but the holes through which the hoop passes are given a bold, raised outline. The hoop acts as the horns.

The bull belongs to the general iconographic repertory of both Crete and the mainland. There is the bull leaping fresco from Knossos and the bull's head rhyton from Shaft Grave IV. Bulls in relief decorate the two cups from a tomb at Vapheio, and several gems are decorated with intaglio bulls. On later Mycenaean pottery, bulls appear as decoration. Bulls are not, however, known on earrings from the mainland. The closest examples of bull's head earrings from Crete are conical pendants with horn-like hoops. The cones are covered in granulation and terminate in large bulbs. Hood identifies the type as Minoan[1]. Amandry also attributes the form to Crete but suggests that there may be Cypriot influences[2].

Exact parallels for this pair come from Cyprus. Karageorghis has found four examples of repoussé bull's head earrings in one grave from Kition[3]. The associated pottery dates the finds to about 1225 B.C., late Helladic III B. All the earrings show variations in length, diameter and repoussé details. These facts suggest that there were several moulds from which the repoussé heads could be produced. These earrings are not unlike the stylized and repetitive floral and marine motifs stamped on beads for necklaces from the mainland during the late Helladic era.

Why this earring type should have originated in Cyprus is not certain. Earrings did remain a popular jewelry item on Cyprus and Crete though they disappeared on the mainland after the beginning of the late Helladic I period.

WEM

[1] S. Hood, p. 205.
[2] P. Amandry, p. 19, no. 3.

[3] G. Karageorghis, *Excavations at Kition*, 1, *The Tombs*, Nicosia, 1974, p. 69-70, no. 134, 140, p. 80, no. 308.

EARLY AND CLASSICAL GREECE

Our knowledge of the period between the destruction of the Mycenaean palaces and the beginning of the ninth century B.C. in the Aegean world is still meager. Around 900 B.C., however, the picture changes, and the ensuing two hundred years which comprise the Geometric period saw the gradual resumption of trade and social contact with the East, and the beginning of colonization in the West. With increasing prosperity and the formation of cities, gold and other metals, always scarce in Greece itself, began to be imported from the eastern Mediterranean. Archaeological evidence from graves and sanctuaries indicates that as early as the mid-ninth century B.C., gold jewelry was used in Greece, especially for burials. More than many other materials, the jewelry reveals early Oriental influence, both in style and in technique [1].

Toward 700 B.C., the orientalizing style of the earlier years gave way to a quieter and more restrained expression. At this time, there was little gold jewelry recorded in Attica. A major center of jewelry was Ephesus in Ionia, near the rich gold-producing areas of Phrygia and Lydia. From places like Ephesus, eastern styles were further spread throughout Greece. Central and northern Greece were subject to additional influences from their northern neighbors, a region of gold deposits. On Rhodes, we have especially Camirus and Ialysus, and some gold jewelry has also been found on the islands of Delos, Thera and Melos [2].

Early in their literary history, the Greeks express their appreciation for finely crafted gold. The following lines by a famous seventh century B.C. Spartan poet are indicative of this:

> ... With wrists snakebound we stand or fall
> Our golden, written serpents stare,
> Lydian bright bands bind our hair
> We stand, contending, jeweled girls ...

Alkman, Hymn to Artemis [3]

---

[1] J. N. COLDSTREAM, *Geometric Greece*, New York, 1977, p. 17-21, 55-72. Graves at the Areopagus and Kerameikos cemeteries in Athens, and at Lefkandi in Euboea have yielded gold earrings with granulation and filigree (fig. 13e), gold rings and diadems (fig. 14a and 16 and fig 19c-d). The author suggests the presence of Phoenician traders and craftsmen around Athens to explain the Oriental influences, in some cases arriving there by way of Cyprus. Toward the end of the ninth century B.C. there is evidence of the further spread of eastern richness and stylistic features at the Teke Tholos Tomb in Crete, where some of the jewelry can be compared with that found previously at Eleusis and Anavysos, p. 99-102, fig. 32; Bernhard SCHWEITZER, *Greek Geometric Art*, trans. P. and C. Usborne, New York, 1971. The author notes that Assyrian influence began its spread toward the west in the first quarter of the ninth century, reaching Syria toward mid-century, p. 18. In his study of the numerous gold bands found in eighth century B.C. graves at Athens, this author suggests craftsmen of Rhodian origin and postulates the spread of orientalizing motifs from Syria and Cilicia by way of the islands of Cyprus, Rhodes and Crete, p. 186-200.

[2] R. HIGGINS, *Greek and Roman Jewellery*, 2nd ed., Berkeley, 1980, p. 95-106.

[3] *Archilochos, Sappho, Alkman, Three Lyric Poets of the Late Greek Bronze Age*, trans. G. Davenport, Berkeley, 1980, Alkman: 6; 2-5. Written for a chorus of Spartan girls dressed as doves to sing at dawn on the feast of the plow, p. 137.

The subsequent Archaic period was an era of active trade and interchange throughout the Greek world, particularly for those of the powerful aristocratic class. It was notably against their displays of luxury and excess that the renowned poet-legislator Solon of Athens in the years 594-593 B.C. instituted his democratic reforms, while pleading for moderation and rational control in all matters. Among his actions as archon was the issuance of sumptuary restrictions, in particular against excessive display and expense in regard to funerals[4]. In Sparta, too, Plutarch credits the legendary Lycurgus with the outlawing of "all needless and superfluous arts", and with the calling in of all gold and silver coins, since no gold- or silversmith, engraver or jeweler would linger in a country which had no money[5]. The largely symbolic story of the debate between Solon and the Oriental potentate Croesus of Lydia was a favorite in Greece because it successfully pitted this Hellenic moderation against its eastern antithesis, barbarian luxury and material display. Croesus, who in legend was later to see the error of his ways, is said to have met Solon at Sardis resplendent in every possible variety of "precious stones, dyed raiment and wrought gold". Croesus was said to have dedicated his wife's golden necklace and girdle at the shrine at Delphi, thereby earning the admiration of the Greek populace[6]. In a way, Croesus was donating an *agalma* to the sanctuary, an *agalma* in its original meaning; i.e., a piece of jewelry, as well as a precious possession that one may give to a divinity[7].

Turning to the archaeological evidence for the Archaic period, we find that the major sources for modern museum collections of gold jewelry are Rhodes, Cyprus, South Russia, and Sicily and southern Italy. At this time, due to the shortage of gold, Greek goldsmiths found it necessary to work where gold was more plentiful[8]. Late Archaic warrior graves at Trebenischte in Illyria near Lake Ochrid, and at Olbia and Kelermes in South Russia contained gold sheet masks and other ornaments[9]. By 600 B.C., Greek cities were firmly established on the Thracian coast, providing a ready market for resident Greek goldsmiths[10].

---

[4] PLUTARCH, *Solon*, 21.2-5. Modern scholarship suggests that later writers, Aristotle and Plutarch included, characterized those laws enacted later, at the end of the fifth century B.C., as Solonian, thus investing them with the power of antiquity. Additionally, laws enacted before the time of Solon and unrecorded were ascribed to him in later times, as his legend grew: A. R. BURN, *The Lyric Age of Greece*, London, 1960, p. 294-301; R. S. STROUD, *State Documents in Archaic Athens*, p. 20-75, in *Athens Comes of Age, from Solon to Salamis*, Princeton, 1978.

[5] PLUTARCH, *Lycurgus*. While there is some disagreement, most scholars of today see Lycurgus as almost wholly legendary, but symbolic of the Spartan aversion to luxury and decadence; J. R. HOOKER, *The Ancient Spartans*, London, 1980, p. 132-138; P. OLIVA, *Sparta and her Social Problems*, trans. I. Urwin-Lewitova, Prague, 1971, p. 63-70.

[6] PLUTARCH, *Solon*, 27.2-4, "a most august and gorgeous spectacle".

[7] H. BLOESCH, *Agalma, Kleinod, Weihgeschenk, Götterbild*, Bern-Bümpliz, 1943. See also *Anzeiger für die Altertumswissenschaft*, 3, 1950, p. 140-150.

[8] HIGGINS, *op. cit.*, p. 121.

[9] D. C. KURTZ and J. BOARDMAN, *Greek Burial Customs*, London, 1971, p. 316-319; D. M. BUITRON, *Greek Jewelry*, in *Jewelry, Ancient to Modern*, A. Garside, ed., The Walters Art Gallery, Baltimore, 1979, p. 72-93. The author notes the purple film on the gold masks and diadems caused by the burning of the bodies in full paraphernalia at a sixth century B.C. warrior's grave at Chalkidike in northern Greece.

[10] L. CASSON, *The Thracians*, in *Thracian Treasures from Bulgaria*, The Metropolitan Museum of Art, New York, 1977, p. 3-6.

Following the Persian wars, and due to the exploitation of the mines at Mount Pangaeus, gold became more plentiful[11]. Major centers of discovery for the fifth century B.C. are in Eretria, the Peloponnese and in Cyprus, South Russia and Thrace[12]. Excavations at Duvanlij in the Plovdiv district of Bulgaria have provided numerous and striking examples of the work of Greek goldsmiths of the period[13]. For the fourth century B.C., sources are, as before, in Cyprus and South Russia, but there are some changes. Jewelry production in Sicily had declined as Dionysius of Syracuse minted large quantities of coins in an effort to pay the mercenaries needed for his wars with Carthage. Of course, jewelry is still represented on Sicilian coins, but this could be jewelry worn by the aristocratic members of society[14]. At this time, southern Italy became a major center for gold jewelry, especially at Tarentum, where it is believed that clothing was exported in exchange for gold from Egypt. Throughout the Classical period, Near Eastern influences continued to affect jewelry styles, and as the fourth century advanced, gold jewelry became increasingly elaborate, culminating in the decorative Hellenistic style.

Dedicating at sanctuaries was a common activity of both men and women in Greece, and the latter were free to dedicate their jewelry if they wished. The Greek woman legally owned little except her clothing and jewelry. These personal effects were independent of her dowry, and she was permitted to take them with her when she was divorced, widowed or remarried[15].

As far as archaeological evidence goes, most burials are not rich in offerings, especially those of Attica in Classical times. The rich burials were in the provinces where Athenian laws regulating expense were not binding, and where jewelry and gold itself were more plentiful[16]. For those less affluent, cheaper substitutes of terracotta were made in imitation of pieces worn in life[17]. Some jewelry, in particular the funerary diadems, are of special manufacture and design[18]. In the fifth century B.C. the dead were sometimes wreathed to signify victories in life, and some of these wreaths were delicately crafted in gold[19].

Sculpture, vase painting and literature provide additional evidence that jewelry played its part in the cults and rituals connected with death. Schanz notes Pausanias' description of a sculptural group in Achaia, long-vanished, in which the

---

[11] BUITRON, *op. cit.*, p. 72-93.

[12] HIGGINS, *op. cit.*, p. 122-123.

[13] I. WENEDIKOW and I. MARASOW, *Gold der Thraker, Archäologische Schätze aus Bulgarien*, Mainz, 1979, p. 89-97, 106-109.

[14] For a catalogue of some of these coins, see G.K. JENKINS, *Coins of Greek Sicily*, British Museum, London, 1966.

[15] D.M. SCHAPS, *Economic Rights of Women in Ancient Greece*, Edinburgh, 1979, p. 70-102.

[16] KURTZ and BOARDMAN, *op. cit.*, p. 140-166. The authors note that further excavations in Attica may change this picture. They believe, however, that in Classical times bodies were often buried in nothing more than a shroud. But burial practices differed, and by the fourth century B.C. the richer graves have jewelry *in situ* on the body.

[17] MARSHALL, *BMCJ*, p. 39. The museum has a collection of such terracotta imitations (pl. 42). It is believed that they were offered as dedications at sanctuaries, as well as for funeral use.

[18] D. OHLY, *Griechische Goldbleche*, Berlin, 1953, p. 68. Goldbands, made of thin gold foil, are too delicate to withstand use in life, and may be considered as death cult items.

[19] A. OLIVER, *Jr., Greek, Roman and Etruscan Jewelry*, in *BMMA*, 11, 1976, p. 269-284.

Fig. 1. White-ground lekythos by the Phiale Painter, ca. 440-430 B.C., Munich, Museum Antiker Kleinkunst.

three sisters of a dead warrior are shown slipping off their bracelets as the first manifestation of mourning for their brother [20]. If the removal of ornaments denotes the loss of a loved one, there is some indication that the act of putting on one's jewelry is in some sense a prelude to one's own death and preparation to enter Hades. Several Attic grave reliefs of the fifth and fourth centuries B.C. depict women holding jewel boxes brought to them by their young servant girls. The *Stele of Hegeso* shows Hegeso gazing at her jewelry, perhaps choosing how she will be adorned in death [21]. Fig. 1 illustrates a white-ground lekythos by the Phiale Painter, ca. 440-430 B.C., on which a woman is shown putting on a diadem prior to her

[20] H. L. SCHANZ, *Greek Sculptural Groups, Archaic and Classical*, New York, 1980, p. 88-89; *Pausanias' Description of Greece*, 5, trans. J. G. Frazer, 1898: 7. 26. 3. The role of jewelry in ritualistic and cultic practices has an earlier origin in the ancient Near East. In the ancient Sumerian-Akkadian myth, the goddess Inanna-Ishtar, at each successive stage in her descent to the underworld, divests herself of a single ornament until all are removed and she has reached her destination. See «Descent of Ishtar to the Nether World», *The Ancient Near East, An Anthology of Texts and Pictures*, 1, J. B. Pritchard, ed., Princeton, 1958, p. 80-85, ANET 106-109.

[21] K. F. JOHANSEN, *The Attic Grave-Reliefs of the Classical Period*, Copenhagen, 1951, p. 19, fig. 5; p. 17, 18, 61, 155-157. On occasion, the dead are depicted holding a taenia or funeral vase instead of jewelry; the meaning in these instances is clear.

Fig. 2. Volute-krater by the Karneia Painter, end of the 5th c. B.C., Tarentum, Museo Archeologico.

departure for the underworld. Hermes, the messenger god, waits to guide her on the journey into Hades [22].

More information is gained from vase paintings and coins, which can be dated with some certainty. Only occasionally do we see jewelry on men, although the mythological figure, Eros, is often festooned with it and certain young dandies adorned themselves with such things as metal anklets. Thucydides scoffed at the rich old men who fastened a knot of their hair with a tie in the form of a golden grasshopper [23]. Men did, however, wear amulets for magical purposes, as talismans against an uncertain fate. Plutarch notes that when Pericles was dying of the plague, he allowed the women caring for him to hang an amulet around his neck, although when well he would have considered the practice foolish [24]. Signet and swivel rings with engraved semi-precious stones were popular for men, although Aristophanes ridiculed some who wore them as "fops, signet-and-jewel bedecked" [25]. Nevertheless, in earlier times the Athenian kouroi sometimes wore a single plain ornament, perhaps a necklace. In Cyprus, where Oriental influences were strong, there was less restraint, and we find male sculptural figures adorned with earrings, heavy necklaces and bands which encircle the upper arms [26]. Fibulae were used

[22] P. E. Arias and M. Hirmer, *A History of 1000 Years of Greek Vase Painting*, New York, 1960, p. 364-365, pl. 41, 42, in Munich, Museum Antiker Kleinkunst, inv. no. 2797; Kurtz and Boardman, *op. cit.*, p. 207. The authors note that the «adornment of Hades» is referred to by ancient authors: Euripides, *Medea*, 980 and *Alcestis*, 613, 631-632.

[23] Thucydides, 1.6.

[24] Plutarch, *Pericles*, 38.

[25] Aeschylus, trans. G. M. Cookson; Sophocles, trans. R. Jebb; Euripides, trans. D. P. Coleridge; Aristophanes, trans. B. B. Rogers, Encyclopedia Britannica, Chicago, 1952; Aristophanes, *Clouds*, 335.

[26] J. L. Myres, *Handbook of the Cesnola Collection of Antiquities from Cyprus*, The Metropolitan Museum of Art, New York, 1914, p. 194, no. 1251, p. 199, no. 1266, p. 220, no. 1356; Marshall,

Fig. 3. Silver diadrachm from Pandosia, obverse, head of Hera facing, ca. 400 B.C., Museum of Fine Arts, Boston.

universally to fasten clothing and were necessary in particular for the loose, short chlamys of the warrior.

On vase paintings through the sixth and fourth centuries B.C. we see jewelry worn by young brides and matrons at home and on ceremonial occasions, and by cavorting maenads and courtesans. There are necklaces, snake bracelets and delicate earrings (fig. 2)[27]. Hetairai and flute girls serve and entertain at symposia, dressed in filmy attire or nude. Most wear amulets and chains around their necks, arms and ankles, and all wear earrings either of the disc type or those with elaborate hanging pendants[28]. While clothing for women is simple, coiffures are carefully arranged with long hair lifted and secured by means of hairbands, diadems and ornaments. Coins often provide additional detail on jewelry and the manner in which it was worn. On a silver stater from Pandosia in Magna Graecia, ca. 400 B.C., Hera is splendidly arrayed in a crown with palmette motif, she wears

BMCJ, p. 165, fig. 46, terracotta figure wearing spiral earrings; p. 166, fig. 47, Archaic sculptured relief wearing "leech" earring through ear; p. 167, fig. 48, a terracotta statuette with "leech" earring through nose.

[27] ARIAS and HIRMER, *op. cit.*, pl. 231, p. 387-388, volute-krater by the Karneia Painter, end of fifth century B.C., in Tarentum, Museo Nazionale Archeologico, inv. no. 8263.

[28] For an overview of women and ornament in the Archaic period, see J. BOARDMAN, *Athenian Red Figure Vases, The Archaic Period, a Handbook*, London, 1975 and J. BOARDMAN, *Athenian Black Figure Vases*, New York, 1974. For hetairai in attendance at komoi, see J. MARCADÉ and W. ZSCHIETZSCHMANN, *Eros Kalos, Studien über die erotischen Darstellungen in der Griechischen Kunst*, Hamburg, 1962. For headgear hetairai were required to wear to identify them as prostitutes, illus. p. 158.

an earring composed of an inversed granulation pyramid (fig. 3)[29], and acorn necklace.

In literature, women are sometimes judged worthy or otherwise by their ability to resist those who would seduce them with gold and precious jewels. Earlier, Homer vividly described the splendor of the gifts offered to the patient and incorruptible Penelope by her suitors. The moral is clearly drawn: virtue is approved and justly rewarded[30]. In contrast, we have the legend of the treacherous and doomed Scylla, who is induced by the bribe of a golden necklace to pull out of her father's head the immortal hair on which his life depends. As a result of her greed, Megara falls, and she herself is punished by being turned into a seabird[31]. The theme of the maiden corrupted by gold recurs in the fifth century B.C. drama, *The Libation Bearers* by Aeschylus, in which the chorus sings of the havoc wrought by the passions of unscrupulous and foolish women[32]. Again, in his *Agamemnon*, Aeschylus expresses his fear of beautiful and dangerous women when he characterizes Helen with the words:

> ... The windless water's witchery
> Was hers; a jewel in the Crown
> Of Wealth that sparkles soft was she ...[33]

Jewelry, in particular brooches and pins, is sometimes referred to in a context of violence in ancient literature. Herodotus describes how the women of Athens, whose husbands had been killed in the battle against the Argives and Aeginetans, murdered the lone survivor on his return by striking him repeatedly with the brooches which fastened their dresses. They were punished for this act by being made to wear the linen tunic of Ionia, which did not require fastenings. The Argives and Aeginetans, in turn, commemorated their victory by decreeing that their women, henceforth, wear brooches half again as large, and that they dedicate only brooches in the temples of their goddesses[34]. Finally, in *Oedipus Rex*, Sophocles has Oedipus destroy his own eyes by piercing them again and again with golden brooches taken from the robe of his dead queen Jocasta[35].

One may sense a certain ambiguity in the minds of the Greeks of the Archaic and Classical periods concerning gold and fine jewelry. Literature and art suggest that they were captivated and sometimes mesmerized by the splendor of beautiful objects. Yet due to their perception of themselves as more spiritual, more capable of restraint than others, there are frequent instances of denial. That denial was most often focused on their eastern neighbors, the Persians, on whose taste and customs they had so often drawn.

Morag MURRAY

[29] G. SELTMAN, *Masterpieces of Greek Coinage*, Cambridge, 1949, fig. 32a, silver didrachm from Pandosia, ca. 400 B.C., obverse, head of Hera.

[30] *Odyssey*, 18. 290-301, 23. 205-245. Brooches, it seems, were an appropriate gift. Penelope received no less than twelve of them, in pure gold, to fasten her gloriously embroidered robe.

[31] M. GRANT, *Myths of the Greeks and Romans*, New York, 1962, p. 150, 316. In some versions of the legend, it is a gift of Cretan gold bracelets which brings about the tragedy.

[32] AESCHYLUS, *Choephoroe*, 610-618.

[33] AESCHYLUS, *Agamemnon*, 43-45, supra, n. 25.

[34] HERODOTUS, 5. 87, 88.

[35] SOPHOCLES, *Oedipus Rex*, 1263-1281.

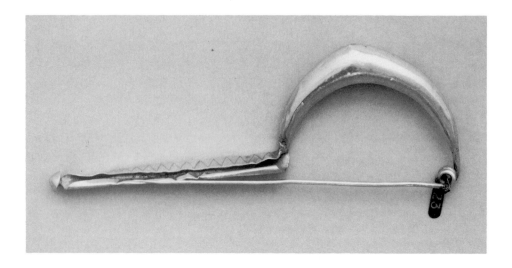

7
Bow fibula

Archaic, South Italian, 6th c. B.C.
L. 13.2 cm; h. 4.6 cm.
The Museum of Fine Arts, Houston.
   Acc. no. 41.10.
Gift of Mr. and Mrs. Nicolas de
   Koenigsberg.

This large and well-preserved fibula is made from yellow sheet gold, with a hollow bow. There are some minor dents along the length of the sheath where the pin is held. The bow expands toward the top, where a small swelling in the metal creates the illusion of a pointed arch. The sheath forms a slender triangle which terminates in a small conical capsule. The inner face of the sheath, left open to receive the pin, is decorated along its upper surface for the full length of the sheath with a row of triangles formed by zig-zag incisions in the metal. The style is simple, with clean lines and balanced proportions.

Bow fibulae of this kind may have ultimately derived from a much earlier type such as the late ninth century B.C. fibulae from the Kerameikos [1]. The large bow made it possible for the wearer to secure and pin a considerable amount of material. They were worn by both men and women.

Almost identical is a fibula in Tarentum, said to have come from Ruvo. It is dated to the sixth century B.C. [2]. Another of similar design is now in Berlin, and was found in a grave in Ruvo. It differs in that it has two blue glass rings which encircle and hang freely from its sheath, which has a larger conical capsule than the Houston fibula, and serves to keep the rings in place [3]. Two smaller fibulae from Ruvo of the sixth century B.C. are of the same design, except that their sheaths are ornamented with small gold shields in the form of roses [4]. Of the same date and from the same area, now in Naples, are two fibulae of a similar type, but with more elaborate decoration. Both have a large golden, richly decorated pomegranate suspended on a chain of interwoven links and loosely attached to the tongues of the fibulae [5]. The presence of the pomegranate, an acknowledged chthonic attribute and symbol of the underworld, suggests that the latter fibulae, and perhaps also the one from Houston, had religious connotations [6].

Since the parallels with known provenance come from southern Italy in the sixth century B.C., it is likely that the same is true for the Houston fibula. The town of Ruvo was not far from Tarentum, one of the main centers of metalworking and trade in Magna Graecia from the sixth century B.C. on.

MM

[1] SCHWEITZER, p. 211-216, fig. 123-126, pl. 236-237, p. 298. Zig-zag lines similar to those on the Houston fibula are among the geometric motifs which decorate these early fibulae.

[2] BECATTI, p. 179, pl. LXVI, no. 267.

[3] GREIFENHAGEN, 1, p. 89-90, pl. 68, no. 5, color pl. VIII.

[4] SIVIERO, pl. 32; also in BREGLIA, p. 29, no. 37-38, no. 24880, 24881.

[5] SIVIERO, pl. 14, 15, no. 24845, 24846. The former has similar incised triangles on the inner surface of its sheath; also in BREGLIA, p. 29, no. 39, 40, pl. V, no. 3, 5.

[6] MUSCARELLA, p. 82-86. The author suggests that since many more fibulae have been found in graves and sanctuaries in Greece and surrounding areas than could have been worn in life, they may have been put there as gifts to the deities, or for the use of the deceased in the netherworld. Attic grave stelae from the sixth century B.C. frequently show the deceased with right hand extended, holding a pomegranate, see JOHANSEN, p. 79-88, pl. 37, 39.

[7] LANGLOTZ, p. 48-53.

8
Swivel scarab ring

Greek, provenance unknown, 5th c. B.C.

L. of scarab 1.8 cm.

Courtesy of the Walters Art Gallery, Baltimore.

Acc. no. 42.124.

Formerly in the collections of Morrison and Robinson, purchased from Kelekian in 1909.

Bibliography:

The Morrison Collection, Christie, Manson and Woods, London, 1898, p. 11.

Exhibition of Ancient Greek Art, Burlington Fine Arts Club, London, 1904, p. 208, pl. 110, M. 130.

Catalogue of the Collection of Engraved Gems ... Formed by Charles Newton Robinson, Christie, Manson and Woods, London, 1909, p. 6

WALTERS, 1979, no. 269.

This swivel sealstone ring with hollow gold hoop and sard scarab is in excellent condition. The sard is a dark, translucent orange, its flat side incised with a griffin which crouches on a simple ground line, amply filling the oval field. The hollow hoop gradually narrows as it approaches the discs which form the ends. Wire is passed through the discs and through the perforated scarab, and is then wound around the shanks.

Such rings were usually worn with the carved beetle back facing out, but could be swivelled around when the wearer wished to use the seal. Occasionally, they were hung on a chain and worn around the neck as amulets. Seal rings were among the votive offerings presented to the gods in the temples [1].

The carnelian and the sard were the most common gems in ancient glyptic art [2]. Scarab forms such as this are derived from Egypt, but techniques and materials reached the Greek artist from the east, probably from Phoenicia by way of Cyprus [3]. During the fifth and fourth centuries B.C. gem engraving was at its zenith in the Greek world.

The griffin on this ring is similar to those found on Greek and Persian gems of the fifth century B.C. [4]. With its sinuous neck, curving open jaws, upright ears and forehead knob, it is stylistically akin to the bronze griffin heads of seventh century B.C. Greece [5]. Griffins were thought to have apotropaic qualities and appeared in grave and sanctuary furnishings. As mythological guardians of treasure, they were thought to watch over the stores of precious metals and coins, and were a fitting emblem for a sealstone [6]. A similar recumbent griffin with serpentine, maned neck in the hellenized style appears on a scaraboid of blue chalcedony [7]. Yet another parallel in the Graeco-Persian style appears almost running rather than crouching [8]. An Etruscan ring of similar type is less finely crafted, with an engraving that crowds and overlaps the field [9].

MM

[1] RICHTER, 1920, p. xxviii-xxx.

[2] *Ibid.*, p. lv.

[3] BOARDMAN, 1968, p. 13.

[4] WALTERS, 1979, p. 90.

[5] J. BOARDMAN, *Style and Civilization, Pre-Classical from Crete to Archaic Greece*, New York, 1967, p. 78, fig. 42.

[6] I. FLAGGE, *Untersuchungen zur Bedeutung des Greifen*, Ph. D. diss., Köln, 1975, p. 27-34. On griffins, see also J. N. COLDSTREAM, *Sphinxes and Griffins from Geometric Knossos*, in *Antichità cretesi, Studi in onore di D. Levi*, 2, Catania, 1980, p. 161-164; C. DELPLACE, *Le griffon de l'archaisme à l'époque impériale. Étude iconographique et essai d'interprétation symbolique*, Brussels, 1980.

[7] BOARDMAN, 1977, fig. 5.

[8] BOARDMAN, 1975, fig. 100.

[9] HOFFMANN and von CLAER, fig. 117.

9

Armlet with lion's head finials

Cypriot, 6th c. B.C.
Diam. 9 cm, thickness 1.3 cm.
Anonymous European Loan.

The gold armlet forms three-quarters of a circle, with ends terminating in lions' heads facing each other. The hoop is thick, tubular and undecorated, with a light and unidentified core material inside. There is no collar masking the juncture where the finials fit over the hoop. The armlet is in good condition, with an irregular reddish-brown patina. There are minor dents and wrinkles in the hoop and some ruptures in the material of both finials, particularly in those areas which border the hoop.

The faces of the lions are fierce in demeanor, similar to the naturalistically rendered lions of Assyria, but their ears and manes are more schematic than realistic. There is considerable variation in the detail of execution of the lion heads. Final A, to the left, has a flattened, turned-up nose with opened nostrils. The eyes do not protrude. The eyebrows are rendered with curved, incised lines, while the cheekbones are underlined with two horizontal, flat incisions. The cheeks, however, are almost invisible. There is a curved crease underlining the cheeks. The temple is wide and the lips are shown by an encircling wire. The incisors are rendered and the teeth between them are drawn. The chin is round. The mane begins above the forehead and is slightly convex forming a crest near the ears. The mane encircles the face and is delineated at the edges by a fine, narrow groove. This mane has a geometric design and is made of narrow rows of triangular punchings which schematize the locks rendered in flat relief. The ears have a triangular form but the tops are round. The inner side of one is apparent. They are set into the mane and have the same decoration.

Final B, on the right, has a less animated lion's head. The nose is less turned up and the eyes are round and rendered in relief. The arch of the eyebrows is produced by slanting

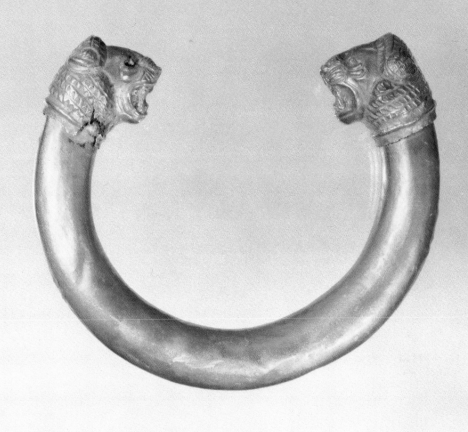

incisions. The cheekbones are also underlined by two horizontal incisions, but they are thicker. The cheeks, as in Finial A, are almost non-existent; the mane begins very close to the mouth. The cheek is as in the first lion, but with an incision over the upper lip; the mouth and teeth are the same. The chin appears to be flatter and the mane has triangles outlined at its end. One of the ears lies flat while the other is turned revealing the inside.

This type of bracelet is known in Cyprus [1] and seems to have antecedents in Iran earlier [2]. The style of lion's head is close to a lion's head from Iran in the Schimmel collection, attributed to the Vth cent. B.C. [3] and moreover related to another piece from Urarta, in the Museum of Erevan [4], dated to the eighth cent. B.C. The technique used here for punching the mane is unparalleled.

CL

[1] L. P. DICESNOLA, *Cyprus, its Ancient Cities, Tombs and Temples*, New York, 1878, p. 311.

[2] *Walters*, no. 26. Bracelet dated 8th cent. B.C.

[3] See J. SETTGAST (ed.), *Von Troja bis Amarna*, Mainz, 1978, no. 182.

[4] See e.g. G. AZARPAY, *Urartian art and artifacts*, Berkeley-Los Angeles, 1968, p. 38, fig. 9.

10
Pair of Boat Earrings

Greek, provenance unknown, 4th c.
B.C.
H. 3.1 cm; w. 2.5 cm.
Williams College Museum of Art,
Rogers Collection.
Acc. no. E27.

These hollow gold "askos" or "leech" ear-rings are in good condition, with some minor damage. There is some denting and rupture of the metal on both faces of earring "B". The ornamental motif which closes the hollow end of the crescent of earring "A" is damaged, and three of the granules which decorate the outer edge are missing. On both earrings, along the inner curve of the crescent there are protruding ridges, and pieces of metal which have broken off, the apparent remains of the support for a part which is now missing. The overall color is yellow gold, with isolated areas of reddish coloration.

Two sheets of gold were beaten into crescent-shaped moulds and then soldered together to form the hollow body. As the crescent narrows, encircling bands decorated and bounded by twisted filigree wires rise in five tiers to the ends of the tubes. From one end rises the tapering gold wire which pierces

the ear, the other closes in a bud or flower form which is outlined in filigree.

A graceful leaf design applied in filigree accentuates the hoop as it rises. Running along the outer curve of the crescent where the sections are joined, appears a row of granulation balls, surmounted by a second row of slightly smaller balls of granulation. On either side of this decorative "sur" is a double row of wire which is twisted at opposing angles to give the effect of braided wire. A single row of plain wire is placed adjacent to them. A matching arrangement of wires runs along the inner edge of the crescent on either side of the area where the missing part of the earring would have been placed.

Identical floral patterns in fine filigree wire punctuated by tiny gold globules decorate both faces of the crescents. Nine-lobed palmettes spring from the inner edges of the bands which encircle the tubes of the crescents. A stylized floral motif with spiraling tendrils and interspersed leaves occupies the central portion near the outer arch. Many of the granules are now lost as a result of wear, but the fine twisted wire for the most part retains its textured, beaded appearance.

The history of the boat earring in its most simple form begins in the Bronze Age, and the type, usually decorated, continues through the Archaic and Classical periods. They retained their popularity through the fourth century B.C., but are seldom seen in Hellenistic times [1]. A pair in Athens, thought to be of the Archaic period, are undecorated except for a row of "spurs" along their outer edges [2].

Palmettes in filigree such as those on the Williamstown earrings are characteristic of the Classical period, and appear on earrings in London, from Tarentum and from Kalymnos [3]. A pair in the Stathatos Collection in Athens, of fourth century B.C. date, are outlined with two rows of granulation along their outer edge, and have almost identical filigree palmettes [4]. An earring in Baltimore, dated a little before 320 B.C., with a sphinx seated in the hollow of its crescent, has the same palmette motif, spirals, small gold granules and running "spur" as the Williamstown earrings. There are spiral motifs on the Walters earring which are somewhat similar to those on the central portion, outer arch, of the Williamstown earrings. However, additional motifs in filigree and granulation, as well as enamelling, completely fill the decorative fields [5]. A very decorative pair of boat earrings, covered with filigree and appliqued motifs, come from a grave in Thessaly and are dated in the fourth century B.C. Palmettes and spiral motifs can be found in the crowded field, and the hoop, as it emerges from the tube, is decorated with a leaf in filigree similar to that of the Williamstown earrings [6]. Another pair, also from Thessaly, have the same nine-lobed palmette at both ends, and are dated in the latter third of the fourth century B.C. [7].

This earring can be dated with some certainty in the fourth century B.C., since palmettes of this style are common during that time, and because of parallelism with askos earrings with a figure inside. Its craftsmanship and design are of high quality, which is typical of Greek jewelry of the Classical period. Since its surface decoration is more restrained than is usual for late fourth century B.C. examples of the type, it seems safe to date it, tentatively, in the first half of that century.

MM

[1] HIGGINS, 1980, p. 125, 126. Boat earrings of the more elaborate kind with hanging pendants are commonly seen on coins of the fifth and fourth centuries B.C.

[2] SEGALL, pl. 8, no. 5. For a further example from the Archaic period with filigree in a simple triangular and scroll pattern, see BECATTI, pl. 75, no. 296,a,b. The granulation «spur» on these earrings is identical to that of the Williamstown earrings.

[3] MARSHALL, *BMCJ*, p. 179, pl. 30, no. 1657-1658, from Tarentum. These earrings have a triple outlining row of granulation. From Kalymnos, with pendants attached, p. 179, pl. 30, no. 1660-1661.

[4] AMANDRY, 1963, p. 218, pl. 33, fig. 122, no. 154-155. The crescent of this earring is closed with a heavy, knob-like protuberance, and it lacks the grace in styling of the Williamstown earrings.

[5] WALTERS, 1979, pl. 237.

[6] MILLER, p. 3-24, from Homolion Grave A, pl. 2a-c, 3a,b.

[7] *Ibid.*, from Homolion Grave B, pl. 10a,b.

11

Spiral earring

Greek, provenance unknown, 4th c. B.C.

H. 3.4 cm; w. 1.75-2.14 cm; thickness of spiral 0.3-0.4 cm.

Museum of Art, Rhode Island School of Design.

Acc. no. 23.360.

Bibliography:

HACKENS, p. 58-60, no. 18, fig. 18a-e.

See additional illustration p. 189, fig. 36b.

This spiral earring of gold-plated bronze is in very good condition, with minor damage to one of the gold caps and some loss and discoloration of the enamel. There is evidence of wear in the beaded filigree of the central decoration zone, and in the granulation triangles which border the zone.

Closing the hollow ends of the spiral is a three-sided granulation pyramid on a base sheet, tipped by a large, and then small, ball of granulation. Below this is a row of beaded filigree, then a series of egg motifs which once held blue and green enamel. Another row of filigree borders the central zone, in which there are S spirals and almond shapes in filigree with gold granules in and around them. Below this are two strands of twisted filigree, bordered on both sides by plain wire. Between the decoration zone and the body of the earring is a row of granulation triangles.

Spiral earrings came to the Greek world in the seventh century B.C. from the Orient. By the Archaic and Classical periods, the various regions had developed their own distinctive styles [1]. Some, especially those with shorter spirals, were apparently worn several at a time, arranged on a ring or band [2]. Spiral earrings on Cypriot sculpture are shown on the upper lobe of the ear, in combination with disc or "leech" earrings on the lower lobe [3]. They occur on coins less often than the disc or boat types, but are seen occasionally. Fig. 4 illustrates a coin of 460 B.C. from Lycia on which is shown a female head wearing spiral earrings with pyramid decoration, similar to the Providence earring [4].

As stated by Hackens, this earring and the

one in New York which may be the other one
of the pair, have a number of parallels which
were found in southern Russia, many of
which are now in the Hermitage[5]. Earrings
of this distinctive style seem to be found
chiefly in that region, and perhaps are the
work of one group of craftsmen. A pair of
earrings and other jewelry items in the
de Massoneau Collection, from southern
Russia, have the same decorative features as
the Providence earring, and are dated early in
the fourth century B.C.[6]. A similar date, or
perhaps somewhat later, is suggested for this
earring[7].

MM

[1] Higgins, 1980, p. 122-124.
[2] Marshall, *BMCJ*, p. 176, fig. 56, Cypriot
terracotta head, wearing several of a type of spiral
earring common in the fifth century B.C.
[3] N. Leipen, *The Loch Collection of Cypriot
Antiquities*, Royal Ontario Museum, Toronto,
1966, p. 50, fig. 163, female head wearing long
leech-type earrings and multiple spiral earrings on
upper lobe, ca. 600 B.C. It is doubtful that earrings
as large as the Providence earring would ever be
worn directly through the ear, but certain crudely
fashioned terracotta figures of Bronze Age Cyprus
wear several spiral earrings in each ear, passed
through holes in the upper and lower lobes; see
Myres, p. 374.
[4] C. Seltman, *Masterpieces of Greek Coinage*,
Cambridge, 1949, fig. 14a.
[5] Hackens, p. 58-60. The British Museum has
an example from Kerch, also. An earlier version
with open spiral is found in Thrace.
[6] Greifenhagen, 1, pl. 20, no. 6, 7, earrings,
and pl. 19, no. 4, 5, ram's head bracelet, finials. See
also, pl. 42, 44.
[7] Hackens, p. 58-60.

*Fig. 4. Silver diadrachm from Lycia, obverse,
head of Aphrodite Tetraskeles, early 5th c.
B.C., in the British Museum.*

12
Diadem

Greek, said to be from a tomb near
Phigaleia.
L. 22 cm; h. at center 3 cm; central
field 3 × 3 cm.
Smith College Museum of Art, North-
ampton, Massachusetts.
Gift of Phyllis Williams Lehmann in
memory of Karl Lehmann, 1961.
Acc. no. 1961:27.
Bibliography:
Smith College Museum of Art Bulletin,
no. 41, 1961, fig. 12.

This diadem is made of thin sheet gold,
mounted with two modern screws through
holes in the center of the pelte-shaped termination of the palmette. It is in very good
condition, with edges only slightly bent
except for the corner on the right, which is
bent upwards. There is a wrinkle from edge
to edge through the palmette on the left, and
a slight wrinkle to the right of the rosette.
More wrinkles can be observed to the left of
the rosette on the right, and another to the
right of the kneeling figure in the central
section. The surface of the gold in the diadem
has a reddish-gold tinge.

The embossed design was created by
impressing sheet gold on a matrix or die
made of wood, stones or bronze, and tapping
it with a soft hammer. Two moulds were
used, one for the central section and one for
the lateral ornamentation.

In the central section is a representation of
a figure kneeling to the right, with shoulders
and chest turned frontally. With his out-
stretched left arm he holds a bow, the string
of which might be the horizontal line above
his left knee. In that case, his right arm is
pulling the string. If the line does not indicate
a string, he may be placing his right arm on
his hip and merely holding the bow like an
attribute. His costume, as well as the two
dotted rosettes that serve as filling ornaments
in the field can be found in Greek art from
the seventh century B.C. on [1].

Even though one can find parallels for
some individual motifs of the lateral ornamentation in Greek Archaic painting, as well
as in the acroteria of grave stelae [2], the best
comparisons for this piece come from the
fourth century B.C. One may again look at
architectural ornamentation [3] or vase painting [4], and especially at fourth century B.C.
gold diadems [5]. Of interest especially here
is the decoration of fourth century B.C.
Tarentine jewelry [6].

Although a discrepancy between the central motif and the lateral ornamentation is
not usually found in fourth century B.C.
diadems, archaizing elements do occur, for
example, in a pair of earrings now in the
museum in Pforzheim [7].

Another unusual feature are the bent edges
around the object: in funerary diadems sofar
known, edges are flat. This object seems to

have been designed to be mounted on a (flexible?) support.

There is one other diadem which seems to be embossed in the same mould: it is in Copenhagen, while a parallel piece in the Canellopoulos collection, Athens, shows some minor variations both in the decoration and in the attitude of the archer. Both pieces, as well as other related materials, have been published by R. Laffineur, who has presented other arguments against their authenticity [8].

MM

[1] *Greek Art of the Aegean Islands*, The Metropolitan Museum of Art, N.Y., 1979, p. 139, fig. 88 for similar belt and kilt, and p. 140, fig. 89 for boots; *Dädalische Kunst auf Kreta im 7. Jahrhundert v. Chr.*, Ausstellungskatalog Museum für Kunst und Gewerbe Hamburg, Hamburg, 23. Sept.-27. Dez. 1970, p. 28, pl. 5, for helmet; P.E. ARIAS and M. HIRMER, *Mille Anni di Ceramica Greca*, Munich, 1960, p. 44-45, fig. 16-17, pl. 4, for costume worn by the figures on the Chigi vase; BOARDMAN, 1968, pl. 4, no. 62, 63, for kneeling figures found on Archaic gems; H. PAYNE, *Necrocorinthia, A Study of Corinthian Art in the Archaic Period*, Oxford, 1931, pl. 21, no. 8, early Corinthian aryballos with kneeling figure in field of rosettes.

[2] P. JACOBSTHAL, *Ornamente Griechischer Vasen*, 1 and 2, Berlin, 1927, p. 214, pl. 37a, pl. 38b, for spiral ornament; RICHTER, 1959, p. 71, fig. 75-76, for grave stelae of the sixth century B.C.

[3] J. TRAVLOS, *Pictorial Dictionary of Ancient Athens*, New York, 1971, p. 321, fig. 421, for palmettes and scrolls on a monument dated 394 B.C.

[4] JACOBSTHAL, p. 215, pl. 55a for seven-leafed palmette with elongated center frond, and p. 220, pl. 105b,d, for lyre form with palmette enclosed.

[5] For pre-Classical diadems, see T. HACKENS, *Un bandeau funéraire- en or de style protoattique*, p. 1-12, and R. LAFFINEUR, *L'orfèvrerie rhodienne orientalisante*, in *Aurifex 1, Études d'orfèvrerie antique*, T. Hackens, ed.,Louvain-la-Neuve, 1980; for diadems with typical fourth century B.C. style scrolls, volutes and palmettes, see GREIFENHAGEN, II, p. 12-13, pl. 3, and p. 121, pl. 82; also in G. VON ZAHLHAAS and H. FUCHS, *Ein Diadem aus Sizilien*, in *Archäologischer Anzeiger*, 4, Berlin, 1981, p. 577-582, fig. 1-3; and also G. Neumann, *Ein frühhellenistisches Golddiadem aus Kreta*, in *AthMitt*, 80, 1965.

[6] *Taranto*, in *Enciclopedia dell'arte antica*, 7, Rome, 1966, p. 603-617, fig. 735.

[7] SEGALL, 1966, p. 37-8, pl. 24.

[8] R. LAFFINEUR, *Collection Paul Canellopoulos: bijoux en or*, in *BCH*, 104, 1980, p. 454-456.

Fig. 5. Butterfly necklace, Greek, 1st c. B.C., Walters Art Gallery, Baltimore.

LATE CLASSICAL TO HELLENISTIC

Since early Classical times, Macedonia strove to become part of the Greek world. This desire to maintain ties with Greece was displayed by Alexander I, forebear of Alexander the Great, the first Macedonian to participate in the Olympic games. By the time of Philip II (359-336 B.C.) even the most eminent Greek writers were attracted to the court at Pella. Aristotle accepted Philip's invitation to educate his son Alexander, and by the time of Alexander's reign, Pella was the major center for scholars and artists from southern Greece and Asia Minor, thus rivaling the reputation previously held by Athens.

At Pella, there was an unusual outburst of artistic activity. The simple houses of the fifth century were, at least for the aristocracy, replaced by villas expensively equipped with furniture, statuary and mosaic floors. Jewelry from this period should be seen in the context of such lavish expenditure [1].

Literary sources frequently refer to Persia and her influence on Greece. Pliny mentions the conquest of Asia and the introduction of luxury (*Natural History*, 34.34). and Diodorus' description of Alexander's burning of Persepolis is characteristic of the Greeks' impression of Persia as an exotic place where gold and jewels were plentiful [2]:

> "It was the richest city under the sun and the private houses had been furnished with every sort of wealth over the years ... Here much gold and silver was carried off and to little gold, and many rich dresses ... with gold embroidery became the prize of the victors ... The Macedonians gave themselves up to this orgy of plunder for a whole day and still could not satisfy their boundless greed for more ... Alexander took possession of the treasure ... the vaults were packed full of silver and gold. The total was found to be 120,000 talents ..."
>
> Diodorus, 17.69-71.

Athenaeus also seems to be in awe of the luxurious Hellenistic Kingdoms. As he describes a procession at Alexandria sponsored by Ptolemy II. Athenaeus quotes Callixenus of Rhodes:

> "The women had on embroidered tunics [and they were] covered with much gold jewelry ... [there was] a satyr crowned with a gold pine wreath ... [followed by an] elephant [with] trappings of gold and round its neck an ivy crown of gold ... followed

---

[1] Note Diodorus' description of the funeral chariot which carried Alexander's remains from Babylonia, where he died, to Alexandria:

> [Alexander's sarcophagus] was placed beside the carriage that was to carry it, over which a vaulted gold roof decorated with scales studded with jewels was constructed, eight cubits wide and twelve cubits long; beneath the roof and running around the whole work was a gold cornice, rectangular in design, with goat-stag protomes done in high relief, from which gold rings two palms wide were hung, and through which, in turn, there ran a processional garland splendidly decorated with flowers of all sorts and colors.   (DIODORUS, 18.26-28)

Also see Diodorus' account of the burial of Hephaistion (DIODORUS 17.115).

[2] See Diodorus' description of a feast for the generals of Alexander's army in Persepolis: according to Diodorus, "Persia furnished in plenty everything needed for luxury and enjoyment" (DIODORUS, 33.289-281).

by 500 young girls dressed in purple tunics with gold girdles ... Negro tribute bearers [carried] sixty bowls full of gold and silver coins and gold dust ... Then there were statues of Alexander and Ptolemy, crowned with ivy crowns made of gold ... After them 2,000 steers ... with gilded borns [and] gold stars on their foreheads ... Upon the trone of Ptolemy Soter lay a crown made of 10,000 gold coins ... [there were] seven gilded palm trees twelve feet high ... a gilded thunderbolt sixty feet long [and] a gilded temple measuring sixty feet all round ... [There were] 3,200 gold crowns shown in the procession ... [and a] crown of gold 120 feet in circumference adorned with precious stones".

Athenaeus, 197-203.

Other ancient writers such as Arrian tell us that this growing orientalism was resented by the Greeks, but oriental influence survived in Macedonia [3].

From the time of Philip, one finds a striking increase in the availability of gold. When Philip conquered Amphipolis and the Pangaion region in 357 B.C., he gained access to gold and silver mines [4]. The Pangaion mines were well known among the ancients [5], but the gold mines of Philippi were "scanty and insignificant before Philip increased their output so much by his improvements that they could bring him a revenue of 1,000 talents" [6] (Diodorus, 16.8.5).

From these mines [Philip] soon amassed a fortune. With the abundance of money, he raised the Macedonian kingdom ... to a greatly superior position, for with the gold coins he struck ... he organized a large force of mercenaries, and by using these coins for bribes induced many Greeks to become betrayers of their native lands.

Diodorus, 16.8.5.

Although short of funds at the beginning of his reign [7], Alexander financed his campaign by exploiting the gold mines already tapped by Philip. Another source of wealth was the plunder of Persia, where the treasure of Darius alone was said to

---

[3] Alexander adopted Persian dress which was, according to Arrian, part of a conscious policy of cultural fusion uniting East and West:

[Alexander's] adoption of Persian dress was ... a matter of policy ... by it he hoped to bring the Eastern nations to feel that they had a king who was not wholly a foreigner ... That was also no doubt, why he included a proportion of Persian troops in Macedonian units, and made Persian noblemen officers in his crack native regiments.   (ARRIAN, 7.30)

The fusion of Persians with Macedonians is exemplified by the famous mass marriage at Susa; best known from Arrian's account:

Here at Susa [Alexander] held wedding ceremonies for his companions; he also took a wife himself, Barsine, Darius' older daughter ... The marriage ceremonies were in the Persian fashion ... There proved to be over 10,000 other Macedonians who married Asian women; Alexander had them all registered, and every man of them received a wedding gift.   (ARRIAN, 7.5).

[4] No elaborate methods were needed to recover and prepare gold. Hellenistic miners could gather gold from the pockets of river beds and from alluvial sands deposited by flooding or shifting rivers. For more information on the mining of gold, see R.J. FORBES, *Studies in Ancient Technology*, 7, Leiden, 1963, p. 127. See also J. F. HEALY, *Mining and Metallurgy in the Greek and Roman World*, London, 1978. H. HOFFMAN and P. DAVIDSON, *Greek Gold, Jewelry from the Age of Alexander*, Boston, 1966, p. 18-23.

[5] The wealth of the Pangaion gold and silver mines is mentioned by Pliny, Herodotus, Theophrastos and Strabo. See essay by D. TZAVELLAS, p. 163-169.

[6] According to Diodorus, Philip enlarged his kingdom, more by gold than by arms (DIODORUS, 16.13.2, 15.16.4).

[7] A.P. BELLINGER, *Essays on the Coinage of Alexander the Great*, American Numismatic Society, New York, 1963, p. 35-80.

have been worth 10,000 talents. It is not a coincidence that most of Alexander's conquests throughout Asia Minor and Iran included all their rich gold deposits[8]. Alexander's empire also engulfed Egypt and the Nubian gold sources.

Archaeological evidence from burials on the Greek mainland, nearby islands and places such as Ialysus and Thebes, shows modest use of gold jewelry. The Erotes tomb in Eretria, for example, does not seem to have been a lavish burial[9], and jewelry from this tomb does not seem to have a distinct local style; it shows the influence of the eastern part of the Greek world.

Gold headbands may have been made specifically for burial in the Hellenistic period, as one was found *in situ*. Most of the jewelry found in tombs on the Greek mainland, however, were simple ornaments of baser metals[10]. Terracotta imitations were used when precious metals were unavailable.

Unlike the modest burials of the Greeks, the Thessalians used gold more plentifully in tombs. The jewelry recovered from the Pelinna graves, for example, includes a necklace, a finger ring, a bracelet, a pair of earrings and several gold wreaths. The quantity of gold found at Pelinna as well as the stylistic similarities of the jewelry point to Macedonian or Persian influences. The jewelry from Pelinna, a town which had no real significance until Philip II[11], may in fact, have originally belonged to veterans of the armies of Philip or Alexander. Although there is too little evidence to say who might have owned the jewelry and to what social class the owners belonged, the rich use of gold suggests they were army officers.

Crossing the border into Macedonia, one finds even richer tombs than those in Thessaly. The tomb "of Philip II" in Vergina, for example, included gold wreaths and diadems that are more lavish than anything unearthed in Pelinna. Very rich burials similar to that of Philip II have been discovered in other areas of ancient Macedonia such as Amphipolis and in south Russia, Thrace, Scythia and Tarantum.

Eros, Aphrodite and Dionysus are frequently represented on jewelry as well as on plain and precious objects buried with the dead. Eros often holds a *tainia*, a woolen ribbon which, like the wreath, was actually found in tombs or sometimes painted on the walls[12]. It may have been included as a gift for the gods. These victory symbols signified the special achievements during the lifetime of the deceased.

Aphrodite's connection with burial iconography, as Segall has pointed out[13], can perhaps be explained by a reference from Parmenides:

---

[8] See map, FORBES, *op. cit.*, 8, Leiden, 1964, p. 164.

[9] See K. KURUNIOTIS, *Goldschmuck aus Eretria*, in *AthMitt*, 38, 1913, p. 289-328.

[10] D.C. KURTZ and J. BOARDMAN, *Greek Burial Customs*, Ithaca, New York, 1971, p. 162-169.

[11] See S.G. MILLER, *Two Groups of Thessalian Gold* (*University of California Publications in Classical Studies*), 18, Berkeley, 1979, p. 25, n. 147.

[12] B. SEGALL, *Zur griechischen Goldschmiede-Kunst des 4. Jahrhunderts V.Chr.*, Wiesbaden, 1966, p. 37.

[13] *Ibid.*

... but under her (the earth), there is a lovely path, a horrible muddy, tunnel-like path. This leads ... to the lovely fields of Aphrodite ...

Parmenides, Fragment 20.

In Athens, the sumptuary laws of Demetrios of Phaleron in 316-317 [14], as well as the lack of gold in mainland Greece, could explain the fact that one does not find many gold objects buried with the dead. Looking back to the Classical period, however, one finds many literary sources which refer to the adornment of the body with jewelry in preparation to enter Hades (see article by Murray). One also finds representations of adorning the body on vase paintings and grave stones. The cost of the grave stones was certainly not insignificant, but the burials were generally modest in jewelry.

At the beginning of the Hellenistic period, mainland Greeks appear to continue this practice of artistic restraint even though the literary sources traditionally refered to adornment. However, the rest of the Greek world preferred more lavish burials, at least for the upper classes.

The Macedonians may have misinterpreted this symbolic representation of jewelry in Greek culture. They possessed natural gold resources and imported jewelry that could be melted down and refashioned so that with their abundance of gold, they interpreted literally a ritual which was used mainly symbolically by the Greeks. Furthermore, the peoples who were their northern neighbors, as well as their partners in trade to the east and west, appear to have adopted this new practice of lavish burials.

From the tombs of these areas, one finds jewelry with an interesting mixture of types and styles. For example, the Herakles knot (cat. no. 21), introduced in Egypt in the second millenium, was not known in Macedonia before Alexander [15]. Traditionally, the knot symbolized strength and the power of love, but Alexander may have adopted it because of his association with Herakles. It may also have alluded to the Gordion knot. The Herakles knot was usually found on a thigh-band, but was also found on diadems, necklaces, fingerrings and bracelets.

The thigh-band (*periskelis*) was worn above the knee under a diaphanous garment, with the Herakles knot worn at the front of the thigh as a closure [16]. The pennanular, or broken-circle bracelet became popular after it was introduced by the Persians, and Hoffmann believes that both the diadem and thigh-band came into fashion during the Hellenistic period due to Persian influence.

Bracelets were worn in pairs according to the Persian tradition, and the notion of the jewelry ensemble may also have been prompted through contact with the

---

[14] It is unclear whether Demetrios' restrictions referred to the construction of new tombs, as well as forbidding elaborate sculptured tomb monuments and the types of monuments that could be erected. It appears though, that Demetrios' restrictions were observed, for it is not until the second century B.C. that relief monuments of some size and magnificence reappear. See M. BIEBER, *The Sculpture of the Hellenistic Age*, New York, 1955, p. 64 and KURTZ and BOARDMAN, *op. cit.*, p. 162-169.

[15] H. HOFFMANN and P. DAVIDSON, *Greek Gold, Jewelry from the Age of Alexander*, Boston, 1966, p. 6.

[16] A terracotta statue of Aphrodite illustrates how the thigh-band was worn. See HOFFMANN and DAVIDSON, *op. cit.*, fig. D opposite p. 8.

Persian Empire. The ensemble must have been worn on special occasions by a member of the ruling family, a priestess or the wife or a high public official. A typical ensemble might include a diadem, one or more golden frontlets, earrings (ranging from simple hoops with animal or human head finials, to elaborate sculptural earrings), one or more necklaces, bracelets fibulae and thigh-bands [17].

Jewelry shows traces of surviving regional styles, but regional styles were increasingly fused. Therefore, Higgins regards Hellenistic jewelry as basically homogeneous [18]. Indeed, jewelry from this period reflects the "fusion and diffusion" of Hellenistic culture [19].

Persian jewelry is itself a mixture of regional styles and is, therefore, difficult to define in precise terms. The Persian artisan borrowed and skillfully adapted to his own particular purpose the styles of other peoples [20]. The Greek goldsmith's interpretation of current Achaemenid motifs was slightly more naturalistic, whereas Persian jewelry was more decorative, ornamental and abstract. The Persians preferred geometric or natural foliate forms, while the Greeks' main concern was the human body. Thus, when abstract Persian motifs were incorporated into Greek jewelry, they were usually combined with human forms.

Through exposure to Persia, Egypt and other eastern and northern countries, an abundance of gems and semi-precious stones entered the Greek market and affected jewelry style. Achaemenid jewelry had long distinguished itself by its brilliant use of polychrome glass enamels and inlays. In 200 B.C., garnets, carnelians, pearls, emeralds and plasma, a green variety of chalcedony, became popular (see article by Lemaigre). The garnet seems to have been the most popular of the stones, but when possible, the Greeks preferred combinations of colors such as juxtaposed garnets and emeralds.

Eventually, color was used not only as an accent, but as an integral part of the design. A third century B.C. medallion with the bust of Aphrodite (cat. no. 4), for example, can be compared with a similar second century B.C. medallion from Delos which uses not just one type of gem, but several contrasting colors [21].

The use of color combinations became more elaborate during the first century B.C. [22]. For example, a butterfly necklace from Olbia in the Walters Art Gallery (see fig. 5) uses five colored inlays for dramatic effect. The central portion of the necklace is made up of a violet stone in the center, and blue-green glass in the flanking rectangular and oval settings. The butterfly pendant has an emerald for its

---

[17] *Ibid.*, p. 57.

[18] R. HIGGINS, *Greek and Roman Jewellery*, 2nd ed., Berkeley, 1980, p. 153-157.

[19] F. W. WALBANK, *The Hellenistic World*, Cambridge, Mass., 1982, p. 60-70. See also, R. LACQUER, *Hellenismus. Akadem. Rede zur Jahresfeier der Hessischen Ludwigsuniversität am 1. Juli 1924. Schriften der Hessischen Hochschulen Univ.*, 1924.

[20] Babylonian, Egyptian and even Greek influence can be traced back to the campaigns of Cyrus. Under Darius, Persia came into closer contact with Egypt, but many Greek craftsmen and artists worked at the Persian court, so many conflicting styles survived under both Cyrus and Darius.

[21] See T. HACKENS and E. LÉVY, *Trésor hellénistique trouvé à Délos en 1964*, in *BCH*, 89, 1965, p. 537-538, pl. 19.

[22] Polychromy becomes progressively richer, until by the beginning of the second century, the goldwork is often reduced to the status of a foil for the display of colorful stones and inlays.

head, a blue stone for its body and gold wings spotted with emeralds. The wings are also decorated with inlays of red, white and green glass [23]. The finials are formed by two lynx heads and the neck is made up of rock crystal beads. The bold geometric forms and the importance given to colored inlays foreshadow the style of the Roman Empire.

In Pliny's time, the image of the Near East was that of a luxurious region. According to Pliny (*Natural History*, 37.12-14), it was Pompey's triumph over Mithradates "that first inclined our taste toward pearls and gems". He continues:

> There were three [golden] dining couches, vessels made of gold and gems set out on nine side-boards, three golden statues representing Minerva, Mars and Apollo, thirty-three crowns made of pearls ... there was also a portrait of Pompey made of pearls ... that portrait, I emphasize, was made of pearls; what was really celebrated was the triumph of luxury and the conquest of restraint.

Margaret BARRY

---

[23] Some of the stones are modern replacements, but the original is known from a nineteenth century description and photograph, see Walters Art Gallery, *Jewelry: Ancient to Modern*, A. Garside, ed., New York, 1979, p. 283.

13
Medallion

Hellenistic, provenance unknown, 3rd c. B.C.

Maximum diam., 3.9 cm; max. relief 1.8 cm.

Williams College Museum of Art, Rogers Collection.

Acc. no. E43.

The emblem is exquisitely worked in repoussé from a single sheet of gold. The form, in high relief, is encircled by a ring of beaded wire which conforms to the contours of the bust-length male and female figures.

At the back of the medallion, there is a small gold loop which was made separately and attached at the top along the central axis. At the backside, there are worn attaches of three other loops and it is clear that there remains only one of four original loops through which leather cross-straps were threaded. This arrangement made it possible to wear the medallion over the garment in the center of the chest. The two small holes at mid-section on either side of the medallion are later modifications. According to Hackens, the addition of the holes made it possible to wear the medallion on a chain as a pendant. It is also possible that the holes were

made in order to accommodate a pin which would secure the medallion to the garment as a brooch.

The hands and torso of both figures are rendered more generally than the heads and accessories, which are finely chased. The man's head, which is damaged on the right side, is tilted gently toward the woman as if about to kiss her. His right arm reaches around from behind in order that his right hand may touch her exposed breast. His tunic has slipped from his left shoulder and gathers in soft folds in the bend of his arm as he reaches up to touch her chest. The woman holds a gold cup in her left hand, her right arm is raised and bent behind her head. She inclines intimately toward the man in response to his gestures. In both of the figures the hair is swept back and secured by a floral wreath. The woman's hair is curled into a bun at the back, from which several strands escape and fall loosely around her neck. The jewelry worn by the woman is of a type particularly common during the mid- and late Hellenistic periods. She wears a spiral snake bracelet on the inside of her right arm, a hoop earring and heavy rope braid pendant necklace.

The features of the man and woman, the full, fleshy cheeks, the almond-shaped eyes, tight mouths and weak chins, characterize these figures as particular individuals and suggest that the medallion is an exceptionally rare double-portrait, which may have been commissioned by a member of the royal family or aristocracy to commemorate their marriage. The iconography of the *Hieros Gamos* has a long history in Greek art. A

small wooden figurine from Samos[1] and a terracotta statuette from Metapontum[2] are among numerous examples of the figures of Zeus and Hera shown in the same manner of embrace. Zeus reaches around to touch Hera's breast. This motif was also popularized in erotic displays of symplegma. The figures of Dionysus and Ariadne can be seen in similar attitudes in a terracotta from Delos[3], on a late fourth century bronze mirror in the Louvre (no. MNC632) and later in Pompeiian wall paintings[4]. An interesting, but more distant parallel can be seen on an Etruscan terracotta funerary urn from the third century B.C., now in a private collection in Paris[5].

Although there are no exact parallels for this unique piece, closely related to this type of medallion is a small, single-figure relief pendant in the Stathatos Collection, Athens (no. ΣT 234)[6] and the bust of Aphrodite with Eros from Delos[7], both dating from the mid-third century B.C. The absence of elaborate inlays in concentric ornamental zones, typical of later medallion-discs (cat. no. 14) suggests a similar date for this example.

MJA

[1] K. SCHEFOLD, *Die Griechen und ihre Nachbarn*, Berlin, 1967, p. 162, fig. 18b.

[2] J. BOARDMAN and E. LA ROCCA, *Eros in Greece*, London, 1978, p. 88.

[3] J. MARCADÉ, *Eros Kalos*, Geneva, 1962, p. 43.

[4] G. M. A. RICHTER, *Ancient Italy*, Ann Arbor, 1958, p. 126, fig. 245.

[5] Reproduced in *Architectural Digest*, November, 1982, p. 173.

[6] MILLER, pl. 21e.

[7] E. LÉVY, *Nouveaux Bijoux à Délos*, in *BCH*, 92, 1968, p. 528-535, fig. 8.

14
Medallion-Disc:
Bust of Aphrodite with Eros

Hellenistic, from Pagasai in Thessaly, mid-late 3rd c. B.C.

Maximum diam. 7 cm; max. relief 2.3 cm.

Museum of Art, Rhode Island School of Design.

Acc. no. 29.256.

Bibliography:

P. AMANDRY, *Medallion en or du Musée de Providence*, in *AJA*, 59, 1955, p. 219-222, pl. 64-65.

P. AMANDRY, *A Greek Gold Medallion*, in *BullRISD*, 12, no. 3, 1955, p. 7, fig. 1-5.

M. GRAMATOPOL, *Un medallion de type thessalien du Musée archéologique de Constanza*, in *Mélanges Marcel Renard*, III, Brussels, 1969, p. 264-271;

HOFFMANN-DAVIDSON, 1965, p. 224-225, no. 91.

HACKENS, 1976, p. 66-70, fig. 22a-h.

The medallion-disc with relief bust, unfinished in this example, is a particularly common jewelry type during the fourth through second centuries B.C. Numerous medallions have been unearthed from tombs

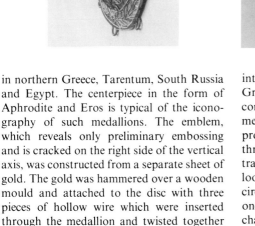

in northern Greece, Tarentum, South Russia and Egypt. The centerpiece in the form of Aphrodite and Eros is typical of the iconography of such medallions. The emblem, which reveals only preliminary embossing and is cracked on the right side of the vertical axis, was constructed from a separate sheet of gold. The gold was hammered over a wooden mould and attached to the disc with three pieces of hollow wire which were inserted through the medallion and twisted together at the back. The figure of Aphrodite wears a diadem and is partially draped. The winged figure of Eros, situated on her right shoulder, reaches across her chest in a playful attempt to loosen the knot which secures her peplos.

The high relief of the central emblem contrasts sharply with the relatively flat patterns of the concentric zones. A ring of beaded wire separates the figure group from the sloping sides of the medallion. This zone is decorated with palmettes which are outlined in filigree and inlaid with dark blue enamel. The enamel has turned black over time. Each of the ten palmettes is isolated within a half-circle of filigree and characterized by a central diamond shape surrounded by six smaller leaves arranged symmetrically. Seven granules grouped together to form rosettes occupy the interstices between the palmettes. The flat outer rim is embellished with a tightly drawn floral motif, which extends in opposite directions from a lozenge-shaped garnet mounted on the axis of the medallion at the top. Whereas the interest in the highly modeled figure is a Greek contribution to the pre-established conventions of the medallion-discs, the ornamental motifs were derived from Egyptian prototypes which had been transmitted through Persian artisans and ultimately transformed by Greek craftsmen [1]. The nine loops placed at regular intervals around the circumference of the medallion may have once served to secure a network of gold chains, now missing [2].

Scholars have not been able to agree on the function of the medallion-discs. The proliferation during this period of terracotta pyxides with lids sculpted in high relief has prompted the suggestion that these medallions were perhaps covers for small metal containers which stored cosmetics and other personal possessions of a precious nature. The most striking examples of medallion-discs used in this manner are in the Stathatos Collection and in the Benaki Museum in Athens [3]. It has also been posited that such medallions were *perammai*, breast ornaments worn over the girdle and held in place by leather cross-straps [4].

A pair of medallion-discs with busts of Athena and Artemis in the Princeton Art Museum (no. 38-49 and 38-50), although somewhat later, are closely related to the Providence medallion. Other stylistic parallels can be traced to examples found in south Russia now in the Hermitage and Fitzwilliam Museums [6].

MJA

[1] For a discussion of the absorption and mutation of Egyptian and Persian prototypes by Greek artists, see SEGALL, 1945, p. 2-11.

[2] A comprehensive description and evaluation of the state of preservation of this piece can be found in HACKENS, p. 66-70.

[3] AMANDRY, 1953, pl. 39, 234; cf. SEGALL, 1938, pl. 14, no. 6.

[4] HIGGINS, 1980, p. 171.

[5] HOFFMANN-DAVIDSON, p. 266-268, fig. 124-124c.

[6] Stylistic and iconographic continuities between medallions from several regions may be the result of the transmission of bronze and plaster jewelers' moulds from Galjub and Memphis throughout the Hellenistic world. See SEGALL, 1945, p. 11, fig. 10; cf., MILLER, 1979, pl. 21.

15

Gold and amber necklace

Hellenistic, South Italy, 4th c. B.C.
L. 44.15 cm.
Virginia Museum of Fine Arts, The Williams Fund.
Acc. no. 79.17.

The preserved length of this necklace, now on a modern string, is comprised of a series of fifteen regularly spaced triple rosettes. Each layer of petals is trimmed in twisted gold wire. A single gold granule sits in the center of each of the smallest of the rosettes. Alternating with each rosette at the front of the necklace are six double lotus blossoms. Each blossom is decorated with filigree and a single small rosette which is situated centrally, at the juncture of the two blossoms. Ten hollow cylindrical tubes of equal length wrapped with two single strands of twisted wire provide the spacers between the rosettes at the back of the necklace. Both ends of the necklace terminate in conical finials. The finials are closed with a half sphere and divided horizontally into three zones. Each zone is decorated with an abstract filigree pattern. The two conicals meet a final rosette at the back. A series of fragile amber pendants (see Lecomte article on amber, p. 211 ss.) are suspended by triangular gold loops from the alternating series of rosettes and lotus blossoms. Five pendants of approximately equal size flank both sides of a much larger central pendant. The tight rhythm of the rosette-lotus blossom combination, which is further articulated by the heavy pendants, emphasizes the front of the necklace.

Pendant necklaces with repeating series of rosettes separated by lotus blossoms have a long history in Greek jewelry. Numerous variants in gold, silver and terracotta are known. The earliest examples, those with acorn and coin pendants dangling from single rosettes date from the fifth century B.C., and have been found in tombs in Eretria and Nymphaeum [1]. Other parallels from the early fourth century have been discovered in Homolion and Panticapaeum (Hermitage Museum, no. TT.F854.22) [2]. The more elaborate late fourth century necklaces of this type with triple layers of rosettes and figurine pendants can be seen in a closely related example from Tarentum now in the British Museum (no. 1954) [3]. Although the chains of both necklaces are quite similar, the conservative simplicity of the pendant type in this example suggests a date from the mid-fourth century.

MJA

[1] HIGGINS, 1980, p. 129.
[2] MILLER, p. 10-12, fig. 4-5.
[3] MARSHALL, *BMCJ*, pl. XXXV.

16a
Fragments of a crown

Hellenistic, provenance unknown.

Dimensions: leaves of five teeth: L. 47-44 mm, max. w. 47-36 mm, min. w. 6-4 mm; leaves of four teeth: L. 39 mm, max. w. 30 mm, min. w. 3 mm; leaves of three teeth; L. 39 mm, max. w. 32 mm, min. w. 2 mm; leaves of two teeth: L. 38 mm, max. w. 30 mm, min. w 3 mm; leaf of indented border: L. 32 mm, max. w. 26 mm, min. w. 4 mm; oval leaves: L. 39 mm, max. w. 18 mm, min. w. 1 mm.

Anonymous European Loan.

These disparate leaves, sixteen in number, do not seem to have belonged to the same crown. The leaves of five teeth and of four teeth, which have finely embossed veins, spread fan-shaped from the base of the leaf to the teeth. The oval leaves resemble olive leaves. As for the other leaves, it is impossible to connect them to a particular species. They are similar in that the sessile leaves, without stalks, have a hole which allows them to be fixed to the stem and in that they are all so thin one can compare the gold leaf to an aluminum leaf.

All these leaves bear, to differing degrees, red and brownish concretions. One can see the presence of tears on several leaves.

A more homogeneous funerary crown, with only multiple teeth leaves, from Macedony has been published by R. Laffineur, who dates the object in the IVth cent. B.C. [1].

MD

[1] R. LAFFINEUR, *Collection Paul Canellopoulos: bijoux en or*, in *BCH*, 104, 1980, p. 404-406.

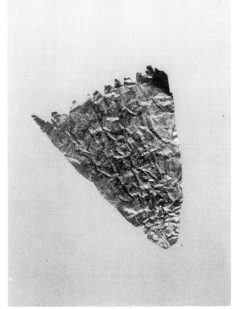

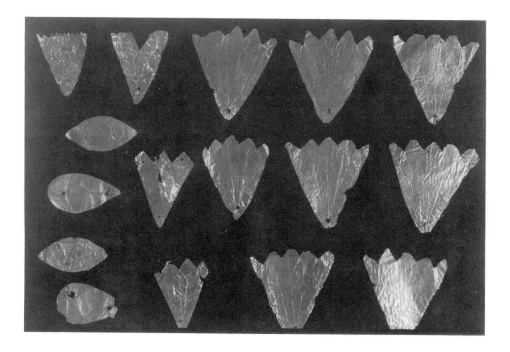

16b
Fragments of crown

Hellenistic, provenance unknown.
Dimensions: leaves of three teeth: L. 46 mm, max. w. 33 mm, min. w. 4 mm; leaves of five teeth: L. 50 mm, max. w. 35 mm, min. w. 5 mm; triangular leaf: L. 37 mm, max. w. 37 mm, min. w. 4 mm; diamond-shaped ornaments: L. 72-60 mm, w. 38-34 mm.
Anonymous European loan.

These leaves and ornaments may have formed a funerary crown. The extraordinary thinness of the leaves supports this hypothesis. The leaves of three teeth, worked in repoussé, are a little thicker and are decorated with three quite broad and well-indicated veins. The other leaves, except for the small triangular leaf, also seem to have been provided, originally, with veins. These leaves and the ornaments are now rather pleated.

The leaves and ornaments have holes that were used to fix them to a stem. One notes on the majority of the leaves and ornaments the presence of blackish, brownish and greyish concretions. Some of these leaves can be compared (as in the previous case) with the leaves of the crown of the P. Canellopoulos collection.

It is interesting to note that the borders of several leaves are cut in a uniform manner. Other leaves have irregular and rough borders. This is a criterion for authenticity. The leaves with regular borders are imitations. The leaves with irregular borders are, however, authentic. These pieces are rarely homogeneous, but the reconstruction proposed in the exhibit is a likely hypothesis.

MD

17
Pair of bull's head earrings

Hellenistic, provenance unknown, late
4th c. B.C.
Diam. 4.5 cm × 3.5 cm.
Williams College Museum of Art,
Rogers Collection.
Acc. no. E29.

The hoop of the earrings consists of a twisted band of plain gold alternating with a double strand of beaded wire wrapped around a central core. The beaded wire runs around two-thirds of the hoop and tapers into a plain pin for passing through the ear. The length of the pin, one-third of the hoop, suggests that the earrings were to be worn upside down [1]. The pin is secured by a small hook which protrudes from the bull's chin. Two paired bands of twisted wire separate the collar into three decorative zones. The first zone, a ring of pointed leaves, initiates the transformation from the hoop into the head of the bull. The central zone is decorated with repeating scrolls of filigree, which are accented above and below with tear drops, also of filigree. The third zone is a row of filigree petals. The bull's heads were made separately, each from two sheets of gold,

which were worked in repoussé, folded together and tucked into the collar. They are not reinforced. The seam is visible under the chin and behind the horns, which were also made separately. The eyes and the ears are marked out by small perforations in the gold sheet. They were not originally articulated with inlays of colored gems or glass. The absence of color in favor of a highly modeled surface characterizes these earrings as being from the fourth century. In the early Hellenistic period Greek artisans emphasized the decorative and expressionistic potential of the gold itself.

Animal head finials introduced into the iconographic repertory of the Greek goldsmith as a motif repeated throughout jewelry ensembles were adapted from the highly stylized animal forms, which were a standard feature of Achaemenid design. In contrast to the eastern and far eastern prototypes, which maintain an intentionally ambiguous dialogue between ornament and the image, the Greek craftsman never obscured the distinction between that which is abstract and that which is representational.

Several variations of gold hoop earrings

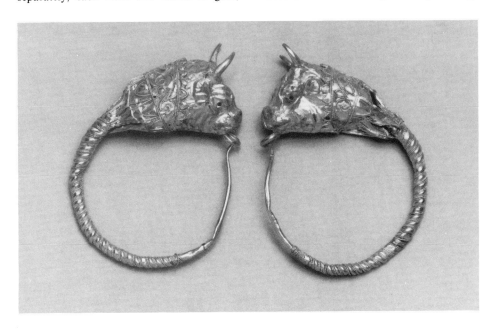

with animal finials can be traced throughout the Hellenistic world. The most common of these, the lion's head, first appeared in tombs in Amphipolis, Salonika and Syracuse in the early fourth century [2]. Elaborated versions of the lion's head earrings in which the tapered end terminates in a second smaller head have been found in Tarentum, Capua and Ithaca [3]. Hoops which terminate in the heads of bulls, goats, lynx, gazelle and less frequently in the heads of griffins continue to be seen into the first century A.D., primarily in the regions of South Russia, Olbia and Cyprus. This example may have originated in a Cypriot workshop which disseminated similar earrings throughout Egypt [4] and Syria [5].

Parallel earrings with bull's head finials from Cyprus date from the late Hellenistic period. These examples are coloristically elaborated with beads of stone and glass which have been threaded on to the hoops.

Such earrings can be found in the Walters Art Gallery [6], the Museum of Art, Rhode Island School of Design [7], the British Museum [8] and in the Staatliche Museen, Berlin [9].

MJA

[1] This can be seen on Etruscan terracottas. See A. ANDRÈN, *Architectural Terracottas from Etrusco-Italic Temples* (*Acta Instituti Romani Regni Sueciae*, vol. 6), Lund-Leipzig, 1939, pl. 156, no. 525.

[2] HIGGINS, 1980, p. 159-160.

[3] *Ibid.*

[4] A similar pair found in Egypt can be seen in the Benaki Museum; see SEGALL, 1938, p. 69, pl. 21, no. 71.

[5] HACKENS, p. 79.

[6] WALTERS, 1979, pl. 252.

[7] HACKENS, p. 77-84, fig. 26-29.

[8] MARSHALL, *BMCJ*, pl. XXXI-XXXII.

[9] GREIFENHAGEN, II, pl. 44, fig. 7-8 and 13-18.

18
Disc earring with Victory pendant

Hellenistic, provenance unknown, late 4th c. B.C.
Diam. of disc 1 × 0.9 cm; h. of pendant 2.5 cm.
Anonymous European loan.

The earring is comprised of three parts: a hook, disc and figurine pendant. The hook, which is tapered at the end and bent into a loop, is soldered into a second strip of gold which runs down the central axis of the back of the disc. The end of the hook wraps through a loop at the top of the figure and winds around itself. The disc is made from a single sheet of gold. The rims have been raised and trimmed with a double ring of twisted wire. A simple rosette with nine filigree petals and a single gold granule is situated within the plate of the disc. The figure suspended from the disc is constructed from two sheets of gold. The front of the form is embossed with a figure of Victory wearing a chiton. The back is simply a sheet of plain gold which was hammered to match approximately the embossed form. The two halves are fitted together by overlapping seams. The wings which stretch up and out from the body were made separately and soldered on at the back.

The Victory or Nike figure was as popular a motif as the Eros figure throughout the Hellenistic period. This earring is among early examples of the disc-pendant type, others of which have been found in tombs in Thebes, Kerch and Kyme. Late Hellenistic examples are characterized by elaborate discs, embellished with filigree and precious stones from which dangle finely chased and etched animated figurine pendants.

Numerous parallels and variations can be cited. Those which are most closely related are a pair of third century earrings in the British Museum [1] and a pair from Pangaeus, in Macedonia, now in the Staatliche Museen, Berlin [2].

MJA

[1] MARSHALL, *BMCJ*, pl. XXXII, no. 1845-1846; see also no. 1849-1850 and 1910-1911.
[2] GREIFENHAGEN, I, pl. 12, no. 7-8; cf., pl. 13, no. 1; cf. G. DEMORTIER article in this catalogue for analysis of this piece p. 226.

19

Hoop earring with Eros

Hellenistic, provenance unknown, late 4th-2nd c. B.C.
Diam. 1 cm; height of Eros 1.1 cm.
Anonymous European loan.

The nude figure of the winged Eros is bent backwards to form the front of the hoop. The braided rope of gold is attached to Eros' head and passes first through a semi-circular loop soldered to his feet and then between his legs. The transition from the head of the figure to the rope is disguised by a small rosette which is delicately folded around the top of the hoop. The front of the elongated figure is cast from a single sheet of gold; there is no corresponding posterior. The facial features, eyes, nose and mouth are carved in some detail; the arms and torso, however, are only summarily executed. The hands are attached at the hips. The wings were embossed separately and soldered behind each shoulder. Both wings stretch directly back from the body, following the contour of the arms. Eros wears a filigree banderole, which passes diagonally from his right shoulder to his left hip. Small globules of gold hang at irregular intervals from either side of the strap.

Although the Eros figure was a common motif in Hellenistic jewelry, this particular earring type occurs with less frequency than do the great variety of Eros pendant earrings. Several closely related examples and a number of variants have been discovered sporadically in regions as far north as southern Russia and as far south as Crete. The most precise parallel to this piece is a pair of earrings in a private collection, which repeats exactly all the features of this earring with the exception of the gold braided hoop which, in this example, is of plain wire[1]. In a number of late fourth century earrings, such as the pair in the Stathatos Collection, Athens[2], a precious stone has been substituted for the rosette. Other parallels can be found in the Museum of Art, Rhode Island School of Design[3], the British Museum[4] and in the Staatliche Museen, Berlin[5].

MJA

[1] See Sotheby's «Fine Antiquities», auction catalogue, May 1982, no. 201.
[2] AMANDRY, 1958, p. 211, no. 29; cf. HIGGINS, 1980, p. 161, pl. 47i.
[3] HACKENS, p. 91, fig. 34a-b.
[4] MARSHALL, *BMCJ*, pl. XXI, no. 1714-1715.
[5] GREIFENHAGEN, 1, pl. 21, no. 8-9; 11, pl. 43, no. 1, 9, 10, 13, 17.

20
Finger ring

Hellenistic, provenance unknown, late
3rd c. B.C.
Maximum diam. 2.28 cm; max. w.
1.3 cm.
Museum of Art, Rhode Island School
of Design.
Acc. no. 25.116.
Gift of Ostby and Barton Co. in
memory of Engelhardt Cornelius
Ostby.
Bibliography:
HACKENS, p. 93, fig. 36a-d.

The ring is solid cast and has no bezel. The broad face of the ring is incised with the bust of a winged Eros. The head of the figure is shown in profile and is more deeply engraved than the chest, which is seen in three-quarter view. The wings and the hair of the intaglio are finely chased. Four rows of short curls cap the forehead; the hair becomes longer and falls around the neck at the back. Parts of the arms are also indicated. A delicate single strand of garland lies obliquely across Eros' chest.

Although Eros figurines continued to be popular as earring pendants into the second century B.C., the heavy, simple style and the absence of polychromy in this signet ring suggest a date of late fourth-early third century B.C. The most closely related, although not exact, parallels for this example can be found in Paris in the de Luynes Collection (no. 528), in the British Museum [1] and in the Staatliche Museen, Berlin [2]. A similar ring type with the figure of Eros riding a dolphin can be seen in the Ionides Collection [3].

MJA

[1] MARSHALL, *BMC Finger Rings*, pl. XLIII, no. 126 and no. 1103.
[2] GREIFENHAGEN, 1, pl. 58, no. 6.
[3] BOARDMAN, 1968, p. 95, fig. 29.

21
Herakles Knot

L. 5.5 cm; diam. of knot 2.2 cm.
Williams College Museum of Art,
Rogers Collection.
Acc. no. E45.

In this example, the knot is of the simple, flat type, constructed from two separate loops of sheet gold which interlock with one another. Each loop, an approximate mirror image of the other, is trimmed on the inside and outside by a braid of twisted wire. The face of the knot is decorated with double strands of twisted wire organized in a rhythmic, spiralling pattern. The spirals are studded at regular intervals above and below by circlets of gold. A small rosette comprised of eight petals and a single gold granule provides the centerpiece of the knot. Two palmettes of unequal size stretch out from either side of the rosette. The interiors of the two flat collars which sheath the terminals of the arms of the knot are decorated by small rosettes, which repeat exactly the central motif. The rosettes are placed asymmetrically between double strands of twisted wire. On the right, the passage of the knot into the collar is concealed by a row of pointed leaves. A pair of single gold spirals which are fastened to the back of the knot extend from above and below each of the collars. Two large, wide semi-circular loops protrude from

the ends of the collars. These loops were probably intended to support a heavy gold chain or band.

The Herakles knot was introduced in Egypt in the second millenium as a decorative motif of secondary interest believed to have amuletic potency. The knot became particularly popular as a symbol of strength, power and love during the Hellenistic and Roman periods. It is by virtue of its popularity as a decorative and symbolic motif that it has become an appropriate form for imitation.

Stylistically, this piece is consistent with Herakles knots which appear frequently during the late fourth and third centuries B.C. as the central ornament on diadems, necklaces, thigh bands, finger rings and bracelets [1].

There are several reasons, however, for suggesting that this example is among numerous modern-day forgeries. Hoffmann, in his investigation of forgeries, argues that the backs of modern Herakles knots are characterized by milling marks, faint parallel lines produced by a steel roller [2]. Under microscopic investigation, marks, somewhat marred by scratches, resemble those noted by Hoffmann. But it is the lack of technical symmetry and iconographical consistency which confirms this knot to be a forgery. One notes specifically the random assemblage of

sumptuous ornament and the lack of control experienced by the forger during the heating process. This problem caused the filigree wire to change arbitrarily in thickness and flooding to occur in the joints. Hoffmann has also noted that the arms of authentic knots typically have tapered ends; in this example, however, the diameter of the arms is uniform throughout[3]. These technical imperfections and irregularities suggest that perhaps the forger was consulting recent publications on metalworking without understanding or observing the compositional principles which govern original examples.

The absence of elaborate figurines, animal head finials, and precious gems in this example suggests that the forger was perhaps looking at a late fourth century example, such as the distant parallel now in the Staatliche Museen, Berlin[4].

MJA

[1] Elaborate Herakles knot bracelets are particularly rare, the only known authenticated example was in the Staatliche Museen, Berlin (now lost, can be seen in BECATTI, p. 444, pl. 23), in the Cairo Museum and in a private collection (see HOFFMANN-DAVIDSON, p. 152, fig. 54a-f). An unusual bracelet was recently auctioned in Europe, see Galerie Koller, Zurich, *Collection d'Orfèvrerie antique*, November, 1982, p. 28, no. 30 (the description suggests that the mounting is a modern bracelet).

[2] HOFFMANN, *Greek Gold Reconsidered*, in *AJA* 73, 1969, p. 447-452. Cf. GREIFENHAGEN, review of HOFFMANN-DAVIDSON, *Greek Gold*, in *Gnomon*, 40, 1968, p. 695-700.

[3] *Ibid.*, p. 448.

[4] *Ibid.*

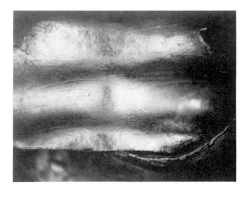

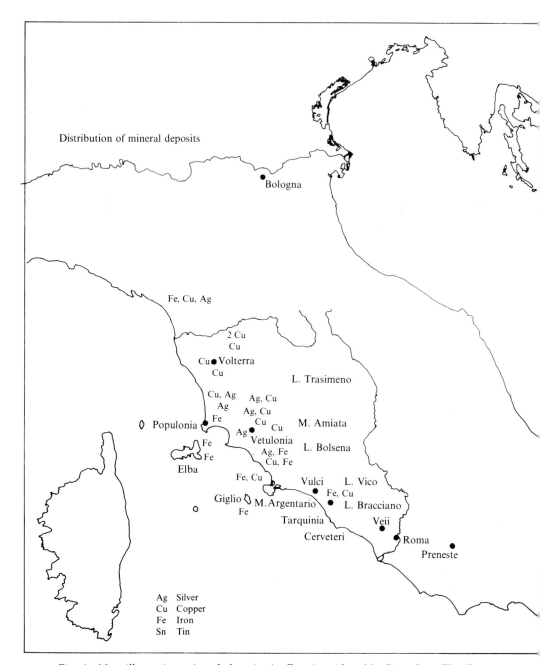

Distribution of mineral deposits

Bologna

Fe, Cu, Ag

2 Cu
Cu
Cu● Volterra
Cu

L. Trasimeno

Cu, Ag   Ag, Cu
Ag   Ag, Cu
Fe   Cu   Cu   M. Amiata
Populonia ●   Ag ●
Fe   Vetulonia
Fe   Ag, Fe   L. Bolsena
Elba   Cu, Fe

Fe, Cu   Vulci   L. Vico
Fe, Cu
Giglio ◊   M. Argentario ●   L. Bracciano
Fe   Veii
Tarquinia
Cerveteri   ● Roma
Preneste

Ag   Silver
Cu   Copper
Fe   Iron
Sn   Tin

Fig. 6. Map illustrating mineral deposits in Etruria. After M. Cristofani, The Etruscans.
A new investigation, *London, 1979, p. 54.*

ETRURIA

One distinctive feature of jewelry recovered from excavations in the region of Etruria is the technological virtuosity of those craftsmen in their handling of gold. Refinement of granulation, filigree, repoussé and engraving, combined with a penchant for overall decorative schema, are hallmarks of the Etruscan style. Refinement of technique and complex decorative patterns are expressed through many forms of objects in various media. Both domestic and foreign goods found within the tombs [1] exhibit a complexity of design which suggests that foreign traders may have developed wares to satisfy Etruscan taste.

Within the tombs a vast array of quality objects has been unearthed suggesting a people of great wealth. At the end of the eighth century B.C. and throughout the seventh century B.C. exceedingly rich graves appear in Etruria. Burial sites from Vetulonia and Chiusi in the north to Caere, Tarquinia and Praeneste in the south all contain tombs of splendid wealth. A sudden profusion of bronze objects, terracotta, bronze and iron figurines, and gold jewelry is found in excavations of these sites displaying a marked contrast to the simpler Villanovan burials of the preceding two centuries [2]. The rapid accumulation of riches in Etruria was dependent upon the geographic nature of the region and the early unification of villages into urban centers.

The physical geography of Etruria ranged from the Apennine mountains, rich in forests and woodlands, to the alluvial coastal plains of the Maremma, ideally suited to agriculture. During the eighth century B.C., numerous primitive villages became consolidated into larger socially differentiated centers, an environment in which an artisan class could flourish. While the geography of Etruria aided greatly in the development of the civilization, many scholars believe that the greatest contribution to wealth and culture lay in the geological features — vast deposits of copper, tin and iron — making the region one of the richest metallurgical centers in the Mediterranean.

Geological surveys reveal the wealth of these deposits (see fig. 6). Copper and iron are present in the middle elevation ranges, such as the Colline Metallifere in the north, Mounts Amiata and Cetona in central Etruria and the Tolfa mountains to the south. The actual beginning of mineral exploitation at sufficient levels to attract foreign trade is disputed [3], yet a date in the seventh century B.C. seems logical for the beginning of the systematic exploitation of mineral deposits.

---

[1] Information on Etruscan culture is to be gathered mainly through archaeological excavations, particularly of tombs, since no definitive Etruscan literary source has been recovered that would give an indication of contemporary culture. Brief mention is made of Etruria in later Greek and Roman writings.

[2] By reviewing early gold jewelry in northern European museum collections, von Hase has found gold fibulae that are from Villanovan tombs. He suggests that they are of domestic production. Yet stylistic comparisons place these pieces in the eighth century B.C. when Phoenician traders could have brought foreign goods to Villanovan sites. F. W. VON HASE, *Zur Problematik der frühesten Goldfunde in Mittelitaliens*, in *Hamburger Beiträge zur Archäologie*, 5, 1975, p. 99-182.

[3] When these rich mineral resources were actually mined in ancient times is difficult to determine.

An abundant supply of timber near the mining sites facilitated the smelting of ore without the expense of shipping unrefined metals. The many unskilled laborers needed for the hand-sorting of ore for roasting could be supplied by the cities, their labor coordinated by a few skilled workers who would direct the smelting process[4]. This early organization of the society into strong economic groups is most likely responsible for the inability of the Phoenicians and Greeks to establish their own mining colonies within Etruscan territory[5].

One of the centers that benefited from the exploitation of regional mineral resources was Vetulonia which in ancient times lay near the sea-lagoon of Lake Prilius, its protected harbor. The presence of several rich graves including the *Tomba della Straniera*, the *Tomba del Duce*, the *Circolo dei Monili* and the *Tomba del Littore* supports the contention that a small group of powerful individuals controlled the economic and political direction of the city. The mineral wealth of the city, combined with its accessible harbor, prompted extensive trading with other civilizations of the Mediterranean basin.

The Phoenicians were the first people to set up numerous colonies in the western Mediterranean for the purposes of trade. While Phoenician traders may have come to Etruria to trade wares for Etruscan metals, several of their own colonies were situated to take advantage of mineral deposits. Settlement of the Balearic island of Ebusus (Ibiza) and a trading-post at Gades (Cádiz) gave the Phoenicians access to the gold and silver of the Iberian coast[6]. Gold from the Segura and other rivers of the Sierra Nevada was extracted through washing in sluices. The production here was considerable, though even greater deposits were exploited in Galicia and the Asturias. Trading colonies were established on the island of Sardinia to receive these metals. The closest trading partner with the Etruscans was the city of Tharros, located on the west coast of the island to receive precious metals from the western settlements. The workshops of Tharros contributed to her status as the wealthiest Sardinian city and the most important trading center in the Carthaginian west. The key exchange between Tharros and the cities of northern Etruria would have been a trade of gold and tin for Etruscan

---

One reason is that these areas have not, except in a few cases, been extensively excavated. More importantly, later mining may have disturbed any archaeological evidence for the earliest, systematic, large-scale exploitation of these regions. Consequently, varying dates have been suggested — Grant, for instance, proposes a date of the eighth century B.C., whereas Cristofani and Minto, who have conducted excavations in mining and ore-processing areas, feel that the early sixth century is a more probable dating for such systematic mining. See M. GRANT, *The Etruscans*, 1980, p. 14; M. CRISTOFANI, *Ricerche archeologiche nella zona 'industriale' di Populonia*, in *Prospettiva*, 16, 1979, p. 74-76; A. MINTO, *I Materiali archeologici*, in *StEtr*, 11, 1937, p. 305-341.

[4] P. G. WARDEN, *The Colline Metallifere: Prolegomena to the Study of Mineral Exploitation in Central Italy*, in *Crossroads of the Mediterranean*, (*Archaeologia Transatlantica*, 2), Louvain-la-Neuve, 1983.

[5] A. RATHJE, *Oriental Imports in Etruria in the Eighth and Seventh Centuries B.C.: Their Origins and Implications*, in *Italy Before the Romans*, D. and F. R. Ridgway, eds., London, 1979, p. 179.

[6] The leading Iberian silver mining regions were Castulo and Mastia (Cartagena). Castulo was known in ancient times as *mons argentarius*. The Phoenicians also established outposts in southwest Britain (Cornwall) for the procurement of tin, as the British Isles were a major source for this metal in antiquity.

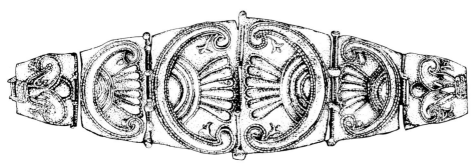

Fig. 7. Bracelet from Tharros, gold, 7th c. B.C., British Museum. After Marshall, BMCJ, *no. 1542.*

Fig. 8. Bracelet from Tharros, gold, 7th c. B.C., Museo Nazionale, Cagliari. After Becatti, no. 227.

Fig. 9. Bracelet from Tarquinia, gold, 7th c. B.C., British Museum. After Marshall, BMCJ, *no. 1358.*

bronze implements and weapons, as tin was a valuable ingredient in Etruscan bronze.

An investigation of objects discovered in tombs reveals the importance of Tharros as an intermediary in the trade between Iberia and Etruria. Two exceptional gold bracelets from Tharros have stylistic similarities to jewelry from both Aliseda in Iberia and several sites in Etruria. The first, a six-segment bracelet in the British Museum (no. 1542) is embossed with large palmettes and lotus blossoms that are outlined in granulation. The second, from the Museo Nazionale, Cagliari, has identical motifs with the addition of a central rectangular panel embossed with Egyptian motifs. Identical palmettes and lotus motifs are found on numerous pieces from the Aliseda hoard. These same forms appear in Etruria as shown by the repoussé designs on a pair of bracelets from Tarquinia now in the British Museum (no. 1358-9).

A similar comparison can be made for swivel scarab rings which are found at Aliseda and in Etruria. At both locations there are rings with spiral attachments so they could hang as pendants, showing a close artistic heritage. The presence of Egyptian motifs in both Iberian and Etruscan art can be explained by the role the Phoenicians played in spreading eastern motifs to the west. It was the Phoenicians who carried the Egyptian techniques of filigree and granulation to the western Mediterranean.

Iconographic similarities exist as well between Carthaginian and Etruscan jewelry. The motif of a crescent moon encircling a solar disc which appears frequently on Carthaginian examples is also found as a pendant motif on a necklace from Vulci (see figs. 10 and 11). In addition, the "Master of Animals" motif is common in both cultures (see cat no. 22).

There were also Phoenician and Carthaginian trading centers (emporia) in Etruria, notably at Graviscae, a port of Tarquinia and at Punicum and Pyrgi, ports of Caere[7]. The large quantities of gold jewelry that appear in southern Etruscan tombs in the seventh century may be explained by the proximity of these Phoenician emporia to the major urban centers of the south. Although the great mineral wealth lay to the north, perhaps gold was exchanged for the region's abundant agricultural products. Jewelry within tombs such as the Regolini-Galassi at Caere the Barberini and the Bernardini tombs at Praeneste show close parallels with Phoenician models[8].

Another important trading partner with Etruria was the great emporium of Pithecusae (Ischia). The Phoenicians may have begun their development of trading settlements by establishing a colony at Pithecusae prior to Greek arrival there in the eighth century B.C.[9], but it was under the Euboean colonists that trading center experienced its most intensive relationship with the Etruscan mainland.

It is no coincidence that the emporium of Pithecusae grew rapidly just as the Etruscan city-states were drawing together, for the consolidated centers of wealth were ideal points of exchange. This revival of Greek interest in the west after the fall of Mycenaean Greece corresponded to the Geometric period of Greek art. This style, characterized by maeander and zig-zag patterns in horizontal bands, was soon to be found in conjunction with orientalizing motifs from the Near East on crafts throughout the Mediterranean. Greek colonies in Asia Minor were responsible for spreading oriental design to the west, as well as supplying, as is the case of Al Mina (Syria), gold from the eastern interior[10].

Pithecusae, with its central location off the southern Italian coast, became a leading center for the fusion of design and the dispersal of wares throughout the Mediterranean. Like most emporia of ancient times, it attracted craftsmen and

---

[7] M. GRANT, *op. cit.*, p. 132, 150-155.

[8] L. PARETI, *La Tomba Regolini-Galassi*, Vatican City, 1947; C. D. CURTIS, *The Barberini Tomb*, in *MAAR*, 5, 1925, p. 9-25; C. D. CURTIS, *The Bernardini Tomb*, in *MAAR*, 3, 1919, p. 9-90.

[9] M. GRANT, *op. cit.*, p. 35.

[10] Al Mina was located at the mouth of the Orontes in northern Syria and was probably the earliest and most important of Greek settlements in the east. It was important as a supplier of gold as well as copper and iron, a distinction it shared with the city of Chalcis. See J. BOARDMAN, *The Greeks Overseas*, 2nd. ed., London, 1980, p. 38-40.

Fig. 10. Necklace from Vulci, gold, 7th c. B.C., Antikensammlungen, Munich. After Higgins, 1980, pl. 33B.

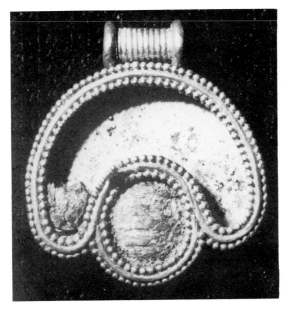

Fig. 11. Carthaginian pendants, gold, 7th c. B.C., Musée National de Carthage. Cfr Br. Quillard, Bijoux Carthaginois (Aurifex 2), pl. IX, no. 6(B).

merchants of all races to its harbors and workshops. When Strabo (5.4-9) describes the prosperity of Pithecusae as being dependent upon *chryseia* (χρυσεῖα), he most likely meant goldsmiths' workshops as opposed to gold mines[11]. Geological investigation has not detected major sources of gold on the island of Ischia, while archaeological evidence has unearthed craftsmen's tools, as well as miscastings to help support the presence of a gold workshop.

Similarities in gold jewelry, particularly fibulae with elongated catchplates (see cat. no. 22) found at both Pithecusae and Etruscan sites, suggest that most of the

---

[11] That Χρυσεῖα should be translated as "goldsmiths' workshops", as opposed to "gold mines", was first suggested by Buchner in 1972 and is discussed in G. Buchner, *Early Orientalizing: Aspects of the Euboean Connection*, in D. and F. R. Ridgway, *op. cit.*, p. 135-137.

gold arriving in Etruria may have been in the form of finished ornaments. The Euboeans at Pithecusae would have been familiar with the Greek motifs, both Geometric and eastern, as well as a tradition of working in gold which they could have developed in their early colonies in Asia Minor. The sudden appearance of numerous spectacular pieces of gold jewelry within Etruscan tombs, combined with the lack of a native tradition in gold working, suggests that most of the orientalizing gold jewelry found in Etruria in the seventh century was of foreign manufacture [12].

Early orientalizing goldwork is represented in tombs throughout Etruria, and the closeness of form and similarity of decoration suggest a single place of production. While some scholars suggest a southern Etruscan city [13], Pithecusae, with its organized commercial structure, would seem a more likely candidate [14].

As the importance of Pithecusae grew, the need for additional agricultural goods prompted the founding of a second colony on the mainland at Cumae. Spectacular gold ornaments have been recovered on this site which show parallels to the works from Pithecusae. Comparisons also exist between works from Cumae and Etruscan finds. Comb fibulae from Cumae, such as those in the Museo Nazionale, Naples, are found at numerous sites in Etruria [15], their decorative schema all possessing similar components. As Ischia grew too small to hold the growing populations, perhaps small workshops of goldsmiths moved to other emporia in the region, such as Cumae, as the excavations suggest.

Very near to Vetulonia lay the emporium of Populonia, which, even after it had achieved city status, never gained true independence from Vetulonia. As is common throughout the western Mediterranean, emporia attracted a variety of cultures to one region for the purpose of trade, so it does not seem unreasonable to suggest that a gold workshop of Greek craftsmen trained at Pithecusae may have been in residence near Vetulonia. That Greek workshops with a common training may have been established in the key cities and emporia is further suggested by the closeness of jewelry types at different locations in Etruria, though decorative techniques vary slightly. A preference for a silhouette granulation style existed in the north, while in the south an outline granulation style was preferred. This subtle difference in stylistic approach may show the preference of a particular workshop which had established itself in the Etruscan city and set a particular character for the jewelry produced in that area. Thus, gold jewelry produced within Etruria may have been of Greek manufacture. This challenges the popular belief that the Etruscans were quick to imitate and absorb outside influences and make them their own.

Etruscans were great workers of iron and bronze. Earlier scholarship suggested that since the Etruscans were superb metallurgists, their work in bronze would naturally lead to work in gold. While it cannot be denied that motifs may have been

[12] *Ibid.*, p. 137.

[13] I. STRØM, *Problems concerning the Origin and Early Development of the Etruscan Orientalizing Style*, Odense, 1971, p. 89, 106, and P. G. GUZZO, *Su due classi di affibbiagli etruschi del sec. VII a. C.*, in *StEtr*, 36, 1968, p. 298-301.

[14] BUCHNER, *op. cit.*

[15] Comb fibulae can be found in the following Etruscan tombs: the Tomba Barberini and the Tomba Bernardini, Praeneste; the Tomba Regolini-Galassi, Caere; Tomb 2, Falerii; Tombs 3, 32 and 38, Narce; and also in tombs in Marsiliana and Picenum. STRØM, *op. cit.*, p. 100-101.

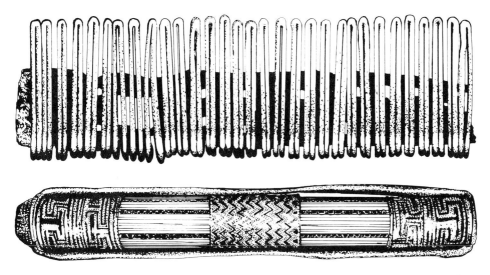

Fig. 12. Comb fibula from Caere, gold, 7th. c. B.C., British Museum. After Higgins, 1980, pl. 39B.

transferred between the cultures, it seems unlikely that a sudden flourishing of native Etruscan goldsmiths would rise out of the smelting trades — an ironmonger is not a goldsmith.

As various Greek cultures expanded toward the west (Corinthians, Phocaeans, Athenians), their colonies and colonists within the emporia influenced the appearance and availability of crafts within Etruria. By the middle of the sixth century B.C., Etruscan trade had reached from the Tyrrhenian Sea to the Adriatic. As Etruscan cities on the western coast of Italy demanded more direct trading routes with the eastern Mediterranean, emporia were established on the east coast of Italy, particularly at the mouth of the Po river, to receive goods that would be transported to the west by overland routes.

By the sixth century these emporia had become such cosmopolitan centers that it is hard to decipher through excavation exactly which civilization was responsible for the founding of the settlement. Both Spina and Adria, emporia near the mouth of the Po, contained varied populations of Etruscans and Greeks. While Spina is considered an Etruscan and Adria a Greek emporium, their characters are remarkably similar. Gold jewelry unearthed at Spina, although an Etruscan settlement, should possibly be considered of Greek manufacture, for the more severe sculptural qualities of the workmanship and representation of Greek iconography (see cat. no. 28) show close ties to Hellenic artistic style.

Is there, indeed, a tradition of native Etruscan goldcraft, or is a great deal of the gold jewelry discovered in Etruria the creation of itinerant Greeks establishing workshops at key Etruscan cities and emporia? As future archaeological investigations are undertaken and more comprehensive, comparative studies are made between various jewelry deposits, a more thorough understanding of Etruscan culture and its relationship to other Mediterranean peoples may come to light.

Ivette M. Richard
Richard W. Sadow

22
Fibula

Etruscan, provenance unknown, 7th c.
B.C.
L. 9.8 cm; h. of bow 1.6 cm.
Museum of Art, Rhode Island School
of Design.
Acc. no. 30.051.
Formerly collection of Dr. Ludwig Pol-
lak, Rome.
Museum appropriation and special gift.
Bibliography:
HACKENS, p. 22-34.
G. M. A. HANFMANN, *The Etruscans
and Their Art*, in *BullRISD*, 27, no. 1,
1940, p. 10-11, fig. 10-11.
L. E. ROWE, *The Gold Fibula*, in
BullRISD, 22, no. 1, 1934, p. 13-17.
R. S. TIETZ, ed., *Masterpieces of Etrus-
can Art*, Worcester, 1967, p. 20, illus.
p. 119.
See additional illustrations, infra p. 189.

Except for a minor dent and scratches on
the front face of the bow, and some other
indentations, this fibula of *sanguisuga* or
mignatta type shows little modern restoration
of damage. Some flooding of the granulation
with solder near the pin suggests that the pin
has been reattached in modern times. The
pin, enclosed in an elongated catchplate, is
attached to one end of the bow, while the
catchplate itself is attached to the other end.
Cylindrical elements, with circular plates at
each end, are used as attachments for the pin
and sheath to the bow. These cylinders, along
with the bow and catchplate, are decorated
with *pulviscolo* granulation. Distinctive is the
handling of the granulation. While many
figures are rendered in silhouette granulation,
some features such as the faces of the
sphinxes, the wings of the main figure and
some of the animals are worked in the outline
style. Very possibly from Vetulonia [1], where a
preference for plain-granulation existed, the
combination of two styles of granulation on
the fibula indicates influences of the more
advanced orientalizing style.
A variety of granulated patterns and
figures cover the fibula. Masking the lateral
seam of the bow, and on the flat section along

the top of the sheath, two related geometric
patterns are used. On the upper part of the
bow and on part of the sheath is a pattern
composed of double elongated "z's". The
simpler rendition of this design, using a single
row of granulation is found on the underside
of the bow and on the narrower section of the
sheath.
The remaining surfaces of the fibula are
filled with various human and animal figures.
On the sheath is a file of animals running
toward the bow, including a sphinx, horse,
feline, griffin, stag, goat and dog. These
animals are rendered in a more naturalistic
manner than on parallel fibulae from Vetulonia. This type of animal file is derived from
Near Eastern examples. Beneath this, on the
underside of the sheath, a tiny fish carefully
outlined in granulation, swims in a sea of
stylized waves.
Both front and back faces of the bow are
composed of animals grouped around a
central figure. These are a combination of
fantastic and naturalistic creatures. The two
beasts flanking the central figure are prominent in the design. One is a lion; the other,
a sphinx, has a triangularly-shaped head outlined in granulation. Four curls of hair frame
the head and curl inwards, reminiscent of
Hathor locks, perhaps indicating an Egyptian
or more generally, an oriental influence.
Many other animals surround the central
group. On the front face of the bow, a griffin
and a sphinx stand opposite one another
below the central figure. Outline granulation
is used again in the pointed wing of the
griffin. To the right of the sphinx is another
animal, not readily identifiable. To the
extreme left, near the cylindrical element,
appears yet another griffin above a reclining
dog. It is in this area that damage from
resoldering is visible.
Looking underneath the bow two more
animals can be seen. These two, a stag at the
right and another animal on the left, are
antithetically arranged with their hind legs
overlapping.
The back face of the bow constitutes a
slight variation. Beneath the central figure, a

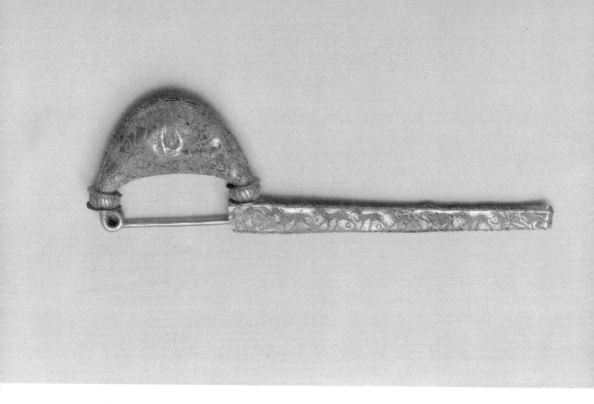

dog attacks a sphinx. Behind the dog on the right, one sees a mountain goat with vegetal motifs beneath it. Opposite this, to the extreme left of the bow, are two super-imposed animals of similar type. The tail of one is spiral, of the other, short. Below, toward the underside of the bow, a griffin attacks a goat.

The focus of the composition is the central double-headed figure, with long curled wings and symmetrically upraised arms. Whether the figure is male or female has been questioned. It is often described as a female deity, but most recently Hackens labels it as male[2]. This seems to be supported by Bonfante's analysis of garments represented on monuments of the Orientalizing period[3]. A long Daedalic chiton was worn by both men and women, but it was always worn belted by women. Here the garment hangs loosely, indicating a male figure.

In addition, the headdress of this figure resembles a type on male figures of the seventh century. The "feather-crown" is found on many bronzes and terracottas from Etruscan tombs[4]. Many Egyptian Bes figu-rines found in Etruscan tombs and through-out the eastern Mediterranean during the seventh century are represented with similar headdresses. Bonfante points out that this

type of headdress is traditionally associated with soldiers, musicians, dancers and with animal-tamers[5]. A seventh century example from the Palace of Ashurbanipal at Nineveh shows such a musician and animal-tamer wearing a feather-crown[6].

The connection of a feather headdress with animal-taming is especially significant. The arrangement of the central figure between two animals and surrounded by other crea-tures of great variety would suggest a "Master of Animals" iconography. It follows a long tradition, going back to Mesopotamia, and it was part of the Near Eastern reper-toire. Examples of such figures also exist in Etruscan art[7]. However, the figure on the fibula, being both winged and double-headed[8], is rather unique, since one finds eastern examples of winged bifrons and winged "Master of Animals", each within their separate iconographic settings.

The dual nature of this figure creates difficulty in iconographic interpretation. This conglomeration of figures and patterns and the composite nature of the main figure, all carefully arranged on the fibula, suggest a merger of various eastern traditions for decorative purposes.

IMR

¹ According to HACKENS, p. 25-33, the closest parallels are Vetulonian — two fibulae of the Poggio della Guardia; two fibulae, a pin and a gold bracelet in the Tomba del Littore; and the remaining bow of a fibula from the Costaccia Bambagini. He includes parallels from Chiusi, Rusellae, Bologna and Vulci. On stylistic and technical grounds, he dates it to the end of the seventh century.

² HACKENS, p. 21, 33.

³ L. BONFANTE, *Etruscan Dress*, Baltimore and London, 1975, p. 32-34.

⁴ E.H. RICHARDSON, *The Recurrent Geometric in the Sculpture of Central Italy, and its Bearing on the Problem of the Origin of the Etruscans*, in *MAAR*, 27, 1962, p. 186-188, and fig. 64-66, 72-75.

⁵ BONFANTE, p. 69.

⁶ R.D. BARNETT, *Assyrische Palastreliefs*, Prague, 1960, fig. 54.

⁷ Cf. STRØM, p. 209, no. S III 9 (an embossed gold sheet from Caere, Regolini-Galassi Tomb) and S III 24 (from Vetulonia, Tomba del Duce); G. CAMPOREALE, *Sul motivo del cosidetto Despotes Theron in Etruria*, in *ArchCl*, 17, 1965, p. 36-53, pl. 14-18; MARSHALL, *BMCJ*, no. 1356, (a bracelet from Praeneste); HIGGINS, 1980, pl. 37A.

⁸ Such double-headed figures have their origin in the east. This representation may anticipate Janus, although Janus is not associated with "Master of Animals" iconography. See P. ACKERMAN, *The Oriental Origins of Janus and Hermes*, in *Bulletin of the American Institute for Iranian Art and Archaeology*, 5, no. 3, 1938, p. 216-225.

23
Pair of bracelets

Etruscan, provenance unknown, 7th c.
B.C.
W. 2.5 cm; diam. 3.9 cm; w. 2.4 cm;
diam. 4.0 cm.
Courtesy of the Walters Art Gallery,
Baltimore.
Acc. no. 57.395-6.
Bibliography:
J. V. CANBY, D. BUITRON and A. OLI-
VER, *Ancient Jewelry in Baltimore*, in
Archaeology, 32, 1979, p. 53-56.
WALTERS, 1979, p. 70, fig. 222.

This pair of bracelets, remarkably well
preserved, is part of a set of four [1]. Plain
wires outlined with twisted wire alternate
with undulating wires, and they are joined
together to form a wide band of openwork
filigree. The two ends are banded by narrow
strips of filigree which run along the width of
the bracelet providing a border. From the
border, a double strip of openwork filigree
extends to form a hook and eye clasp [2]. This
combination of very fine twisted and smooth
wires and waved patterning is aptly called
trina-lacework.

Usually found in pairs, Vetulonian bracelets were worn by both men and women.
Sometimes the pairs consist of matched
bracelets of the same size. Other times, one
bracelet is larger than the other, one worn on
the upper arm, the other at the wrist.

Although very similar to other bracelets
found in Vetulonian tombs, this pair varies
from the "Vetulonian" type [3]. Two pairs of
gold filigree bracelets from the Circolo dei
Monili, provide comparisons [4]. Whereas the
Walters' bracelets are composed of alternating strips forming one wide band, the
examples from the Circolo dei Monili are
characteristically divided into three units,
with the long central section extending to
form the clasp. Each of the three units is
terminated with a separate semilunar boss.
Other bracelets of this type have finials of
human heads, circular or triangular bosses,
or repoussé strips [5]. The reserved style of
the Walters' bracelets may indicate a closer
affinity to the Geometric period prior to the
emerging orientalizing influences.

Bracelets of similar form, but made of gold
sheets rather than openwork filigree are
found in southern Etruria [6]. These bracelets
are decorated with repoussé, granulation or a
combination of these techniques. Intricately
and elaborately ornamented, these repoussé
bracelets lack the delicacy of their northern
counterparts.

IMR

24
Two pendants

Carthaginian, provenance unknown,
7th-6th c. B.C.
A: H. 0.8 cm; w. 0.7 cm;
B: H. 1.1 cm; w. 0.7 cm.
Anonymous European Loan.

[1] The other pair, also at the Walters Art Gallery (acc. no. 57.393-394), are slightly larger than these bracelets found in groups of four are not unusual. One such example is a set of four gold filigree bracelets found in the Circolo dei Monili, a Vetulonian tomb.

[2] On one of the bracelets (acc. no. 57.395), the clasp has broken off and the extending double strip of filigree has been glued to the end of the bracelet.

[3] For a description of "Vetulonian" type, refer to L. BANTI, *The Etruscan Cities and their Culture*, London, 1973, p. 257.

[4] *Ibid.*, fig. 64c.

[5] There may be some connection between Vetulonian filigree bracelets and jewelry found in Iberia. Filigree was also a technique used, although vegetal patterning was preferred over geometric motifs. Corollaries exist between bracelets in Iberia and Etruria in finial motifs. See G. NICOLINI, *The Ancient Spaniards*, Farnborough, Hants, 1974, p. 190-195. A pair of bracelets, probably Vetulonian, shows other similarities. Here the central finial is composed of a lunar crescent below a sunburst motif, reminiscent of Phoenician/Carthaginian examples. Sotheby Parke Bernet, Inc. auction catalogue, Dec. 9, 1981, no. 271.

[6] See HIGGINS, 1980, pl. 36, who illustrates two Tarquinian examples. KARO, 2, 1902, p. 97-114, describes the various bracelets found in Vetulonia and elsewhere in Etruria.

These two dissimilar gold pendants exhibit stylistic similarities with Carthaginian necklace pendants. Both pieces have tubular loops of wire. Pendant A has a four-ring loop of unornamented wire; pendant B is the same with the addition of larger collar terminations. Both types of loops appear with frequency in Carthaginian jewelry.

Two sheets of gold soldered together form the body of the pendants. The pentagonal form of pendant A is margined by a plain wire border; a plain wire ring is soldered to

both faces of the pendant. The shape of this pendant is not common in Carthaginian types. Pendant B represents one of the variations of a common Carthaginian theme. The two circular plates are beaten into convex forms. The back of the pendant is without decoration. The front is shaped by a repoussé crescent reflecting the upper border of the form and a shallow depression which contains a pyramid of four gold granules. The condition of the pendant complicates the understanding of the motif.

Similar pendants to pendant B exist on a late seventh-early sixth century B.C. necklace in the Musée du Bardo [1] (see fig. 11). These pendants have repoussé crescents enclosing granular triangles and a central granular diamond. The lack of a border pattern on these pendants and pendant B provides another parallel. The combination of a

crescent moon and a solar disc is a common theme which traces its origins to Egyptian art. This motif also appears on Etruscan jewelry having been brought to Etruria by Phoenician traders [2].

Pendants such as A and B would have been strung on cords through their loops. The addition of a twisted wire ring on pendant A seems incorrect. Twisted wire was used as ornamentation on Carthaginian jewelry, yet this example of two concentric twisted wire rings used to suspend a pendant has no known parallel.

RWS

[1] Br. QUILLARD, *Aurifex 2*, p. 5-6, pl. IV-V.

[2] The transfer of Phoenician/Carthaginian motifs to Etruria is discussed in the preceding essay, p. 88 ss.

25
Pair of discs

Etruscan, provenance unknown, 6th-
5th c. B.C.
Diam. 3.5 cm.
Field Museum of Natural History.
Acc. no. 2262, cat. no. 239153.1-2.

In excellent condition, this pair of gold
discs combines various techniques favored
in jewelry recovered from Etruscan tombs.
In the center of each gold sheet is a
large "sunflower" composed of three super-
imposed layers of petals. The petals are
covered with fine granulation, which does not
extend down into the central core of the
flower. Each of the petals is outlined with a
plain wire and in some cases this outline of
wire does not meet the background sheet
exactly at the outermost edge. The petals are
slightly convex and in one case (acc. no.
239153.1) one of the outer petals seems to
have caused a small puncture to the sheet
behind it. At the center of this concentric
arrangement is a granulated circular boss.

Surrounding the central element are various types of filigree. Two very fine twisted
wires border a thicker beaded wire. In the
next zone, looped wires are arranged to form
compartments around sixteen granulated,
mushroom-like bosses. Another length of
fine twisted wire and then beaded wire define
the outer border.

On the back of the discs rivet-like fasteners
indicate how the central boss and the sixteen
surrounding bosses are attached. A ring of
gold sheet, approximately 0.3 cm in height,
with about the same diameter as the sunflower on the obverse is pierced by four
holes.

The closest parallel for the pair appears to
be in Berlin [1]. They are, however, slightly
smaller than the Field Museum examples
(diam. 2.9 cm). The only other notable difference between the two pairs is that the
flowers on the discs in Berlin cover the central
zone almost completely, revealing very little
of the sheet behind them. The Field Museum

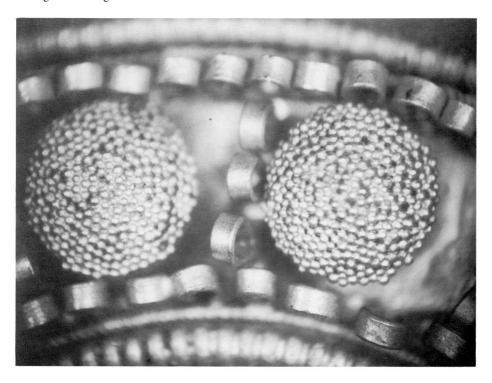

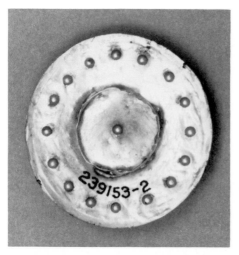

also has another pair of such discs (acc. no. 239154.1-2). However, instead of compartments formed by looped wire around each of the surrounding bosses, spirals of thinner wire encircle them, forming rosettes. A double row of large granules is placed between them. Aside from these close examples, one encounters many other elaborately decorated discs [2].

The function of the discs has been questioned. Ranging from a diameter of 2 to 6 cm, most discs have tubular projections of 1 cm extending from the back. The tube could be put through a hole in the ear lobe and a ring or pin, secured by a safety chain to the side of the disc, could be put through a loop at the end of the tube [3]. This contention seems to be supported by numerous terracottas and wall paintings [4]. They also could have been used as ornaments to fasten a garment, as fibulae [5]. In that case one disc would be placed on each shoulder and connected by a chain.

The Field Museum discs do not have a tube with a loop on the back. Greifenhagen's description of similar discs in Berlin corresponds with those in the Field Museum. He suggests that a wooden plug was used as an attachment. He does not discuss how this would have worked nor how the discs would have functioned. He opposes the notion that these discs were worn as earrings [6].

Although determining the exact function of the discs may not be possible at present, assigning a date in the sixth or early fifth century B.C. seems reasonable. The representations of discs as earrings on terracottas and wall paintings are similarly dated. Fibulae with comparable decorative schema (looped wire, other filigree and rosettes) are also dated to the late sixth and early fifth centuries [7].

IMR

[1] GREIFENHAGEN, I, p. 91, pl. 70, no. 4-5.

[2] Cf. MARSHALL, *BMCJ*, no. 1414-1426; GREIFENHAGEN, I, pl. 70, no. 1-6.

[3] HIGGINS, 1980, p. 140; G. M. A. RICHTER, *Four Notable Acquisitions of the Metropolitan Museum of Art*, in *AJA*, 44, 1940, p. 437-438, fig. 8-9; MARSHALL, *BMCJ*, p. 137.

[4] Cf. A. ANDRÈN, *Architectural Terracottas from Etrusco-Italic Temples*, (Acta Instituti Romani Regni Sueciae, 6), Lund-Leipzig, 1939-1940, pl. 2, fig. 4 (Veii); pl. 6, fig. 15, 16, 18 (Caere); pl. 10, fig. 36, 39 (Caere); pl. 11, fig. 40 (Caere) and pl. 155, fig. 521. For representations on tomb paintings, M. MORETTI, *Pittura Etrusca in Tarquinia*, Milan, 1974, pl. 19, 26, 27, 28. Also see B. VAN DEN DRIESSCHE, *Une forme de boucles d'oreilles portées par les Korai de l'Acropole*, in *Revue des Archéologues et Historiens d'art de Louvain*, 4, 1971, p. 73-96.

[5] MARSHALL, *BMCJ*, p. 137. Marshall illustrates a Boeotian terracotta statue employing discs as fibulae.

[6] GREIFENHAGEN, I, p. 91.

[7] G. M. A. RICHTER, p. 435, fig. 7; GREIFENHAGEN, I, pl. 68, no. 4.

26
Granulated bead necklace

Etruscan, provenance unknown, 6th-5th c. B.C.

L. of beads and spacers, 38.5 cm; largest bead, l. 1.8 cm, w. 1.4 cm; smallest bead, l. 1.0 cm, w. 0.7 cm.

Field Museum of Natural History. Acc. no. 2262, cat. no. 239159.

Thirty granulated gold beads comprise this necklace. Each bead is composed of two fine gold sheets that were beaten into shallow moulds and joined along a transverse seam. A decorative maeander pattern of granulation ornaments each bead; the larger central five beads have three rows of granulation in the pattern, while the remaining beads have two rows of granulation. Around the mid-line and at the two openings of each bead, one gold wire has been soldered. Single rows of granulation follow along the lengths of wire. The beads show some splitting along the seams and several dents. The discoloration of some beads can be accounted for by oxidation of component metals not thoroughly mixed in the preparation of the gold. This particular bead is described by Higgins as "lemon-shaped" [1]. One necklace in the British Museum has two beads similar to those on the Chicago necklace [2].

Between the beads are blue paste discs which ranged from clear turquoise-green to cloudy, pitted white. The necklace is terminated by a series of small gold bands. This arrangement is questionable due to the

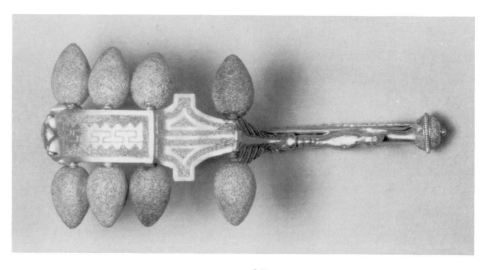

27
Etruscanizing fibula

infrequency with which blue paste appears in Etruscan jewelry.

Beaded necklaces appear frequently in representations on terracottas, bronze mirrors and wall paintings. Their popularity is confirmed by the recovery of numerous beads from excavations, including beads of bronze, terracotta, amber and other stones, silver and gold. However, few all-gold, bead necklaces of this quality have survived.

RWS

[1] HIGGINS, 1980, p. 142.
[2] MARSHALL, *BMCJ*, p. 143, pl. XXII, no. 1453.

Fig. 13. Bow fibula brooch from Naples (Melillo workshop), gold, ca. 1880, British Museum.
After H. Tait and C. Gere,
The Jeweller's Art, *London, 1978, pl. 20.*

Italian, second half 19th c.
Total l. 8.4 cm; max. w. 4.1 cm.
Fogg Art Museum.
 Acc. no. 1925.30.152.
Bequest of Joseph C. Hoppin, Esq.

This distinctive granulated fibula with unique *pulviscolo*, egg-shaped ornaments is an imitation of Etruscan style and reflects the classical revival in jewelry during the nineteenth century. The Victorians created the Greek, the Gothic and the Renaissance revivals, and in jewelry the Archaeological revival—the creation of superbly crafted jewelry based on design motifs from the Classical Age and arranged to contemporary taste.

The popularization of classical adornments in Europe was the result of the first systematic archaeological excavations which began in Italy in the first years of the nineteenth century [1]. These first discoveries of jewelry made their way to the Napoleonic court as the perfect complement to *empire* dressing, and after the appearance of the originals at court, a demand for jewelry *à l'antique* became the fashion for members of European society [2]. To supply this demand for jewelry in the classic mode, goldsmiths began to execute pieces following recently discovered models, the principal proponents of the practice being the atelier of Castellani.

Fortunato Pio Castellani (1793-1865) was established as a goldsmith in Rome by 1814 and by the 1830's was seriously devoted to the archaeological style, consulting with the antiquarian Michelangelo Caetani, *Duca di Sermonatta* (1804-1883). Castellani became familiar with the splendid intricacies of Etruscan jewelry when he and his son Alessandro (1822-1883) were called to advise the Papacy on the purchase of gold ornaments from the Regolini-Galassi tomb which had been unearthed at Cerveteri in 1836[3]. His desire to emulate the delicacy and finesse of ancient goldsmiths in the art of granulation and filigree led to the discovery of craftsmen in the village of Sant'Angelo in Vado (near Orvieto) at the foot of the Apennines who were the inheritors of an unbroken tradition in these techniques since antiquity.

Castellani brought workers from Sant' Angelo in Vado to his Roman workshop to produce those pieces that called for the ancient Etruscan techniques. Some scholars suggest that this story may be an apocryphal tale devised to cover the true rediscovery of granulation techniques[4], which is thought to be Alessandro Castellani's technique of applying granulation and filigree with a colloidal hard soldering by substituting an arsenite flux for borax and using impalpably fine solder[5]. This technique was in practice at the Castellani atelier by the mid-sixties[6] and was demonstrated at the *Exposition Universelle* of 1867.

In addition to being goldsmiths, the Castellani were art dealers and antiquarians as well[7]. Through their lifetimes they amassed superb collections of ancient jewelry that are now deposited in the collections of the British Museum, the South Kensington Museum and the Museo Nazionale, Naples. These large collections of ancient originals most certainly provided the inspiration for the jewelry which was designed throughout their notable career, and may have been responsible for attracting the finest talents in archaeological jewelry such as Carlo Giuliano (1831-1895) and Giacinto Melillo (1846-1915) to the atelier.

After the abortive 1848 revolution in Rome, the Castellani were exiled to Naples where they established a workshop. It was there that Carlo Giuliano and Giacinto Melillo received their training in the archaeological style. Giuliano's interest included several revivalist styles and he became known for his mastery of blending the subtle colorings of enamels and cut stones. He was drawn to England by the master goldsmith and jeweler, John Brogdon and established a workshop in London where he spent the remainder of his career[8]. Melillo on the other hand remained in Naples and continued with the execution of etruscanizing pieces that concentrated on the harmonies of balancing sculptural and decorative patterning in gold.

In the collection of the Walters Art Gallery is an outstanding signed necklace by Melillo in the archaeological style (acc. no. 57.1531) which is closely related to an original Etruscan necklace in the British Museum (no. 2273) excavated at Canino and presented to the Museum as part of the Castellani collection in 1872. A granulated fibula in the

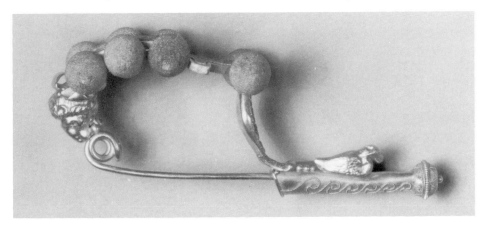

British Museum, also by Melillo, closely parallels sixth century B.C. fibulae in the Naples Museum (no. 24865, 24866, Ficco Collection), except for the inclusion of a putto which straddles the catchplate in a romantic gesture (fig. 13). The Hoppin fibula also shows similarities with the Naples fibulae.

The unique form of the Hoppin fibula may be the result of demands made on the artist by the patron, while pieces that show closer parallels to known pieces which are now in museum collections may have been produced for sale in one of the Castellani shops in London, Rome or Naples. The fibula derives its design from various types of ancient fibulae. The zig-zag and maeander patterns of granulation that decorate the bow of the fibula are common to many seventh and sixth century B.C. types, yet the neighboring passage of granulated triangles and the granular border that follows the picturesque, abstract form of the bow, seem nineteenth century inventions. Also the feather-like motif that connects the bow to the catchplate appears to be a modern fabrication. The eight egg-shaped ornaments, which are completely covered in *pulviscolo* granulation recall a more sober rendition of the irregularly massed groupings of granulated spheres that comprise bows of some seventh century B.C., south Etruscan fibulae. The form derives from necklace elements and its arrangement along the bow may have been prompted by knowledge of an electrum fibula that had been excavated at Cumae [9].

Both the ram's head and the duck which appear in this design are motifs common to Etruscan types. The duck's position is more traditional, being placed upon the catchplate with a wave pattern of granulation representing the river on which it swims, running the length of the tubular catch. The ram's head which is used to make the transition from the bow to the spring of the pin is traditionally positioned as a finial termination for the catchplate. In this instance, the ram's head is placed so that it is not visible when the piece is being worn. A large sphere of gold within its open mouth provides a romantic touch as does the use of the florette that supports the head and the placement of gold spheres to give transitional passages a more *finished* appearance in keeping with nineteenth century taste. The finial on the catchplate is a half-domed bead with decoration in granulation and beaded wire. This type of finial is common to late sixth-early fifth century B.C. fibulae often found in southern Etruria.

The closeness of motifs between the Hoppin fibula and numerous examples in the Museo Nazionale, Naples suggests familiarity with the collections and that this piece is of Neapolitan manufacture. The quality of the workmanship and the balance of the design suggest the hand of a skilled master, such as Melillo, and a date which corresponds to the height of his technical abilities, ca. 1880. The Hoppin fibula should not be considered as a forgery, but rather as a forthright imitation of the ancient Etruscan style with a romantic nineteenth century flavor.

RWS

[1] Excavations at Pompeii began in 1748 but it was not until 1860 that scholarly excavations began. A systematic search of Etruscan sites began in the nineteenth century stimulated by some spectacular Etruscan finds in the 1820's.

[2] To the north of Rome, the estates of the Princess of Canino, wife of Lucien Bonaparte, yielded a rich harvest of gold jewelry. The princess dazzled Roman society in the 1830's by wearing a parure of original Etruscan gold to ambassadorial functions ... from Mrs. HAMILTON GRAY, *Tour of the Sepulchres of Etruria, in 1839*, London, 1841, 2nd ed.

[3] WALTERS, 1979, p. 237.

[4] S. BURY, *Alessandro Castellani and the Revival of Granulation*, in *Burlington Magazine*, 117, 1975, p. 667.

[5] W. BURGES, *Antique jewelry and its Revival*, in *Gentleman's Magazine*, 162, London, 1863, p. 405.

[6] Alessandro Castellani's research into the rediscovery of granulation may have reaped results at a far earlier time had he not participated in the 1848 rebellion in Rome which landed him in the Castel Sant'Angelo until 1858 when he was released by feigning madness.

[7] The death notice of Alessandro Castellani in the *Times*, London, 13 June 1883, discusses his contribution as an antiquarian and the sale of pieces from his collection to the British Museum in 1872 and 1873 as the most significant aspects of Castellani's life.

[8] A review of Giuliano's career is presented in M.L. D'OTRANGE, *The Exquisite Art of Carlo Giuliano*, in *Apollo*, 59, 1954, p. 145-152.

[9] G. PELLEGRINI, *Tombe greche arcaiche e tomba greco-sannitica a tholos della necropoli di Cuma*, in *Monumenti Antichi*, 13, 1903, p. 228-229.

28
Bulla

Etruscan, Spina, 5th c. B.C.

Max. h. 4 cm, h. of body 3 cm, max. diam. 2.6 cm.

Courtesy of the Walters Art Gallery, Baltimore.

Acc. no. 57.371.

Purchased by Henry Walters from Sangiorgi, 1930.

Selected bibliography:

G. M. A. HANFMANN, *Daidalos in Etruria*, in *AJA*, 39, 1935, p. 189-194, pl. xxv.

A. ANDRÈN, *Oreficerie e plastica etrusca*, in *Opuscula Archaeologica*, 5, 1948, p. 94, fig. 6.

BECATTI, p. 186, no. 186, no. 316, pl. 78.

R. S. TIETZ, ed., *Masterpieces of Etruscan Art*, Worcester, 1967, no. 56.

WALTERS, 1979, p. 67, no. 209.

The body of the bulla is composed of two plates, the lower one on which the figures are represented and the circular upper one, joined by a seam at the line where the relief begins. The two parts were necessitated by the need for access to the interior chamber for the execution of the repoussé figures which were later incised with great care. To the top of the bulla two rings are obliquely soldered on either side of the opening to the bulla interior. A central ring is attached to the spike-like stopper, from which two tubular forms extend to meet the other two rings. The opening in the bulla, the attached rings, the tubular pieces of the stopper and the gold globular termination of the bulla are all ornamented with beaded wire. This bulla which was found near Spina is similar in form to bullae worn by both men and women in painted representations [1].

On each side of the bulla appears a winged figure facing right. The two are identical in type except for the attributes which they carry. Both are positioned in an archaic manner to fill the field with frontal torso and double-contour legs and head in profile. A short, transparent chiton with short sleeves, as was worn by ancient craftsmen, covers their forms in regularly waved lines. The hair is carefully arranged under a broad ribbon. The wings unfold behind the youths and are composed of tiers of intricately described feathers. Over each figure is a deeply incised Etruscan inscription in retrograde. Above the figure that carries a saw and an adze in his bent arms is carved ⊒√ †|Ʌⳡ (*Taitle*); over the other who carries a measuring square and a double-headed axe is ⊒ʃɅ)|⊓ (*Vikare*).

For Hanfmann the figure of *Taitle* is Daedalos; the figure of *Vikare* his young son, Icarus carrying additional attributes of his father. But, there is no physical differentiation between the two figures, suggesting two representations of the same figure[2]. On a stele from Bologna, dated to the first half of the fourth century B.C., is portrayed a figure that follows the same aspect as those on the bulla[3]. In addition to the saw, the figure carries both the axe and a measuring device in its right hand combining attributes from both sides of the bulla. Indications of who this figure is may be determined by analyzing other representations that bear the inscription of *Taitle*.

In the British Museum, there is an engraved gem that bears a *Taitle* inscription[4]. A beardless winged youth faces right over a row of wave patterning with a saw in his left hand and an adze in his right. His head is thrown back in the traditional iconographic symbol of death. A second gem in the British Museum shows a winged nude youth running right with a saw and an adze which bears no inscription[5]. Another inscribed gem, this example from the collection of H. Dressel,

Berlin, presents a nude youth who fills an amphora at a spring. His attention is distracted by a turtle in the lower right of the gem[6]. No representations presently known bear *Vikare* inscriptions.

In the collection of the Walters Art Gallery is a pair of gold bullae which are similar in size and shape to the bulla[7]. One of the pair was purchased at the same time from the same source, making the suggestion that the three bullae are from the same necklace a plausible one. The pair is ornamented with palmettes that are arranged in a manner that is common to many Attic vases found at Spina[8].

This gold bulla represents a jewelry type that appears with some frequency from the end of the sixth century B.C. Bullae, which are hollow pendants, were used either as amulets to hold some form of charm or, as in this example, as perfume containers. Investigation of residue from within the bulla has been found to be labdanum which was used to fix scents of delicate perfumes as well as for its own odor (Pliny, *Natural History*, 8.7).

RWS

[1] On a terracotta antefix from Praeneste, late sixth-early fifth century B.C., a woman wears a necklace with three acorn-shaped bullae. A banqueting male figure from a fresco in the Tomba della Caccia e Pesca, Tarquinia, ca. 530 B.C. has suspended around his neck bullae of several forms including the acorn shape. The similarities of southern Etruscan representations with actual bullae from Spina suggest that this emporium acted as an intermediary in the exchange of goods from the eastern Mediterranean to southern markets. Antefix in J. KEITH, *et al.*, *The Pomerance Collection of Ancient Art*, New York, 1966, p. 115, no. 135. Fresco in M. CRISTOFANI, *The Etruscans. A new investigation*, London, 1979, p. 38-39.

[2] On late Classical, early Hellenistic and Imperial Roman gems, when representations of Daedalos are more frequent, there is a clear distinction between mature bearded father and youthful son. Daedalian iconography of these periods is predominantly Daedalos making wings or Daedalos attaching wings to Icarus' back. Numerous examples can be seen in *Antike Gemmen in Deutschen Sammlungen*, Munich, 1969, 4 vols.

[3] E. BRIZIO, *Sepolcrii etruschi nel Giardino Margherita*, in *Notizie degli Scavi di Antichità*, ser. 4, 7, 1890, p. 140-142, pl. 1,3.

[4] WALTERS, 1926, p. 82, pl. XI, no. 663.

[5] *Ibid.*, p. 89, pl. XII, no. 727.
[6] FURTWÄNGLER, p. 219, pl. LXIV, no. 27.
[7] WALTERS, 1979, p. 67, no. 210.
[8] Examples of this motif are provided in N. ALFIERI and P.E. ARIAS, *Spina, die neuentdeckte Etruskerstadt und die griechischen Vasen ihrer Gräber*, Munich, 1958, p. 31, pl. 12, 13 and p. 62, pl. 108-111.

29
Pair of earrings

Etruscan, provenance unknown, 4th c. B.C.
H. 3.25-3.4 cm, max. w. 1.3-1.35 cm.
Museum of Art, Rhode Island School of Design.
Acc. no. 25.107a,b.
Museum appropriation and special gift.
Bibliography:
M. A. BANKS, *Gold Earrings*, in *Bull-RISD*, 22, no. 1, 1934, p. 17-18.
HACKENS, p. 40-41.

A curved gold plate which tapers into a hook at the back comprises the upper part of these earrings. Two intertwined wires outline the tongue-shaped earrings as well as vertically divide the front surfaces. Below this, three large hollow caps (now dented) are visible from the front. A fourth is attached to the back for structural purposes. The hole in each of these spheres, seen from the back, was necessary in the manufacturing process to prevent explosion.

Interspersed around the spheres are granules (not as fine as the granulation found in cat. no. 22 and 25) and smaller hemispheres. Some of the hemispheres are soldered on hollow side out, while others are convex side out. A cluster of four small balls with granules hanging from them is found below each of the three spheres.

The closest parallel to these is in Berlin[1]. Both pairs have a curved plate for the upper section, with clustered decoration below. This ornamentation of the lower section is closely related to that of leech-type earrings, which in the fourth and third centuries B.C., became very elaborate (cat. no. 130). The development of this type can be traced back to the fifth century B.C. with a leech decorated beneath with a single cluster of small balls and granules, similar to the decoration described above[2]. Eventually an ornamented horseshoe was placed above the leech, covering the fastening of the earring[3]. Variations of the type occur and one unusual example can be found in the British Museum[4]. The size is remarkable in that particular pair (h. 14.2, w. 6.4 cm). Whether such a pair would have been worn daily or reserved for funerary purposes is not known.

The function of the Rhode Island School of Design's earrings is also not clear. The very sharp edges of the hook suggest that they were perhaps intended to be funerary objects.

IMR

[1] GREIFENHAGEN, I, pl. 73, no. 9.
[2] MARSHALL, *BMCJ*, pl. XLIV, no. 2243-2250.
[3] *Ibid.*, no. 2251.
[4] *Ibid.*, no. 2256.

30
Pair of leech earrings

Etruscan, provenance unknown, 4th-3rd c. B.C.
H. 4.7 cm; w. 2.8 cm.
Museum of Art, Rhode Island School of Design.
Acc. no. 25.106a,b.
Museum appropriation and special gift.
Bibliography:
M. A. BANKS, *Gold Earrings*, in *Bull-RISD*, 22, no. 1, 1934, p. 17-18.
HACKENS, p. 37-39.

The final development of the leech earring is represented by this pair. Formed from two sheets, the leech is joined together carefully on the center, with the joint visible only under magnification. Twisted wire provides a border around the outer edges. Wider at the bottom, this ring is convex toward the front and breaks through the sheet to the back.

Above the central element is an elaborately decorated horseshoe-shaped plaque. Granules separate the leech from an unadorned crescent. The next zone, consisting of ten embossed discs depressed in the center, is outlined by three twisted rectangular strips of gold. This same filigree encloses the next band as well. Here hollow hemispheres, some of them now dented, are soldered to the background. A double strand of filigree formed from four wires twisted two by two, surrounded by a plain wire on the outer edge, completes the decoration of the horseshoe.

The lower section of the earrings is a cluster of decorative forms (hence the alternative name *orecchino a grappolo* for this type). The main elements are five large embossed caps. Most of these have been dented. They are surrounded by smaller caps and granules.

The embossed elements on the front are soldered to a base sheet. Holes in the sheet behind the hemispherical caps prevented them from bursting while being soldered. However, evidence of repairs to these earrings in antiquity is visible at the back and it seems that brazing and bursting of the gold sheet did occur during these repairs [1].

Numerous comparable pieces can be cited, as these are a common type [2]. The type is also often seen on both terracottas and tomb paintings of the Classical and Hellenistic

periods in Etruria [3]. Probably one of the most famous images of Etruscan tomb painting is the woman wearing this type of earring in the *Tomba dell'Orco* in Tarquinia [4].

IMR

[1] HACKENS, p. 37.

[2] Cf. BECATTI, no. 412a,b, now in Rome at the Villa Giulia; GREIFENHAGEN, I, pl. 73, no. 1-3; G.M.A. RICHTER, *Handbook of the Etruscan Collection*, New York, 1940, p. 54, fig. 172; MARSHALL, *BMCJ*, p. 255-256, pl. XLIV, no. 2252-2258.

[3] For representations on terracottas: M.A. DEL CHIARO, *Etruscan Art from West Coast Collections*, Santa Barbara, 1967, p. 37, fig. 24, 25, 28; A. ANDRÈN, *Architectural Terracottas from Etrusco-Italic Temples* (*Acta Instituti Romani Regni Sueciae*, 6), Lund-Leipzig, 1939-1940, p. 57-58, no. IV: 6-7, pl. 20, fig. 66, 67. For tomb paintings see: M. MORETTI, *Pittura Etrusca in Tarquinia*, Milan, 1974, pl. 83, 85. Cf., M. ANDRÈN, *Una matrice fittile etrusca*, in *StEtr*, 24, 1956, p. 207-219, who discusses a mould for terracotta leech earrings which would be applied to the terracotta heads. He not only deals with examples of terracottas with this type of earring, but also with the earring type itself.

[4] MORETTI, pl. 83.

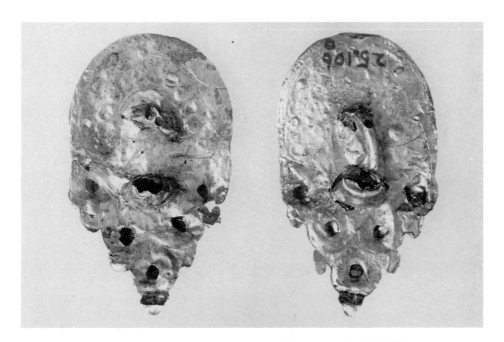

Fig. 14. Funerary monument of Aththaia, daughter of Malchos, limestone, Palmyrene, 2nd half of 2nd c. A.D., Museum of Fine Arts, Boston, gift of Edward Perry Warren in memory of his sister.

ROMAN SYRIA

Alexander the Great conquered Syria in the years 333-332 B.C. and initiated an interplay of eastern and western culture which permeated Syrian life for centuries. After Alexander's death the Syrian province eventually passed under the control of Seleucus who founded the key Syrian towns of Antioch, Seleucia Pieria, Apamea and Laodicea. By the mid-second century B.C., Antioch was the center of Seleucid rule. Antiochus IV Epiphanes (215-164 B.C.) urged the hellenization of northern Syria, going so far as to plunder non-Greek houses of worship, particularly Jewish temples [1]. He held Greek festivals and processions, not only in Antioch but in Tyre as well, such as those opening the games at Antioch around 167 B.C. Polybius described the richness of these festivities designed to encourage Greek culture and show royal favor to the towns.

Polybius (200-118 B.C.), as well as Libanius (A.D. 314-393) and Joannes Chrysostomus (A.D. 347-407), provide us with the little we know of jewelry production in Antioch. According to Polybius, Antiochus IV Epiphanes wished to "out-do" the Romans by sending out three thousand Cilicians wearing gold crowns, thousands of horsemen with gold and silver "trappings", and "six hundred of the king's slaves bearing articles of gold plate" [2]. Antiochus "took a lively interest in the work of artists at Antioch" [3], and the city became a center for gold and silver work. Despite Syria's annexation as a Roman province in 64 B.C., northern Syria, with Antioch the commercial and political capital, retained a hellenized culture, while the eastern lands, with Emesa, Palmyra and Edessa "remained what they had been, the residence of priest-kings" [4], and greatly influenced by oriental culture.

There is no evidence to show that Roman customs and fashions affected jewelry prior to the arrival of the Romans in Syria. By imperial times, however, we may assume that Roman customs may also be applied here. We find Pliny demanding that Roman matrons refrain from wearing bracelets on their ankles [5]. The Roman man often loaded his fingers with rings whether for love of the jewels, medical or magical purposes or for astrological divination. Jewelry played a part in the marriage ceremony and in funeral rites. However, the precise effect of romanization on jewelry production in the Graeco-Syrian province is not discernable at a glance, due to the number of conquered cultures involved. The Antiochene workshop under Roman rule must have simply maintained its status, along with rival Alexandria, as a major gold- and silver-working center of the east. Antioch's position at the heart of overland trade routes between the Orient and the West, Egypt and Rome makes her, and northern Syria in general, difficult to characterize

---

[1] G. DOWNEY, *Ancient Antioch*, Princeton, 1963, p. 56.
[2] *Ibid.*, p. 60.
[3] *Ibid.*, p. 61.
[4] M. ROSTOVTZEFF, *The Social and Economic History of the Roman Empire*, Oxford, n.d., p. 248.
[5] E. COCHE DE LA FERTÉ, *Les bijoux antiques*, Paris, 1956, p. 87.

as either Roman, Hellenistic or Oriental, for she embodies a combination of each culture — a fact reflected in Syro-Roman jewelry.

The caravan routes between Egypt, Greece, Asia Minor and Syria had been well-traveled before the Roman takeover, and by imperial times Antioch served as a kind of hub for trade routes radiating into these lands and beyond. According to Charlesworth, the main trade route in the east started from Gaza and kept parallel to the coast until turning eastward, passing over the Carmel and Ephraim mountain ranges and eventually following the Orontes to Emesa, Antioch-on-the-Orontes and the north [6]. "There were not many navigable rivers" in the eastern provinces, but goods could be transported up the Orontes to Antioch's port of Seleucia, and from there to Antioch in a day [7]. Ships from Alexandria and Asia Minor stopped frequently at Antioch's port city on their way to the west. Each year, Batnae in Mesopotamia had a fair to which merchants from as far as China brought their goods by the Antioch-Edessa road [8]. Antioch, "as a place of residence for the opulent merchant shippers of the East" [9] and metalworking center in its own right, and Palmyra, a stopping-place for gold- and silversmiths along the Euphrates route, must have been important centers for jewelry workshops in a region where eastern and western styles converged.

The Romans produced as many types of jewelry as there were purposes for wearing them. Pliny expounds upon the amount of gold worn by Roman men and women.

> Let even men nowadays wear gold bracelets — called 'Dardania' because the fashion came from the Dardani — ... let women have gold in their bracelets and covering their fingers and on their neck, ears and tresses, let gold chains run at random round their waists; and let little bags of pearls hang invisible suspended by gold chains from their owner's neck ... but are even their feet to be shod with gold ...?
>
> Pliny, *Natural History*, 33.4.39-41

Legend goes that Tarquinius Priscus began the custom of the equites, giving his son a gold amulet to be worn as a sign of distinction (Pliny, 33.4.10). While in the Republican period, only diplomatic envoys could wear gold rings (Pliny, 33.4.11); by Imperial times, Horace (*Satires*, 11.7.8-10) derides the practice of wearing several rings on one hand. According to Juvenal, some men even possessed a "light" set of fingerrings for summer and a "heavy" set for winter (Juvenal, *Satires*, 1. 28). Finally, intaglio signet rings were employed for sealing personal documents, and a plain ironring served as a man's betrothal gift to his intended (Pliny, 33.4.12).

---

[6] M.P. CHARLESWORTH, *Trade-Routes and Commerce of the Roman Empire*, Cambridge, 1924, p. 38. For a map of the road system and sea routes of the Roman Empire ca. A.D. 200, see *The Times Atlas of World History*, G. Barraclough, ed., London, 1979, p. 90-91.

[7] *Ibid.*, p. 41.

[8] F.M. HEICHELHEIM, *An Ancient Economic History*, 3, Leiden, 1970, p. 93-94 and 237-238. According to Heichelheim, the most important overland route in the classical world, as early as the first and second centuries B.C., "*began in Ephesus, Antioch or Damascus in turn and* (lead) *via Seleucia on the Tigris through Iran. When it reached Heratus ... it split into a Southern arm leading to the Indus, and several North Eastern arms ... to China*". During the Han Period (ca. 206 B.C. - A.D. 220), "*Chinese traders came regularly in caravans and ship convoys*" to India and then west to "*Parthia, the Roman province of Syria and even Rome*".

[9] CHARLESWORTH, *op. cit.*, p. 46.

Fig. 15. Mosaics of the Seasons, Constantinian Villa, Room 1, Spring and Summer, details, ca. A.D. 320, Princeton University, Department of Art and Archaeology.

Men wore pendants, coronets, brooches and buckles as well. A father hung the *bulla*, a locket containing charms, around his child's neck until the boy took on the *toga virilis* or the daughter left her parent's house to marry. It would thus appear that Haddad may be justified in defending the Antiochenes against a reputation in historical accounts for unchecked love of luxury, as an overt display of wealth and ceremony was common at the time, especially among the Romans [10]. Chrysostomus perpetuated this view of Antioch when he wrote in his *Homilies of St. Matthew*: "Who then, about to marry, inquires about the disposition and nurture of the damsel? No one, but straight way about money, possessions and measures of property" [11]. Haddad also attributes comments in literature about the Antiochene's love of luxury and feasts to propaganda spread by enemy generals like Procopius to encourage their troops in battle against a "soft" army of Antiochenes [12]. Yet, one must wonder at Libanius' condemnation of "military effeminacy" among the northern Syrian soldiers who had become "connoisseurs of gold and gems" [13].

The Antioch mosaic pavements of the Four Seasons in the Constantinian Villa (see fig. 15), excavated in 1935, offer the few remaining Syro-Roman representations of jewelry, along with Palmyrene funerary reliefs. The mosaics have been

[10] G. HADDAD, *Aspects of Social Life in Antioch in the Hellenistic-Roman Period*, Ph.D. diss., University of Chicago, 1949.

[11] *Ibid.*, p. 156-157. The quotation comes from Chrysostomus' *Homilies of St. Matthew*, 31.6.

[12] *Ibid.*, p. 154.

[13] R. PACK, *Studies in Libanius and Antiochene Society under Theodosius*, Ph.D. diss., University of Michigan, 1935, p. 18. Packs adds that "standards of army discipline had been declining for years before Libanius".

given a Constantinian date of ca. A.D. 320 [14], a conclusion supported by the style of jewelry depicted. The personifications of Summer, Autumn and Winter each wear necklaces of black beads, while Spring and Autumn seem to wear pearl earrings in both ears. Levi describes the jewelry around Spring's neck as "a gold necklace, casting a black shadow on the neck, (hung with) a round pendant in blue and green glass tesserae with a black rim" [15]. Summer's tunic is fastened with a large round brooch. These pieces of jewelry, aside from the last, non-specified brooch, are not typically north-Syrian, but indicate Egyptian influence. Black beads are often found on Coptic mummy portraits, a fact made more relevant by Levi's comparison of Coptic portrait style with the rendering of the Seasons' faces [16]. Pearls come to Syria from the east and, thus, represent another non-western influence. Finally, the blue and green glass pendant supports the late imperial dating, for colored paste as a major element in jewelry (as opposed to use as detail on metal pieces) is characteristic of the late Roman and early Byzantine style. The Antioch mosaics, part of which are in the Museum of Art, Rhode Island School of Design, serve as testimony to northern Syria's multi-cultural artistic tradition [17].

Though history provides us with an accurate picture of Antioch as a major north-Syrian jewelry workshop and a Roman provincial capital steeped in Hellenistic culture, we have no pieces of jewelry which can be traced specifically to the Antiochene workshops. One must, therefore, discuss Hellenistic influence on Syro-Roman jewelry keeping Antioch in mind as a major well of Greek stylistic influence with Palmyra as a center where Oriental and Roman styles meet. But if a typically Roman style of jewelry did exist in Imperial times, how did Syrian Hellenism affect it? Coche de la Ferté considers Roman jewelry to be a "composite" of different styles leading up to Imperial times; and later, taking on characteristics of the conquered provinces, especially of the Orient [18]. He points out Roman adaptation of Greek granulation and repoussé, as well as the influence of Greek fresco painting on Roman iconography [19]. He cites the later use of *opus interrasile* and of elaborate polychrome effects by Roman jewelry workshops as oriental techniques.

Pfeiler takes a different view of the question of Roman style by distinguishing between a Hellenistic-Roman (earlier) and an Italo-Roman (second century and later) style [20]. The first style is characterized by Hellenistic naturalism, with organic and animal forms, and colored stones inserted into goldwork in a secondary decorative role, as we find in the pair of earrings in this exhibition (cat. no. 31) [21].

---

[14] *Antioch-on-the-Orontes 2, The Excavations 1933-36*, R. Stillwell, ed., Princeton, 1938, p. 197. The Constantinian date, based on "coins of Constantine the Great (found) sealed underneath the pavement" and other evidence, is supported by R. WINKES in his *Catalogue of the Classical Collection: Roman Paintings and Mosaics*, Museum of Art, Rhode Island School of Design, Providence, 1982, p. 70.

[15] D. LEVI, *Antioch Mosaic Pavements*, 1, Princeton, 1957, p. 230.

[16] *Ibid.*, p. 233-235.

[17] WINKES, *op. cit.*, nos. 39-41.

[18] COCHE DE LA FERTÉ, *op. cit.*, p. 70-71.

[19] *Ibid.*, p. 70.

[20] B. PFEILER, *Römischer Goldschmuck*, Mainz, 1970, p. 2-11.

[21] T. HACKENS, *Catalogue of the Classical Collection: Classical Jewelry*, Museum of Art, Rhode

A Syro-Roman earring displaying colored stone inlay and Greek iconography is the hoop earring with a figure of Eros in the Museum of Art, Rhode Island School of Design (Hackens, no. 44). Italo-Roman work, on the other hand, subjugates the form to the materials, leaving broad surfaces of metal exposed, and relies on geometric, abstract forms and design[22]. Polychrome effects eventually take on a primary role, becoming as important as the precious metal. Recently, El Chehadeh questions Pfeiler's division of Roman style into "Italo-Roman" and "Hellenistic-Roman", taking a more regionalistic stand on the issue[23]. El Chehadeh suggests that certain regions of the Empire produced a particular style of jewelry, with the orientalized Palmyrene jewelry (*infra*) a case in point. He does, however, acknowledge a certain unity of styles within the Empire in the third century due, perhaps, to the use of the stamp technique and mass production of jewelry.

Whether one agrees with Coche de la Ferté, Pfeiler or El Chehadeh, the Hellenistic influence on Syro-Roman jewelry can be determined by comparing pieces from the hellenized and the more eastern-influenced sections of the Syrian province. While a distinction can be made between these two regional styles, a fact which argues in favor of El Chehadeh's regionalist viewpoint, Pfeiler's "Italo-Roman" categorization holds merit for later Roman pieces. A pair of earrings in this exhibition (cat. no. 34), with a close Syrian parallel in the Benaki Museum, Athens[24], displays the abstract, geometric form and broad metal surfaces of Pfeiler's Italo-Roman type. The impact of orientalizing influence on the Roman jewelry in Syria is most evident in a study of the western province, with its major workshop at Palmyra.

Palmyra, the most eastern of the major Roman cities in Syria, retained a semi-autonomous status on the border between the Roman Empire and Parthia. Rome was never to achieve domination over the bellicose Parthians, but for many years prudently settled for a kind of unspoken truce with Parthia, if only in the mutual interest of trade[25]. Palmyra received the benefit of this silent agreement, and in the first century B.C. had already begun its development from a successful trading city into the most important commercial center and neutral zone between Roman Syria and the east. From Palmyra caravan routes stretched in all directions, eastward to Parthia, westward to the Syrian cities of Damascus, Emesa and Antioch and the port cities of Seleucia, Sidon and Tyre, and south to Petra and further into Egypt. Not surprisingly, Palmyra itself was a city comprised of an unusually large number of different racial groups, and during the Roman Imperial period the cultures of Rome, Greece and the East all contributed elements to the Palmyrene way of life. The jewelry which can be associated with Palmyra, largely known through Palmyrene funerary reliefs, reflects certain eastern (as distinct from Hellenistic)

Island School of Design, Providence, 1976, p. 104. Hackens notes the Greek-influenced shape and garnet decoration, while emphasizing the even stronger native Syrian elements in this pair of earrings.

[22] PFEILER, *op. cit.*, p. 106.
[23] J. EL CHEHADEH, *Untersuchungen zum antiken Schmuck in Syrien*, Ph.D. diss., Freie Universität, Berlin, 1972, p. 73.
[24] B. SEGALL, *Katalog der Goldschmiedearbeiten, Museum Benaki, Athen*, Athens, 1938, cat. no. 132, p. 100, pl. 34.
[25] M. ROSTOVTZEFF, *Caravan Cities*, trans. D. and T. Talbot Rice, Oxford, 1932, p. 31.

characteristics while it is also often indicative of styles peculiar to the larger context of Roman jewelry in general.

As an international center of trade, Palmyra must have had jewelry imported from elsewhere which was brought into the city by passing caravans. But the city did have local gold- and silversmiths at least by the second century A.D. These artisans are mentioned on a tariff stone which was set up in A.D. 137 to regulate dues on imports and exports to the city [26]. Furthermore, in A.D. 258 the workshops of gold- and silversmiths of Palmyra honored the powerful Prince Odenath with a statue of the ruler erected at their expense [27]. While actual jewelry has yet to be attributed to Palmyrene workshops, their active production is evident by the richly decorated funerary reliefs.

Palmyrene and indeed all Syrian goldsmiths had to import their gold from outside the province. Syria itself was poor in mineral resources, and no substantial amount of gold was ever mined in the region during Roman times. The surrounding areas to the south, such as the western coast of Arabia and Egypt were rich in gold, however, and it is possible that both could have been sources for some gold used in Syrian jewelry. The Egyptian mines were under Roman imperial control, and their importance was increased by the very fact that the regions of Roman Syria and Asia Minor were devoid of gold [28]. Western Arabia was part of the Nabataean kingdom at this time, but given Palmyra's unique status as a trade center which accommodated both Rome and the east, it seems possible that some gold could have been imported to the city and the province from Nabataea itself. The Syrian crescent-shaped earrings from the Museum of Art, Rhode Island School of Design in this exhibition (cat. no. 31) have, in fact, a close stylistic parallel with a pair of earrings found in a Nabataean grave [29], thus at least some interaction between craftsmen of these regions may be supposed. In addition, a number of gold deposits from Parthia are known [30], and the trade relations between Parthia and Palmyra make this eastern source of gold likely as well. With Palmyra acting as an intermediary, gold from the Parthian Empire could have serviced other Syrian cities along the trade routes such as Antioch.

Our knowledge of actual Palmyrene jewelry types and styles derives largely from the above mentioned funerary reliefs [31]. Since many are dated by inscriptions,

---

[26] CHARLESWORTH, *op. cit.*, p. 49.

[27] J.-B. CHABOT, *Choix d'inscriptions de Palmyre*, Paris, 1922, p. 55. The statue is no longer extant, but a bilingual inscription attesting to its existence and sponsors was found on one of the columns framing the entrance at the tomb Odenath had built for himself at Palmyra.

[28] R.J. FORBES, *Studies in Ancient Technology*, 8, Leiden, 1964, p. 163. See also FORBES, *Studies*, 7, for a list of Roman mines (all metals) throughout Europe.

[29] Nabataean earrings published by A. NEGEV, *Mampsis: A Report on Excavations of a Nabateo-Roman Town*, in *Archaeology*, 24, 1971, p. 169.

[30] FORBES, *op. cit.*, 8, p. 162. He notes that these deposits are not mentioned in ancient texts.

[31] H. INGHOLT was the first to publish his excavations of many of these funerary reliefs, in his *Studier over Palmyrensk Skulptur*, Copenhagen, 1928. Ingholt divided the reliefs roughly into three periods according to date: Period I, prior to A.D. 150; Period II, A.D. 150-200; Period III, A.D. 200-250. These periods have been somewhat modified by D. MacKay on the strength of style and typology of the jewelry represented. See his article, *The Jewellery of Palmyra and its Significance*, in *Iraq*, 11, 1949, p. 160-187. Ingholt's divisions have more recently been qualified by EL CHEHADEH, *op. cit.*, but Ingholt's classifications remain the basis upon which all study of these reliefs is built.

they constitute an invaluable resource for determining the changes in style and taste which took place among the wealthy Palmyrene population from the first to the third centuries A.D.

The reliefs depict both men and women, but the women exhibit the greatest variety and quantity of jewelry types. The earlier reliefs (up until approximately A.D. 130), display a smaller variety and simpler style of jewelry than is found later in the second century and in the third century. Simple diadems and fibulae can be seen on these reliefs, and often a series of keys hang from the fibulae [32]. These keys give the effect of ornamental pendants, although their function is practical. The fashion of carrying keys on fibulae is not found on the later Palmyrene reliefs [33]. Earrings were worn during this early period, and on one relief a woman wears earrings which appear to be granulated balls arranged to look like bunches of grapes [34]. One earring of this type is in the collection of the National Museum, Damascus [35]. A second popular earring type from this period is the unadorned gold loop. The necklaces and bracelets which appear so prominently on later reliefs are not generally seen at this time.

The funerary relief of Aththaia, daughter of Malchos, which dates from the second half of the second century A.D., displays the deceased wearing every conceivable type of jewelry (see fig. 14). The stylistic traits of the individual pieces of jewelry represented show a combination of Roman, Greek and eastern motifs, not surprising for a racially and culturally mixed city like Palmyra. Aththaia wears a long veil over a cloak and tunic. Her earrings with their dangling pendants reflect a universal Roman taste for pendants on jewelry that is seen in hoards discovered throughout the Empire [36]. A Roman fashion popular for both men and women is that of wearing signet rings; Aththaia wears two such rings on the little finger of her left hand. On her right ring finger Aththaia wears another ring of a different type; perhaps a wedding, or more properly, a betrothal ring. The wearing of a ring on this finger to signify marriage had long been a common practice among the Romans [37]. Necklaces and bracelets were popular among Roman women, but while Aththaia wears two of each type of jewelry, these pieces are characterized by certain specifically Syrian elements. Her twin bracelets, which appear to be made of twisted bands of gold or silver alternating with rows of beaded elements which are probably a coarse granulation, are of a type that is found on a very large number of the Palmyrene reliefs. A thickly twisted band of gold is a popular style for Roman bracelets, as is represented in this exhibition by the bracelet from the Virginia Museum of Fine Arts (cat. no. 33), but the addition of granulation or granulated ropes as a decorative element is a local adaptation of this style. Two silver bracelets

---

[32] See, for example, the relief bust of Sēgel, published in MACKAY, *op. cit.*, pl. LV, 2.

[33] *Ibid.*, p. 167.

[34] *Ibid.*, pl. LV, 1.

[35] This earring is published in EL CHEHADEH, *op. cit.*, cat no. 1.

[36] See A. BÖHME, *Frauenschmuck der römischen Kaiserzeit*, in *Antike Welt*, 9, 1978, p. 3-16, and PFEILER, *op. cit.*, for discussions and illustrations of stylistic traits of Roman jewelry organized around the sites where hoards have been found.

[37] See J. CARCOPINO, *Daily Life in Ancient Rome*, trans. E. O. Lorimer, New Haven/London, 1940, ch. 4.

discovered at Dura-Europos conform to this type, as does a bracelet of gold in the National Museum, Damascus[38].

Correspondant to the increase in the amount of jewelry worn by women is the fashion of wearing multiple necklaces. On some reliefs, the total number is as high as five. The alternation of a necklace constructed principally of stones with one made of a gold or silver chain and sporting at least one pendant is seen here, and indeed is not uncommon on other reliefs. It has been suggested that the choker-length beaded necklaces represented on the Palmyrene reliefs are made of pearls, and although Aththaia does not wear a necklace of this type, the use of pearls, which would have been imported from the Persian Gulf[39], is yet another eastern element adopted for jewelry in the border province of Syria. Precious stones were also imported from the east, primarily from India, and these jewels passed by land through Palmyra[40].

The geographical origins of every stylistic element in jewelry cannot always be determined. The crescent-shaped pendant worn by Aththaia is of a type long associated with amuletic powers[41], and is a pervasive type worn throughout the Roman Empire. It is also seen on many Palmyrene reliefs and on a Syrian necklace in Damascus[42]. Palmyra by the late second century A.D. had had sufficient contact with Rome to be receptive to Roman influences of taste, although that taste was naturally complemented by the inclinations of the native Palmyrene craftsmen and their patrons. The large size of Aththaia's jewelry, especially her fibula and diadem adorned with over-sized jewels, and the large quantity worn, suggest a luxury and even a vanity (Aththaia is consciously adorned here for eternity), that equals those Roman women satirized so frequently by ancient authors. Juvenal's *Satires* could as well apply to the female population of Palmyra as to the women of Rome when he admonishes:

> There is nothing that a woman will not permit herself to do, nothing that she deems shameful, when she encircles her neck with green emeralds, and fastens huge pearls to her elongated ears: there is nothing more intolerable than a wealthy woman.
>
> Juvenal, *Satire*, 6. 457-460.

Men on Palmyrene funerary reliefs wear very little jewelry. A signet ring is often seen on the little finger of the left hand, and sometimes a fibula is worn, but the splendor of the men's attire on these reliefs is frequently found on the clothing itself. Costume and jewelry are closely related, and in Palmyra both reflect the tastes of more than one culture. While the style of dress for women and men on a number of Palmyrene reliefs is distinctly Graeco-Roman, there are reliefs in which the men wear clothing which clearly shows a stylistic affinity with Parthian dress[43]. In these

---

[38] See P. V. C. BAUR and M. ROSTOVTZEFF, *The Excavations at Dura-Europos, Second Season*, New Haven, 1931, pl. XLIV, 2 and EL CHEHADEH, *op. cit.*, cat. no. 47.

[39] BÖHME, *op. cit.*, p. 5; and MACKAY, *op. cit.*, p. 171.

[40] M. S. RUXER and J. KUBCZAK, *Greek Necklace of the Hellenistic and Roman Ages*, Warsaw, 1972, p. 202.

[41] R. HIGGINS, *Greek and Roman Jewellery*, Berkeley, 1980, p. 154, notes the use of this type of pendant in Hellenistic times.

[42] EL CHEHADEH, *op. cit.*, cat. no. 42.

reliefs the use of embroidery and the wearing of trousers are taken directly from Iranian costume, and the decorative motifs of the embroidered borders of tunics and trousers often simulate jewels and pearls[44]. It should be noted that Palmyrene men only wore this eastern costume for ceremonial purposes, but the eastern love of rich materials and colored ornament carries over into the jewelry of the Palmyrene women, and is found in the jewelry of the later Roman Empire as a whole. The increasingly polychromatic character of Roman jewelry has been noted by many scholars[45], and is a legacy from the ancient world to Early Christian and Byzantine jewelry.

Little is known of the particular funerary rites and customs practiced by the Palmyrenes, but their funerary reliefs and sarcophagi do furnish some evidence of the part played by jewelry in the funeral. Wealthy Palmyrenes have themselves depicted for posterity in all their splendor so that the representation of their immortalized self will be that self at its best. Thus the later second and third century representations of Palmyrene women wearing a wealth of jewelry assume a ceremonial purpose, and do not necessarily present the everyday appearance of these women. Similarly, the men dressed in luxurious and exotic Iranian costume are not representative of a style of everyday dress. Some funerary reliefs depict the deceased accompanied by a female figure of lamentation, who pointedly wears no jewelry except perhaps for a diadem, and who expresses grief by her bared breasts, self-inflicted wounds and disheveled hair[46]. These unadorned mourners would seem to confirm the distinctly although perhaps not exclusively ceremonial function of the large quantities of jewelry worn by the deceased. The temporal feelings of grief and loss symbolized by the mourners contrast sharply with the serene visages and rich jewelry of the deceased, who have become part of the spiritual world.

Palmyrene funerary relief busts cannot be considered true portraits, as the features of the various deceased are not significantly differentiated from each other[47]. These figures are stylized to conform to certain conventions considered by the Palmyrenes appropriate to their function as memorials. While the explicitly ceremonial and symbolic nature of the Palmyrene funerary reliefs is clear, the depiction of details of clothing and ornament can be nevertheless considered fairly accurate, and thus are invaluable evidence for our knowledge of Palmyrene fashion and taste during the later Roman Imperial period. This taste is shaped by a creative convergence of eastern and western styles of jewelry and clothing which reflects the unique geographical and commercial position of the city of Palmyra under the Roman Empire. The combined influences of east and west affect all of Syria as a Roman province, and Syro-Roman jewelry is a testament to the richly varied cultures of Greece, Rome and the East.

Audrey R. GUP

Ellen S. SPENCER

[43] H. SEYRIG, *Armes et costumes iraniens de Palmyre*, in *Syria*, 18, 1937, p. 4-31, and IDEM, *Palmyra and the East*, in *JRS*, 40, 1950, p. 1-7. See also C. HOPKINS, *Aspects of Parthian Art in Light of Discoveries from Dura-Europos*, in *Berytus*, 3, 1936, p. 1-30.

[44] SEYRIG, *op. cit.*, *Armes et costumes*, p. 19.

[45] PFEILER, *op. cit.*, p. 105; BÖHME, *op. cit.*, p. 13; and COCHE DE LA FERTÉ, *op. cit.*, p. 96.

[46] M. GAWLIKOWSKI, *Monuments funéraires de Palmyre*, Warsaw, 1970, p. 178-179.

[47] M. A. R. COLLEDGE, *The Art of Palmyra*, London, 1976, p. 62.

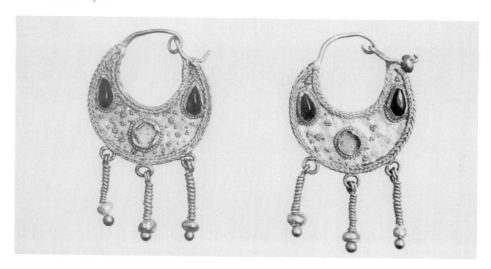

31
Pair of earrings

Roman, found in Syria, 1st-2nd c. A.D.
H. 2.2 cm (without pendants), 3.3 cm
(with pendants); w. 2.2 cm.
Museum of Art, Rhode Island School
of Design.
Acc. no. 19.024a,b.
Gift of Ostby and Barton Co. in mem-
ory of Engelhardt Cornelius Ostby.
Bibliography:
HACKENS, p. 103-104, no. 43.
BullRISD, 7, 1, 1919, illus. only.

This small but finely preserved pair of gold
crescent-shaped earrings are set on each side
with three stones, and further decorated with
granulation and filigree. The middle stone is
missing on all four sides, and the remaining
eight stones are garnets. Three pendants of
gold wire with mother-of-pearl beads at each
end are attached to rings which are suspended from the bottom of each crescent.
These earrings have been given a probable
Syrian provenance [1], and are an excellent
example of the Roman adoption of certain
characteristics of Hellenistic jewelry, which
remained alive in the previously hellenized
province of Syria.

The crescent shape of the earrings is in fact
thought to be of Syrian origin, where the
shape was sacred to the Moon god [2]. The
crescent shape was adopted for jewelry by
the Greeks during the Hellenistic period.
The use of semi-precious stones such as
garnets and mother-of-pearl in the Roman
earrings can also be associated with Hellenistic jewelry, and these earrings have in
fact been classified as belonging to the Syro-
Hellenistic "colored" style of jewelry [3].

In spite of their stylistic affinity with
jewelry from a much earlier period, these
earrings do exhibit certain characteristics
peculiar to the province of Roman Syria and
its environs. The settings of the three stones
on each side of the earrings are surrounded
by rings of tiny granulated beads of gold.
Small clusters of these granulated beads are
placed on the open gold field between the
larger decorative elements of the garnets.
The crescent shape of the earrings themselves
are outlined with two strands of twisted
filigree, which has the appearance of braided
edging and defines the crescent form. This
use of colored stones, granulation and filigree
is found on at least two other pieces of
jewelry from the area of and surrounding
Roman Syria. A pair of Nabataean earrings
shows almost identical decorative elements,
although the earrings are circular rather
than crescent-shaped, and lack pendants [4].
In addition, a silver fibula excavated at
Dura-Europos displays a strikingly similar
decorative pattern, now seen on a different

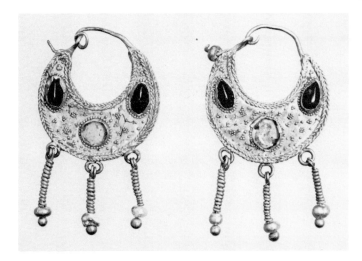

type of ornament [5] (see fig. 16). The fibula is set with garnets, and double strands of twisted filigree outline the fibula's trapezoidal shape, and further cross the surface of the piece in a simple grid pattern. Although no granule clusters are seen here, individual granules dot the surface of the fibula. Thus the decorative scheme relates closely to that of both the Nabataean and the Syrian earrings already discussed.

The earrings are adorned with three pendants, as mentioned above. Although pendants are also seen on the Hellenistic earrings, the use of pendants is frequently seen on many types of Roman jewelry as well. Appreciation of ornamental pendants can also be seen on countless numbers of Palmyrene funerary reliefs. The gold wire pendants attached to the earrings are larger in proportion to the filigree of the earrings proper, and are not as delicately made. These pendants could possibly have been made by another hand and even at a slightly later date, perhaps in response to the popularity of pendants on jewelry which was so pervasive during the Roman Imperial period. The strong Hellenistic tradition in Syria, which decisively influences the style of these earrings, is merged with decorative elements which reveal the presence of Roman taste as well.

ESS

[1] HACKENS, p. 103.
[2] HIGGINS, 1980, p. 154.

[3] HACKENS, p. 10.
[4] A. NEGEV, *Mampsis: A Report on Excavations of a Nabateo-Roman Town*, in *Archaeology*, 24, 1971, p. 169.
[5] For excavation report, see BAUR and ROSTOVTZEFF, 1931, p. 81. The fibula is the property of the Yale University Art Gallery, Dura-Europos Collection, Acc. no. 1929.403.

Fig. 16. Fibula, silver, Yale University Art Gallery, Dura-Europos Collection.

32
Ring

Roman, provenance unknown, 1st-2nd
c. A.D.
H. 1.5 cm.
Bowdoin College Museum of Art,
Warren Collection.
Acc. no. 1923.115.
Bibliography:
S. CASSON, *Descriptive Catalogue of
the Warren Classical Collection of
Bowdoin College*, 1934.
HERBERT, p. 137-138, no. 531.

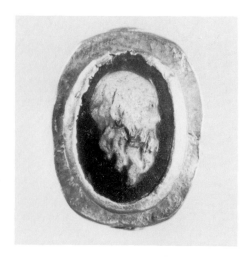

This gold ring is a slightly flattened oval
rising to a flat, rectangular head upon which
an oval sardonyx cameo is set. A white head
of Silenus with pointed ears, flowing beard
and somber expression is carved onto the
dark brown sardonyx ground. A thin layer of
gold covers the edge of the stone in an uneven
setting. This layer is split directly over the
Silenus head. On either side of the ring is a
bust in shallow relief, one of a woman and
the other a man.

A similar ring type, without the raised
stone setting, comes from a grave in Petescia
in Italy and is given an Augustan date by
Greifenhagen[1]. The shape of the ring, especially the flat head with a "ledge" surrounding the cameo, is particularly Graeco-
Roman. It is unusual to find busts in relief on
the sides of a ring during Imperial times.

Pliny comments on the increasing popularity of the sardonyx in Rome since Scipio
Africanus (236-184 B.C.) first wore the
stone[2]. The Bowdoin cameo also reflects a
popular image of the early Empire, adopted
from Hellenistic art, that of the Silenus head.
According to Boardman, Antony "saw himself as a young Dionysos, and his intimate
dealings with the Hellenistic courts of the
Greek world ensured a patronage for gem-
engraving and continued popularity for
Dionysiac subjects"[3]. He notes that Silenus
heads on cameos are particularly popular
through the first century A.D.[4]. Dionysiac
imagery was also kept alive in Italy through
the mysteries of the Bacchic religious ceremonies[5] as well as through the lasting
influence of Greek drama[6]. Parallels to the
type of Silen head on the Bowdoin cameo can
be found on a Campana relief[7], a mould for
an Arretine bowl in Florence[8], and a stucco
relief in the Villa Farnesina[9], all described by
Nilsson. Two undated cameos in Lippold's
collection depict a Silenus profile similar to
that on the Bowdoin gem[10]. A Silenus in
profile on an intaglio in the *Cabinet des
Médailles* in Paris[11] also parallels the
Bowdoin cameo, though in a less refined
style.

The bust reliefs on other side of the ring
are rendered in a coarse, generalized style and
are probably portraits of common citizens.
Nonetheless, the stylistic similarity between
the man's portrait and the portrait of
Vitellius on a Roman coin of A.D. 69[12]
suggests that the two pieces may be close
in date. Both the ring relief and the coin
display their subjects' coarse facial features,

fleshiness and pleased smiles. The woman's portrait stands in a Hellenistic tradition [13].

AG

[1] GREIFENHAGEN, 1, pl. 58,8.

[2] PLINY, *Natural History*, 37.23.85-86.

[3] BOARDMAN, 1968, p. 26. For most recent scholarship on satyr heads, as opposed to Silenus depictions, see T. GESZTELYI, *Satyrbüsten*, in *Acta classica Universitatis scientiarum Debreceniensis*, 14, 1978, p. 65-73.

[4] BOARDMAN, 1968, p. 38.

[5] For a description of artworks depicting the Bacchic mysteries in Italy see M. NILSSON, *The Dionysiac Mysteries of the Hellenistic and Roman Age*, Lund, 1957.

[6] See F. BROMMER, *Satyrspiele*, Berlin, 1959.

[7] NILSSON, p. 89, fig. 18.

[8] G. CHASE, *The Loeb Collection of Arretine pottery*, New York, 1908, pl. I,B.

[9] NILSSON, p. 79, fig. 11.

[10] G. LIPPOLD, *Gemmen und Kameen des Altertums und der Neuzeit*, Stuttgart, 1922, pl. 112, 1,2.

[11] RICHTER, 1968, 2, p. 44, fig. 173.

[12] A. ROBERTSON, *Roman Imperial Coins in the Hunter Coin Cabinet*, I, London, 1962, pl. 30, 19 and 25.

[13] Women are depicted with the same fleshy faces and hair held loosely in a large, high bun on such Hellenistic monuments as the Relief of the Apotheosis of Homer, in the British Museum (ca. 125 B.C.).

33
Bracelet

Roman, provenance unknown, 3rd c. A.D.

Diam. 6.3 cm.

Virginia Museum of Fine Arts.
Acc. no. 64-55-1.

Purchase, The Williams Fund, 1965.

Bibliography:

J. BROWN, *Ancient Art in the Virginia Museum*, 1973, no. 149.

Echoes from Olympus, exh. cat. University Art Museum, University of California, Berkeley, 1974, cat. no. 196, p. 176, illus. p. 183.

A hoop of thick gold wire twisted into a spiral terminates in an oval hinged clasp. This clasp is surmounted by an oval bezel sardonyx in a brownish tone. The bracelet is in excellent condition.

Similar pieces are in the Museum für Kunst und Gewerbe, Hamburg (1926.245) and in the British Museum (no. 2815). A silver bracelet of the same type, but with a clasp comprised of a Heracles knot set with a bezel carnelian intaglio, was found at Dura-Europos [1]. The Dura bracelet indicates Greek influence in Roman Syria as late as the third century. Various adaptations of the spiral-hinge bracelet have emerged from other excavations [2].

MacKay's study of Palmyrene funerary busts reveals that necklaces and bracelets of any kind are absent on busts until nearly A.D. 150, possibly due to Greek influence[3]. Increased trade with India and China between A.D. 150 and 200 may be the reason for more and varied jewelry on funerary busts and stelae[4]. The Palmyrene Stele of Aha (A.D. 161) shows a woman wearing two bracelets of the type found at Dura-Europos. A version of the twisted wire bracelet most common on these later funerary busts combines plain and beaded wires within the spiral. These bracelets became so popular by the third century that they were probably cast to speed up production[5].

A comparison of the Virginia bracelet with the Dura and British Museum pieces again illustrates Hellenistic influence on imperial jewelry, as well as the characteristics Pfeiler considers to be "Italo-Roman". Hellenistic influence in Roman Egypt is indicated by the naturalistic rendering of the serpents' heads in the British Museum piece. Snakes' heads may originally have had a relation to a Bacchic cult[6]. The Virginia bracelet, with its simple clasp, smooth bezel stone and unadorned spiral embodies the geometric regularity and abstract design of Pfeiler's "Italo-Roman" style[7].

AG

[1] Baur and Rostovtzeff, 1931, p. 79.
[2] See Böhme, p. 10 for Lyon bracelet. Other bracelets found at Zagazig (Cairo Museum, no. 59.099) and Villardu.
[3] MacKay, p. 164.
[4] Ibid., p. 170. This increase in trade corresponds roughly with Ingholt's "Period II" in his study of Palmyrene busts.
[5] Baur and Rostovtzeff, p. 79.
[6] Coche de la Ferté, p. 91. He cites Suetonius' Nero, 6, in which Nero's assassins are scared off by a snake, the skin of which is found beside his pillow. According to Suetonius, Agrippina took this as a sign of divine intervention and at her desire "(Nero) has the skin enclosed in a golden bracelet, and wore it for a long time on his right arm".
[7] Pfeiler, p. 106.

34
Two Similar Earrings

Roman, provenance unknown, 2nd-3rd
c. A.D.

H. of (a) 5.8 cm; h. of (b) 5.5 cm.

W. of disc (a) 2.3 cm; w. of disc (b)
2.27 cm.

Museum of Art, Rhode Island School
of Design.

Acc. no. 20.282.

Gift of the Ostby and Barton Co.
in memory of Engelhardt Cornelius
Ostby.

Bibliography:

HACKENS, p. 116-118, illus. 52a,b.

DEMORTIER, this volume p. 221.

The basic element of each earring is a gold
oval shield with two filigree spirals soldered
onto the lower portion and granulation along
the lower edge. A foil ring is soldered to the
loop of six twisted wires attached to the back
of the shield. The loops and ornaments on the
discs show traces of wear. The four spherical
balls soldered to the foil ring are slightly
dented, and the edges of the granulation
curtains attached to the three front spheres
are slightly worn. "Though definitely not a
pair, these two pieces are similar enough to
justify a joint description which shows different techniques producing similar effects"[1].

Several pairs of earrings similar to the
Providence pieces have been found in Syria
and Palestine, including a pair in the National Museum of Damascus (inv. no. 5457)[2]
from Zawieh, a province near Antioch. El
Chehadeh suggests that at least five of these
pairs may be assigned to the same workshop
due to their almost identical structures[3].
He also suggests an evolutionary relationship
between this type of solid gold earring and a
possibly earlier pair[4] in which the round

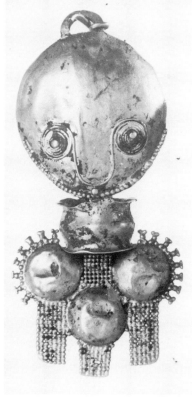

shield begins as a set stone, with the hanging ornaments a reduced version of the ball-and-curtain type [5]. This "evolution" may indicate a gradual "romanization" of the oriental use of precious stones and the Greek preference for fine granulation. The Providence earrings illustrate the broad metal surfaces with linear decoration, the abstract geometric forms and the Hellenistic filigree and granulation techniques which characterize Pfeiler's "Hellenistic-Roman" style [6]. Indeed, two pairs of earrings in the British Museum, very similar to those in Providence, are from Samsun, a region in Asia Minor which lay on the major trade route between Greece and the Orient.

Higgins suggests that this is "an elaboration of the ball-type earring" found at Boscoreale, Pompeii and Herculaneum [7]. While it is possible that the curved hemisphere of the "ball-type" may emerge from late Etruscan earrings [8], Higgins' recognition of a lack of intermediate stages between the two styles gives credibility to El Chehadeh's theory of the evolving style. Although El Chehadeh questions Pfeiler's "Hellenistic-Roman" and "Italo-Roman" classifications, his theory illustrates Pfeiler's approach to the romanization of an originally oriental piece of jewelry.

AG

---

[1] HACKENS, p. 116.
[2] EL CHEHADEH, p. 31-38, illus. 27.
[3] *Ibid.*, p. 36.
[4] *Ibid.*, p. 28-29, illus. 24.
[5] *Ibid.*, p. 31-37.
[6] PFEILER, p. 106.
[7] HIGGINS, 1980, p. 184.
[8] *Ibid.*, p. 184.

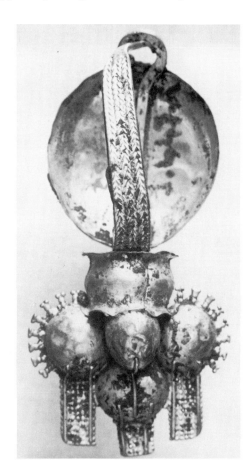

35
Pair of Earrings

Roman, found in Syria, 2nd-3rd c. A.D.
H. 3.34-3.4 cm; max. w. 1.88-1.90 cm.
Museum of Art, Rhode Island School
   of Design.
   Acc. no. 14.016.
Gift of Mrs. Jesse H. Metcalf.
Bibliography:
HACKENS, p. 119, illus. 53a,b,c.
See DEMORTIER, *infra*, p. 223.

Each gold earring consists of a ring of two twisted wires with a convex shield connecting one end of the loop to the other, hooked end. The shield is bordered with three rows of spiral-spool wire. Hackens notes that "the color of the solder" on the five evenly-spaced granules on the innermost row "indicates a different composition from that of the other elements of the ring"[1].

The bottom of each ring is flattened "to allow a good soldering base" for the diamond-shaped boxes attached to the lower side of the rings[2]. The sides of each box are composed of a rectangular sheet of fluted gold foil, folded and soldered along one side. Three granules soldered end-to-end in a vertical row are attached to the bottom of the box. In the base of each box a tiny hole has apparently been punched through from the

inside. The function of this hole is not probably terminal expansion.

Earrings incorporating the shield-like element exist in several collections, but the box addition is very unusual. Similar earrings without pendants are present in Greifenhagen[3] (though a loop on the ring indicates a pendant may be missing), and in the Museum of the University of Indiana[4]. Higgins describes the most common variant of the shield-hoop combination as commonly having "a club as a pendant", in which form it occurs in Tomb 87 and Tomb 95 at Amathus, of the second century[5]. One of these earrings, found in a tomb containing coins of Antoninus Pius and M. Aurelius, is now in the British Museum[6]. Variations on the shield-with-pendant are numerous. Greifenhagen illustrates a pair from Cyprus[7] and a variant type from southern Russia[8] with a stone inlaid in the center of the shield and a granulation pyramid soldered to the club pendant: motifs indicating Greek influence.

A close parallel found in a tomb at Tartara, Syria, and given a second or third century date is in the British Museum[9]. The Worcester Art Museum also owns two pairs of shield-type earrings, one with pendants

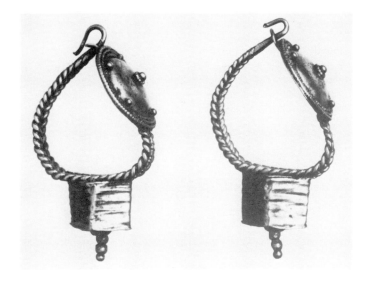

and one without, from Sidon[10]. Finally, the Damascus Museum owns a shield-with-pendant earring with a smooth hoop not in the ring form[11].

An interesting comparison can be made between this entry and the two other shield-type earrings in this exhibition (cat. no. 34), with a pair of earrings from the University of Indiana collection[12] as a kind of "hybrid" of the two styles. The Indiana earrings share the basic shield-and-twisted hoop design with this entry, while they also adopt the filigree spiral decoration on the shield and granulated hanging pendants of cat. no. 34. The Indiana earrings appear to incorporate a miniature version of the box attached to the ring bottom as a base for soldering the pendant of spheres and granules. It might be concluded that workshops in the second and third centuries were experimenting with

multiple combinations of the geometric and linear elements characteristic of late Imperial style. The novel introduction of a box-shaped element affirms this geometricizing trend.

AG

[1] HACKENS, p. 119.

[2] *Ibid.*

[3] GREIFENHAGEN, II, pl. 49,16.

[4] RUDOLPH, pl. 150c.

[5] HIGGINS, 1980, p. 177.

[6] MARSHALL, *BMCJ*, no. 2526.

[7] GREIFENHAGEN, II, pl. 49,27.

[8] *Ibid.*, I, pl. 23,14-15.

[9] MARSHALL, *BMCJ*, no. 2377.

[10] HACKENS, p. 119. Worcester Art Museum acc. no. 1953.48a, b and acc. no. 1953.49,a, b.

[11] ZOUHDI, pl. 15,2 and pl. 14,2 and 3.

[12] RUDOLPH, pl. 166b.

36
Necklace with coin pendants

Roman, provenance unknown, late 3rd-
4th c. A.D.
L. of chain ca. 84 cm; diam. of discs
6.5 cm.
Field Museum of Natural History.
Acc. no. 2262; cat. no. 239195.
Estate of Mr. H. N. Higinbotham, 1941;
collector: E. E. Ayer.

This Roman necklace is composed of four gold chains whose compact herringbone pattern indicates their construction by cross-linking a double loop-in-loop chain[1]. The chains pass through four openwork gold cylinders whose end pieces are decorated to imitate Corinthian capitals. The cylinders act as spacers to keep the three pendants attached to the chains separate from one another. The pendants consist of three gold coins set directly into circular solid gold frames which are each surrounded by a wide outer border of delicate openwork design. The openwork of the two outer pendants shows a pattern of two squares which intersect symmetrically to form an octagonal star shape, with an ivy leaf design filling the matrix created by the squares[2]. The openwork of the center pendant consists of a pure scrolled ivy leaf design, as does the openwork of the four spacers. At the opposite end of the necklace, the four chains pass through two large hollow gold beads which are cast with a lozenge and rosette design, and each chain is attached to the inside of the second bead through which it passes. This complex arrangement of chains allows the necklace to be lengthened or shortened according to the distance between the two beads. The beads themselves act as counterweights to the three pendants. The necklace weighs 400 grams.

This necklace, with its abundance of richly worked gold, is an excellent example of late Roman jewelry. In addition to its elaborate and varied use of gold as a material, the inclusion of coins and openwork, which essentially comprise the pendants, is very characteristic for this time. The use of coins in jewelry has a long tradition in Egypt[3], but

during the second and third centuries A.D., the fashion of placing coins in jewelry, especially as ornamental pendants, becomes increasingly popular, and is frequently seen on Roman necklaces. It is during the Roman Imperial period too that the technique of openwork, known as *opus interrasile*, is revived[4], and its organic lace-like patterns frequently appear. This technique is thought to have its origins in the Orient, and during the third century A.D. flourished under the influence of Syrian workshops[5]. *Opus interrasile* is adopted for use in Byzantine jewelry, where it is often used to form an entire piece[6].

The three coins mounted as pendants depict, from left to right, Otacilia Severa, wife of Philip I (A.D. 244-249), Probus (A.D. 276-282) and Gordian III (A.D. 238-244). The obverse of the coin of Otacilia Severa shows a bust of the empress wearing a diadem, facing right, and the legend reads: M OTACIL SEVERA AVG. The reverse depicts the goddess Concordia seated left, holding her attribute, the patera of sacrifice, and a double cornucopia. The reverse legend is CONCORDIA AVG[7].

The obverse of the coin in the center pendant shows a bust of Probus, wearing a radiate crown and facing right. The legend reads: IMP C M AVR PROBVS AVG. The reverse shows the goddess Roma seated left on a shield, and holding a figure of Victory and a spear. The legend reads: ROMAE AETERNAE[8].

The obverse of the coin of Gordian III shows a bust of the young emperor crowned

with a laurel wreath, facing right. The legend is : IMP CAES M ANT GORDIANVS AVG. The reverse depicts the goddess Liberalitas standing left, holding an account book or abacus, and a cornucopia. The legend is LIRERALITAS AVG II (sic). The spelling error in the reverse legend is not catalogued by Mattingly, and according to the American Numismatic Society, is unique[9].

The three coins form no unified programme, and it may be assumed that they were placed together at a later date than when they were minted for their general historical and decorative value. It has in fact been suggested that by the middle of the third century A.D., coins were preserved in necklaces such as this for the purpose of recording coinage no longer in circulation whose collectible and monetary value was increasing during a period of great inflation[10]. It is argued that this practice was undertaken by jewelers for a private and specialized clientele, who had both a numismatic and an ornamental interest in displaying coins in jewelry[11].

Two well-known necklaces from the Walters Art Gallery, Baltimore, and the Metropolitan Museum of Art, New York, relate closely to the Field Museum necklace[12]. These necklaces have both been given probable Egyptian provenances, and are dated to the early third century and ca. A.D. 225, respectively. All three necklaces have a similar arrangement of quadruple chains ushered through what Vermeule refers to as amphorae-shaped beads[13]. While the Field Museum necklace displays only three

coin pendants, the Metropolitan Museum necklace displays five and the Walters necklace eight. However, the openwork settings of the Field Museum pendants are larger than those of the related pieces. The Field Museum necklace is the only one of the three pieces to have openwork spacers as well. The spacers separating the pendants on the other two necklaces are composed of solid though decorated gold cylinders. The coin of Probus on the Field Museum necklace establishes a later date for this piece than its related necklaces, but even without this confirmation, the presence of such an increased amount of openwork on the Field Museum necklace argues for this later date. The balance struck between the increased gold surface area of the pendants and the lace-like treatment of that surface distinguishes the Field Museum necklace from the earlier and related types discussed here. Its large size and open forms suggest an affinity with Byzantine jewelry, but the style of the necklace remains distinctly Roman.

ESS

[1] See HIGGINS, 1980, p. 16 for description and diagram.
[2] See DENNISON, cat. no. 8, pl. XXVI for a similar border design for a mounted coin.
[3] C. VERMEULE, 1975, p. 29.
[4] HIGGINS, p. 29, notes the presence of openwork of a somewhat different form in early Etruscan jewelry.
[5] COCHE DE LA FERTÉ, p. 93.
[6] GREIFENHAGEN, I, p. 75, pl. 55 and 56.
[7] See H. MATTINGLY, E. A. SYDENHAM and C. H. V. SUTHERLAND, *The Roman Imperial Coinage*, vol. 4, part 3, London, 1949, p. 83, no. 125.

[8] See MATTINGLY, *et al.*, 5, part 2, p. 115, no. 893, pl. V,6 for the closest parallel. The legends and reverse figure are similar on both coins, but the emperor on the obverse of the Field Museum necklace coin wears a radiate crown rather than a laurel wreath.
[9] MATTINGLY *et al.*, 4, part 3, p. 20, no. 42, pl. 1,12, lists this coin with the correct spelling of LIBERALITAS. My thanks to Dr. William Metcalf, Chief Curator of the American Numismatic Society for checking his files for parallels for this error.
[10] VERMEULE, p. 29.
[11] *Ibid.*, p. 6.
[12] WALTERS, 1979, p. 118, no. 328, and VERMEULE, p. 16, no. 26.
[13] VERMEULE, p. 16.

37
Pendant

Roman, provenance unknown, 3rd c. A.D.

Diam. 2.9 cm.

Courtesy of the Dumbarton Oaks Collection, Washington, D.C.

Acc. no. 51.3.

Formerly in the collection of M. Jameson; acquired in 1951.

Bibliography:

Ross, 1965, p. 25-26, no. 23, pl. XXV.

This gold pendant was originally suspended from a necklace, although the loop which attaches the pendant to the necklace is now missing. The pendant consists of an aureus depicting Elagabalus (A.D. 218-219) set in a frame of a repeated triangular design, which Greifenhagen refers to as a schematized lotus-blossom motif[1]. This frame motif was popular in the third century A.D. and can be seen on other mounted coins in the Staatliche Museen, Berlin and in the British Museum[2].

Elagabalus' grandmother, Julia Maesa, was the sister of the emperor Septimius Severus' wife, Julia Domna. The family was from Syria, thus the re-establishment of the Severan dynasty in A.D. 218 also meant a re-affirmation of power for the Roman province of Syria. The coin used for this pendant has been attributed to an eastern, possibly Syrian mint[3], many of which were active under the Severan dynasty.

The reverse of the aureus depicts the emperor's attempt to establish his own eastern religious practices throughout the Roman Empire. The sacred stone of the deity Sol Elagabalus was brought by quadriga to Rome from its original site at Emesa. The emperor Elagabalus adopted the name of the Emesene sun god whose priest he was prior to A.D. 218, and whose cult he was determined to spread during his rule. The association of the Roman emperor with a sun god was firmly established fifty years later under Aurelian. Aurelian's Sol was the universal sun rather than a local deity, but it evolved from the emperor Elagabalus' earlier religious beliefs[4].

The use of coins as pendants to necklaces was very popular in the third century A.D. The related necklace from the Field Museum of Natural History (cat. no. 36) can be compared with this piece for the manner in which coin pendants were attached to the necklace chain.

ESS

[1] Greifenhagen, I, p. 73, pl. 53.

[2] *Ibid.*, inv. no. 30099; and Marshall, *BMCJ*, no. 2727, pl. 59, no. 2939, pl. 68.

[3] A. R. Bellinger in Ross, 1965, p. 25.

[4] H. Mattingly, *Coins of the Roman Empire in the British Museum*, 5, London, 1975, p. ccxxxviii.

38
Necklace

Roman, provenance unknown, 3rd c.
A.D.
L. 42.5 cm.
Field Museum of Natural History.
Acc. no. 2262; cat. no. 239202.

This necklace is composed of a chain of gold wire links, upon which are strung plasma (a green quartz), pearl and gold beads. These beads are strung in a repeated plasma-pearl-gold bead-pearl sequence. This pattern is broken in two places by a missing pearl, and in one place by a missing plasma bead. The fourteen remaining plasma stones are of varying sizes, but most are hexagonal. The gold beads are also of different sizes. These fourteen beads consist of hollow gold cylinders or spools which are covered with delicate spirals of twisted gold wire soldered onto the surface of the spool. Two pendants hang from the chain links on either side of each of the gold spool beads. These pendants are composed of gold and decorated with looped strands of twisted wire of the same fineness as the wire on the gold spool beads. The pendants are cone-shaped, and the twisted wire filigree causes them to resemble elongated flower petals. From each of these cones hang four pearls (although one cone now has only two remaining pearls). These pearls are strung on single gold wires, which have small gold granules at the ends to secure the pearls. Twenty-four of these pendants remain; four are missing. The necklace clasp is a simple hook and eye type, although the eye loop is now missing. The necklace is slightly longer than choker length, although it would have originally been a few centimeters longer with all its beads intact.

The use of colored stones and pearls as both beads and pendants for necklaces is a common practice in Roman jewelry. While the Romans had particular preferences and were aware of the rarity of certain stones, they did not distinguish as we do today between precious and semi-precious stones. Stones were popular because of their variety of colors and, in some cases, because of their supposed amuletic powers [1]. Gold beads are more unusual to find in Roman necklaces, as they are more frequently seen in earlier jewelry such as the Etruscan necklace in this exhibition (cat. no. 26) [2].

The color combination of green and white (emeralds or plasma and pearls) is one of the most popular in Roman jewelry, judging by the many extant necklaces [3]. A necklace of emerald and pearl beads with pendants of pearls and aquamarines in the Staatliche Museen, Berlin [4] may be compared with the Field Museum necklace as a general type, even though it differs in specific stylistic elements. The arrangement of the colored stones as beads and pendants, and the use of a hook and eye clasp are both similar to the Field Museum necklace. Greifenhagen dates the Berlin necklace to the fifth century A.D. and gives it an Egyptian provenance. The Field Museum necklace is undoubtedly earlier. Necklaces with emerald beads found at Pompeii attest to the early popularity of these stones for jewelry [5]. The small size of the beads and pendants on the Field Museum necklace, as well as the perhaps archaistic inclusion of gold beads, also argues for a Roman rather than a Byzantine date.

ESS

[1] RUDOLPH, p. vii.
[2] RUXER and KUBCZAK, p. 207.
[3] *Ibid.*, p. 216. See also the necklace from the Lyon hoard illustrated in BÖHME, p. 10, fig. 16.
[4] GREIFENHAGEN, I, p. 69, pl. 50,1.
[5] HIGGINS, 1980, p. 180.

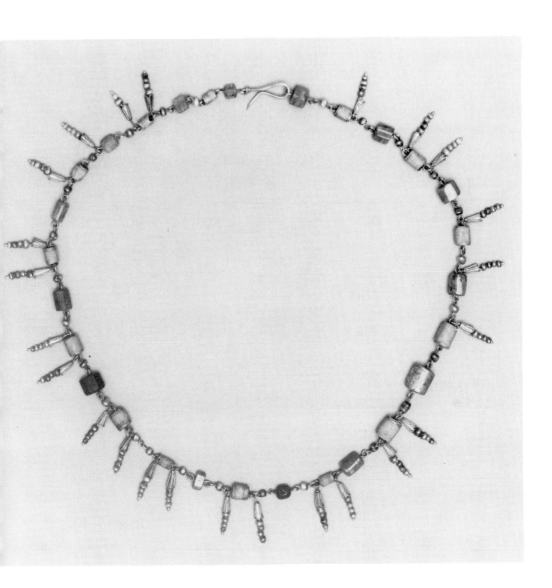

CONSTANTINOPOLIS

Constantine I, the Great (A.D. 306-337), is remembered most for two acts that have shaped the course of history. The first, religious, was his conversion to Christianity and subsequent "Edict of Milan" (313), granting "that every man may have complete toleration in the practice of whatever worship he has chosen"[1]. Second, in the political sphere, he moved the capital east to Byzantium (330), the "New Rome"[2], which during the reign of his hereditary successors came to be called Constantinople. The new imperial capital was to survive until 1453 when it was overrun by the Ottoman Turks.

The "Second Rome" was not built in a day. Indeed, it was not until the end of the fourth century that the Theodosian emperors took up permanent residence there. Moreover, the patriarchate in Constantinople, in contention with the Roman papacy and Alexandrian bishopric, was unable to assert its ecclesiastical jurisdiction over the Eastern Empire until the middle of the fifth century[3].

I. *Gold, Jewels and Artisans*

The former Byzantium, founded a millennium earlier, had long been a major port of call for imports from the east. Strategically located between Europe and Asia, and between the Aegean and Black Seas, it was much closer than Rome to the wealth of the empire, which lay in Asia Minor, Syria and Egypt. As we know from the Theodosian (ca. 438) and the Justinianic (529-534) legal codes, trade, strictly regulated, was very profitable with the Orient through the sixth century. Spices, ivory and jewels were imported from Persia and India. In particular, pearls were procured from the Persian Gulf, emeralds primarily from a mine near Alexandria, and, by way of India, sapphires from Ceylon.

The mines of Illyricum (western Balkans) were the major domestic source of gold, along with mining areas in Asia Minor and present-day Greece. Gold was valuable as the universal medium of exchange throughout the Empire, and on another level it also symbolized one's birthright as a free and equal "Roman" citizen. Justinian I (527-565) legally reaffirmed what had been granted as early as Diocletian's reign, that "the person who received freedom shall at once, and ever afterwards, have the right to wear a gold ring, and be classed as originally freeborn"[4]. The *jus annuli*

---

[1] Lactantius, *On the Deaths of the persecutors*, 48.2-12, trans. in J. STEVENSON, *A New Eusebius: Documents illustrative of the history of the Church to A.D. 337*, London, 1978 (orig. 1957), p. 301.

[2] See G. DAGRON, *Naissance d'une capitale: Constantinople et ses institutions de 330 à 451*, Paris, 1974; and J. E. N. HEARSEY, *City of Constantinople 324-1453*, London, 1963.

[3] Religious parity was achieved at the Council of Chalcedon, A.D. 451. See H.-G. BECK, *Constantinople: The Rise of a New Capital in the East*, in *Age of Spirituality: A Symposium*, K. Weitzmann, ed., New York, 1980.

[4] Justinian I (527-565), *Novels*, ca. 535-565, 6.7.1, trans. from the Greek by S. P. SCOTT in *The Civil Law*, New York, 1973 (orig. 1932), vol. 7 (orig. vol. 16, p. 291).

aurei, or right to wear a gold ring, was thus, theoretically, extended to former male and female slaves[5].

Apparently, gold was in much greater supply during the period under consideration here (330-527) than it had been in the two previous centuries[6]. Toward the end of the fifth century, Anastasius (491-518) added some 320,000 pounds of gold to the imperial coffers[7]. Earlier, Constantine had successfully reformed the currency, establishing the gold *solidus*, 1/72 of a Roman pound (4.5 g), as the monetary standard, which was to last through the eleventh century. Imperial mints in the east with gold issues included Thessalonica and Nicomedia, in addition to Constantinople, Antioch and Alexandria; although from 368 gold coinage was restricted to the imperial residence, with the exception of Thessalonica in the fifth century[8].

Fig. 17. Coin of Theodosius I (379-395), gold, Museum Appropriation, Museum of Art, Rhode Island School of Design.

The mints were administered by the *officium* of the *comes sacrarum largitionum*, or office of the count of the sacred largesses, the latter being the equivalent of secretary of the treasury. In addition to the mints, factories for the making of armor and arms, imperial and military clothing and imperial jewelry were appended to this large financial institution. It was divided into ten departments, the sixth of these, the *scrinii auri massae*, or bullion department, consisted of three main branches: the *aurifices specierum* (goldsmiths), *aurifices solidorum* (minters of gold coins) and

---

[5] Cf. Justinian I, *Corpus Juris Civilis*, (529-534, hereafter *CJC*), 6.8.2, ca. 284-305, and *Digest*, (533), 2.4.10 (3), and 40.10.1-6.

[6] See J. P. C. KENT and K. S. PAINTER, eds., *Wealth of the Roman World, AD 300-700* (exh. cat.), London, 1977, p. 15-19.

[7] *Encyclopaedia Britannica*, 1981 ed., *s.v. Byzantine Empire*, D.M.N., vol. 3, p. 551. Original source could not be located.

[8] See J. P. C. KENT, *Gold Coinage in the Later Roman Empire*, in *Essays in Roman Coinage Presented to Harold Mattingly*, R. A. G. Carson and C. H. V. Sutherland, eds., Oxford, 1956, p. 199-200; J. P. C. KENT, *Excursus on the Comes Sacrarum Largitionum*, in E. C. DODD, *Byzantine Silver Stamps*, Washington, D. C., 1961, p. 44; and A. H. M. JONES, *The Later Roman Empire 284-602: A Social, Economic and Administrative Survey*, Norman, Okla., 1964, vol. 1, p. 437.

[9] *CJC*, 12.24.7, 384. Alternately referred to as 12.23.7. Also, J. P. C. KENT, *The Office of Comes Sacrarum Largitionum*, Ph.D. diss., University of London, 1951 (not available to the author).

sculptores e ceteri aurifices (engravers and other craftsmen)[9]. Employees of the mints and other imperial factories, such as the textile mills, were hereditarily bound to their occupations[10]. Their status in society was considered menial and convict labor in the mines supplied their raw material[11].

In contrast, the skilled artisans who fashioned precious metals into jewelry and other imperial regalia enjoyed a higher social status and imperial favor. Shortly after Constantine's death it became law that:

> artisans who dwell in each city and who practice the skills included in the appended list [e.g., goldsmiths, makers of perforated work, engravers, *barbaricarii*[12], etc.] shall be free from all compulsory public services, since indeed their leisure should be spent in learning these skills whereby they may desire the more to become more proficient themselves and to instruct their children[13].

It is clear from this statute, which appears in both the Theodosian and Justinianic codes, that there was concern that jewelry makers transmit their craft to future generations, and that their numbers remain constant. Thus, any shortage of these skilled craftsmen in the east would probably have been due, in part, to the disruptions of the third century. In contrast to the situation in the west where the later Roman Empire suffered from the continual migration of artisans from urban areas into the countryside, the eastern cities were able to maintain their artisan class[14].

It is also evident from the above decree that the economic importance of these skilled artisans secured their higher social standing, above and beyond any concern with the perpetuation of their craft. Leo I (457-474) proclaimed:

> that those artisans engaged in manufactures for the Emperor, as well as their wives and children, who are also said to be artisans, shall not be required to answer in court, unless before the tribunal of Your Highness, to whose jurisdiction they belong and under whose power they are. Nor shall they, after their term of service has expired, under any circumstances, be liable to civil or curial obligations, or be illegally molested by the illustrious Governors of provinces or their subordinates[15].

Further affirmation of the superior status of jewelry makers over some other imperial factory workmen can be deduced from the fact that with regard to the equestrian order (the second level of aristocracy), the grade of the superintendent of the *aurifices specierum* was *perfectissimi*, whose salary was fifty percent higher than that of the *ducenarii* of the *aurifices solidorum*[16].

Justinian proclaimed that "imperial ornaments must be made in the palace, by

---

[10] *CJC*, 11.7.13, 7 March 426 and 11.9.5, 423-450. For Byzantine mints see W.W. WROTH, *Catalogue of the Imperial Byzantine Coins in the British Museum*, 2 vols., London, 1908.

[11] See Theodosius II (408-450), *Codex Theodosianus* (ca. 438, hereafter *CTh*), 10.20.1, 317 and 10.20.10, 380 or 379; and T.T. RICE, *Everyday Life in Byzantium*, New York, 1967, p. 132.

[12] Administered by the *scrinii ab argento*, the silver bullion department of the *comes sacrarum largitionum*, the *barbaricarii* ornamented arms and armor with silver and, evidently, with gold also. See *CTh*, 10.22.1, 374, and *CJC*, 12.24.7, 384.

[13] *CTh*, 13.4.2, 2 August 33â, trans. by C. PHARR, *The Theodosian Code and Novels and the Sirmondian Constitutions*, Princeton, 1952, p. 390-391. Cf., *CJC*, 10.64.1, 4 August 337.

[14] See A.H.M. JONES, *op. cit.*, vol. 1, p. 762-763 and vol. 2, p. 861.

[15] *CJC*, 11.9.6, 457-474, trans. in S.P. SCOTT, *op. cit.*, vol. 7 (orig. vol. 15, p. 176).

[16] *CJC*, 12.24.7, 384. See also A.H.M. JONES, *op. cit.*, vol. 1, p. 525-526.

the artificers attached to the same, and not indiscriminately in private residences or workshops"[17]. We know that at least by the reign of Valens (364-378) the imperial workshops of the *barbaricarii* were in Constantinople and Antioch[18]. In Constantinople, the jewelers' workshops were set up near the Great Palace. These artisans were responsible for defending sections of the city's walls and could participate in ceremonial processions. Apparently, there was a high degree of specialization in their work from an early date. Goldsmiths and silversmiths worked separately, and those expert in various techniques such as granulation, wire braiding, enamelwork and the making of imperial regalia all had individual workshops[19].

II. *Military, Personal and Religious Adornments*

Imperial gifts of jewelry served a very public and prestigious function. Jewelry makers, therefore, had an important role in the official life of the empire. The emperor gave out many gifts of jewelry to reward individuals for their loyalty, to induce their allegiance and to commend bravery (cat. no. 39). Jewelry was also presented on special occasions in the empire, such as New Year's Day and civil anniversaries.

These gifts were ordinarily bestowed on persons taking up an important office: newly appointed civil or military officers, and foreign emissaries. The Beaurains hoard for example, unearthed in Belgium in 1922, was apparently hidden around A.D. 315. It contains such gifts as gold coins, jewelry and silverware, indicative of an officer of moderately high rank[20].

The three general categories receiving imperial largesses were civil officials, allies and military figures; each earned different types of jewelry. Persons of rank received bronze, silver and gold fibulae or belt buckles depicting the emperor. Civilian groups were given medallions portraying the group's purpose. The more workmanship in a given piece of jewelry and the greater its gold content, the fewer in number and more prestigious were its recipients. The emperor bestowed a rich ceremonial wardrobe on military officials. Items of armor were often decoratively inscribed. The army, without a doubt, received the greatest amount of imperial jewelry[21].

Metropolises that had large army populations during the late empire are present-day sources of numerous fibulae, medallions, rings, belt buckles and other objects. Such evidence indicates that the emperor celebrated important treaties, victories and peace-making by presenting jewelry.

The emperor's largesses were primarily given to men, although the imperial workshops did produce items for the women of the emperor's family and court. Later, during the Justinianic period, the mosaics of San Vitale in Ravenna provide

---

[17]   *CJC*, 11.11.1, 529-534, trans. in S. P. SCOTT, *op. cit.*, vol. 7 (orig. vol. 15, p. 178).

[18]   *CTh*, 10.22.1, 374.

[19]   See T. T. RICE, *op. cit.*, p. 130-131.

[20]   See P. BASTIEN and C. METZGER, *Le trésor de Beaurains (dit d'Arras)*, Wetteren, Belgium, 1977.

[21]   See R. MACMULLEN, *The Emperor's Largesses*, in *Latomus*, 1962, 21, p. 159-166.

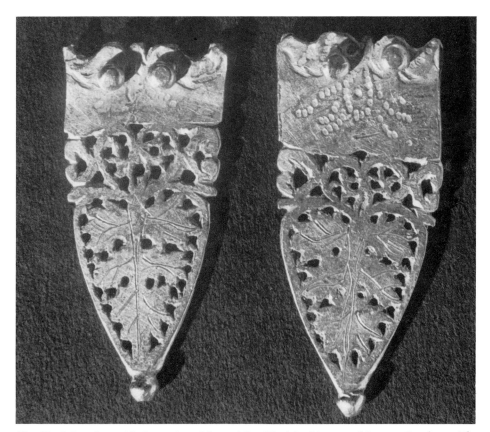

Fig. 18. Belt tabs, gold, Byzantine, 7th c. A.D., Virginia Museum, Museum Purchase: The Williams Fund, 1968.

a way of attributing much extant early Byzantine jewelry to court workshops [22]. In these sixth century mosaics, the empress Theodora and ladies of the court are shown wearing elaborate gold necklaces, bracelets and earrings, studded with pearls, emeralds and sapphires or amethysts. Justinian proclaimed in his *Corpus Juris Civilis* (529-534) that "pearls, emeralds or hyacinths [i.e., sapphires] ... [are] solely reserved for the splendor and adornment of the sovereign" [23]. On pain of death, and under threat of severe fine, he further warned that "no private person shall be permitted to make anything out of gold and jewels [i.e., pearls, emeralds or hyacinths] which is reserved for imperial use and adornment (with the exception of ornaments usually worn by women, and the rings of both sexes)" [24]. One can surmise from Justinian's exemptions to his rule, that the Field Museum gold necklace (cat. no. 44) and others like it, with pearls, green glass beads and amethysts, are not necessarily products of an imperial workshop. Although some Byzantine jewelry of the later sixth and seventh centuries is conservative in nature,

---

[22] See K. R. BROWN, *The Mosaics of San Vitale: Evidence for the Attribution of Some Early Byzantine Jewelry to Court Workshops*, in *Gesta*, 18, no. 1, 1979, p. 57-62.

[23] *CJC*, 11.11.1, 529-534, trans. in S. P. SCOTT, *op. cit.*, vol. 7 (orig. vol. 15, p. 177-178).

[24] *Ibid.*, vol. 7 (orig. vol. 15, p. 178).

the degree of sumptuousness reflects the Justinian age and a later chapter of Byzantine art history.

In addition to the prominent use of colorful gemstones and glass beads, the technique of *opus interrasile* (decorative fretwork, see Fig. 2) was also characteristic of early Byzantine jewelry, and likewise stemmed from the Late Antique period. In this earlier period, openwork was an integral part of medallions using contemporary and often older coins. For instance, objects in the gold treasure of the late Roman period, reported by Dennison and dating from the third to sixth centuries, well represent this practice and technique [25]. However, this interlacing openwork is not restricted to metalsmithing. The tendency to create abstract pattern, to add depth and contrast to surfaces, was also developing at this time in textiles and architectural decoration; for example, the capitals of San Vitale [26]. Later, influenced to some extent by Persian artisans practicing their craft in the empire, Byzantine *opus interrasile* would in turn affect Islamic art. Ennodius (d. 521), Bishop of Pavia, writes in an epigram on the wondrous lace-like quality of openwork (*Carmina*, 2.46-9):

> *Concerning the necklace of Firmina which is enclosed in a 'septicum', so delicate is it*
> Slippery breath flies from the exhausted gold
>
> The wearied metal scarcely touches her white limbs
> The cost of the breathing furnace has diminished its weight
>
> The master has dissolved golden threads through clouds
> His trained hands have enclosed tawny breaths
>
> This breath has wrought strands of precious metal
> One's eyes are in awe of what they have fashioned, nor do they grasp it
>
> It is nothing but I hold it, my right hand persuades my vision
> The aura is drawn from the taut interweavings of limbs [27]

Another substantial body of work includes objects of Christian symbol and ritual, such as marriage rings and belts and pendant crosses. Besides a sum of money, rings were the most popular form of engagement gift [28]. On the rings a couple is typically portrayed with Christ or a cross acting as *deus pronobus*, "confirming the legal action and protecting the marriage" [29]. This innovation is, in essence, more than just a substitution of Christ for Concordia as *pronuba*. In a sermon delivered in Constantinople in 401, Bishop Severianus of Gabala noted that:

[25] See W. DENNISON, *A Gold Treasure of the Late Roman Period*, New York, 1918.

[26] See E. KITZINGER, *On the Interpretation of Stylistic Changes in Late Antique Art*, in *The Art of Byzantium and the Medieval West: Selected Studies*, W. E. Kleinbauer, ed., Bloomington, Ind., 1976, p. 32-48; and *The Development of Interlace and Related Patterns*, in J. TRILLING, *The Roman Heritage: Textiles from Egypt and the Eastern Mediterranean 300 to 600 AD*, Washington, D.C., 1982, p. 104-108.

[27] I am grateful to Prof. M. C. Putnam for this translation from the Latin text in the *Corpus Scriptorum Ecclesiasticorum*, vol. 6, *Magni Felicis Ennodii Opera Omnia*, W. Hartel, ed., Vienna, 1882, p. 572-573.

[28] K. RITZER, *Formen, Riten und religiöses Brauchtum der Eheschliessung in den christlichen Kirchen des ersten Jahrtausends*, Münster, 1962, p. 70.

[29] See E. KANTOROWICZ, *On the Golden Marriage Belt and the Marriage Rings of the Dumbarton Oaks Collection*, in *Dumbarton Oaks Papers*, 14, Washington, D.C., 1960, p. 3-16, plus 37 plates.

When the images of two persons, kings or brothers, are painted, we often notice that the painter, so as to emphasize the unanimity of the couple, places at the back of them a *Concordia* in female garb. With her arms she embraces both to indicate that the two persons, whose bodies are separated, concur in mind and will. So does now the Peace of the Lord stand in the center to teach us how separate bodies may become one in spirit[30].

It is interesting in this regard to compare the Dumbarton Oaks gold marriage ring (cat. no. 42), which dates from the late fourth to fifth century in Constantinople, with the Casket of Projecta, of the late fourth century, from the Esquiline Treasure[31]. This gilt silver casket was found on the Esquiline Hill in Rome and is thought to be a wedding gift. Worked in repoussé, a couple is depicted on the lid within a wreath; however, there is no *pronubus*. Instead, around the rim of the entire lid is the following inscription: "Secundus and Projecta, may you live in Christ"[32]. The rest of the low reliefs illustrate the bathing, dressing and leading of the bride to the traditional Roman wedding.

Jewels were of course used to adorn every manner of liturgical object in the early church. The chalice, the paten, the cross were traditionally enriched with gold and precious gems. We know from Egeria, a Spanish noblewoman who made a pilgrimage to Jerusalem around A.D. 380 (*Travels*, 25.8), that in Constantine's

> Great Church on Golgotha ... the decorations really are too marvelous for words. All you can see is gold and jewels and silk ... and everything they use for services at the festival is made of gold and jewels[33].

But aside from this liturgical use of precious metals and gems, we know the jewelry itself was sometimes found in churches, perhaps given as votive offerings by the faithful. Another and anonymous pilgrim to the Holy Land, in about A.D. 570 from Piacenza in northern Italy, left this report (*Travels from Piacenza*, 18):

> The stone which closed the [Lord's] Tomb ... is decorated with gold and precious stones ... There are ornaments in vast numbers, which (hung) from iron rods: armlets, bracelets, rings, tiaras, plaited girdles, belts, emperors' crowns of gold and precious stones ...[34]

From the founding of Constantinople through the accession of Justinian I, it appears that the use of jewels and precious metal was frequently associated with special occasions. The giving of imperial largess, the entering into the Christian state of matrimony and votive offerings in the church involved gold jewelry. The richness of taste evidenced in this jewelry reflects the values of an aristocratic society. It is a counterpart of the art of the period, as seen in liturgical vessels, ivories and mosaics.

Boyd T. HILL

[30] Trans. by E. KANTOROWICZ, *loc. cit.*, p. 9; cf., C. WEYMANN, *Omonoia*, in *Hermes*, 29, 1894, p. 626-627.

[31] See K.J. SHELTON, *The Esquiline Treasure*, London, 1981.

[32] J.P.C. KENT and K.S. PAINTER, *op. cit.*, p. 44.

[33] Trans. by J. WILKINSON in *Egeria's Travels*, London, 1971, p. 127.

[34] Trans. by J. WILKINSON in *Jerusalem Pilgrims Before the Crusades*, Warminster, England, 1977, p. 83. Cf. G. VIKAN, *Byzantine Pilgrimage Art* (exh. cat.), Washington, D.C., 1982.

39
Victory ring

Byzantine, provenance unknown, 4th c. A.D.

H. 3.2 cm, w. 4.4 cm.

Courtesy of the Walters Art Gallery, Baltimore.

Acc. no. 57.542.

Bibliography:

M.C. Ross, *Notes on Byzantine Gold and Silversmith's Work*, in *Journal of the Walters Art Gallery*, 1955, 18, p. 65-66, fig. 10.

Walters, 1979, p. 152, no. 425.

K. Weitzmann, ed., *Age of Spirituality: Late Antique and Early Christian Art, Third to Seventh Century*, exh. cat., New York, 1979, p. 305-306, no. 278.

Worcester Art Museum, *The Dark Ages*, exh. cat., Worcester, Mass., 1937, no. 79.

The heavy gold ring is composed of a band with foliate carving. At the sides of the band, two leopards carved in the round support almost entirely a circular bezel with scalloped edges. The bezel is set with a nicolo, its vivid blue surface engraved down to a black winged Victory figure.

The symbol of Victory and the weight of the ring suggest that this piece was presented as an imperial gift to reward an exceptionally prominent military personage. Indeed, the magnitude of the gift is clear when one recognizes that the ring's gold content (approximately 90 grams) was at that time equivalent to the ration allowance normally given to three common soldiers for an entire year.

Utilizing the motif of the leopards, Ross dates the ring to the fourth century. The animal motif closest in style to that on the ring is found in two silver handles discovered with the fourth century Traprain Law treasure [1]; one handle bearing a leopard and the other a panther. In addition, a ring with leopards' heads found near Rouen dates to the end of the third century [2], while yet another, now in the British Museum, is designed with rabbits supporting from both sides a coin which depicts the Eastern emperor Marcian (450-457) [3].

Closer in style to the overall ring are two massive gold rings in the Museo di Antichità, Parma [4]. Both bands are carved, and in addition, one has openwork. The bezels of each ring are set with nicolo gems, one of which is engraved with a warrior arming himself. These rings date to the Late Antique period.

BTH

[1] A. Curle, *The Treasure of Traprain*, Glasgow, 1923, p. 79, pl. 31.

[2] A. Alföldi, *Trésor de la fin du IIIe siècle trouvé à Brigetio*, in *Numizmatikai Közlöny*, 48-49, 1949-1950, p. 61, figs. 14-16, pl. 1.

[3] O. M. Dalton, 1901, p. 33, no. 210, pl. 4.

[4] C. Carducci, p. 60, pl. 61.

40

Bracelet

Byzantine, Alexandria or Syria?, ca. A.D. 400.

W. 3.41 cm, diam. 10.53 cm.

Lent by The Saint Louis Art Museum. Acc. no. 54:1924.

Bibliography:

G. A. EISEN, *An Antique Gold Bracelet in Opus Interrasile*, in *Bulletin of The City Art Museum of St. Louis*, 10, October 1925, p. 53-58.

GREIFENHAGEN, I, p. 75-76, figs. 62-62a, pl. 55-56.

C. LEPAGE, p. 10-12.

K. WEITZMANN, ed., *Age of Spirituality: Late Antique and Early Christian Art, Third to Seventh Century*, New York, 1979, p. 307, no. 280.

An especially refined example of *opus interrasile*, this gold openwork bracelet is divided vertically into eight convex panels. In turn, they consist of three horizontal bands, with the upper and lower registers repeating the same motifs. Four of the central panels contain an inscription ΨΥΧΗ ΚΑΛΗ ΥΓΙΑΙΝΟΥϹΑ ΦΩΡΙ which taken together has been translated as: "beautiful soulmate wear (this) in all health"[1]. The motifs of two of the upper and lower registers are repeated three times. The other two of the eight panels are unique. Richly colored leather or other textured material probably lined the inside of this bracelet originally.

The bracelet was discovered around 1913 in Tartous, Mt. Lebanon, Syria, along with a comparable gold bracelet and a bell, which are now in Berlin[2]. They also bear openwork inscriptions, which in consideration of the St. Louis inscription, strongly suggest an engagement gift from the bridegroom.

BTH

[1] Trans., R. Mouterde, Université Saint Joseph, Beyrouth, Lebanon, in a letter of July 12, 1960, in the St. Louis Art Museum's document file.

[2] R. ZAHN, *Amtliche Berichte aus den Königlichen Kunstsammlungen*, 35, 1913-14, p. 85 ff., fig. 43.

41
Necklace

Byzantine, provenance unknown, 5th-
6th c. A.D.
L. 41.6 cm.
Courtesy of the Walters Art Gallery,
Baltimore.
Acc. no. 57.544.
Bibliography:
Walters Art Gallery, 1947, no. 429.
WALTERS, 1979, p. 155, 157, no. 439.

This necklace consists of gold wire links, looped at both ends, that hook together to form the chain. Strung between the loops, pearls alternate with pink quartz drops and green glass beads. The beads are reinforced with rivets at top and bottom.

The openwork discs at the ends are attached to the necklace strand by larger loops. Opposite are a hook and a flattened loop, respectively, by which the discs are fastened. The discs themselves are carved with Greek crosses and foliage. For a discussion of the chromatic range here displayed and its significance, see Hill article, p. 141 ss. and entry no. 44.

The Walters necklace is similar to many fine late Roman ones, excluding the openwork disc clasps. There are two related necklaces in the Dumbarton Oaks Collection[1]. They come from the Piazza della Consolazione Treasure and date to the early fifth century Rome. Strung with pearls, emeralds, cabochon sapphires and chalcedony, they range from 37-40 cm. in length. Another representative comparison piece is the necklace of the Carthage Treasure in the British Museum[2]. Dating to about A.D. 400, it also has pearls, emeralds and sapphires, and is 39.4 cm in length. These uncomplicated strands of gold wire loops are characteristic of the Late Antique period.

BTH

[1] Ross, 1965, p. 1, nos. 1a and 1b, colorplate B and pl. 1.
[2] KENT and PAINTER, 1977, p. 125, no. 186a.

42
Marriage ring

Byzantine, Constantinople, late 4th - early 5th c. A.D.
Diam. 2.5 cm.
Courtesy of the Dumbarton Oaks Collection, Washington, D.C.
Acc. no. 47.18.
Bibliography:
Ross, 1965, p. 48-50, no. 50, pl. 39.

This heavy gold ring was solid cast. The band is rounded on the outside, flat on the inside. The bezel is nearly square, and is pyramidal in form. Its surface is deeply engraved with half-portraits of a man and woman, who are wearing jewelry. Between, but just above them, a cross in lieu of Christ acts as *pronobus* for the couple (see article by Hill, for iconography). There is a Greek inscription along the edge of the bezel: *Aristophanes* [and] *Vigil*[a]*ntia*, that is deeply incised in the *boustrophedon* manner (i.e., in reversed lettering).

Many examples of this type of ring are cited by Ross, including one in the British Museum with almost identical portraits[1].

Although the Dumbarton ring can be attributed to Constantinople on the basis of related pieces with that provenance, the Greek inscription, etc., most of these marriage rings where the provenance is known are from the West. For example, two rings from the Rhineland employ a similar engraving technique[2]. The widespread distribution of this kind of ring is also in evidence in silver objects, for instance, a silver marriage ring in the Schlossmuseum, Gotha, which is quite similar in style and technique, and also dates to the later fourth or earlier fifth century[3].

BTH

[1] Dalton, 1912, no. 127.
[2] Henkel, nos. 98a, 99a, pl. 5.
[3] Schlunk, p. 16, no. 28, pl. 6.

43
Pendant Cross

Byzantine, Constantinople?, 5th c. A.D.
L. 51 cm; cross: h. 2.7 cm; w. 2 cm.
Courtesy of the Dumbarton Oaks
Collection, Washington, D.C.
Acc. no. 50.20.
Bibliography:
Ross, 1965, p. 15, no. 10, pl. 17.
A. KRATZ, *Goldschmiedetechnische Untersuchung von Goldarbeiten im Besitz der Skulpturabteilung der Staatlichen Museen Preussischer Kulturbesitz Berlin (Frühchristlich-Byzantinische Sammlung)*, in *Aachener Kunstblätter*, 43, 1972, p. 156-189.

The cross pendant is suspended from a multiple loop-in-loop chain[1]. There are wire loops at the ends of the chain, one of which is mounted on a "cap". The non-capped loop has a looped wire attached that fastens the chain together.

The arms of the solid gold cross flare outward, and are concave at the ends. The cross hangs on the chain by a ring-like band soldered to its top. There are two globules of granulation at the front and back of this band. There are also clusters of granules on all eight corners of the cross, and also four single instances surrounding the bezel. The bezel is set with smooth natural glass, or else a pale green glass paste. Radiating outward are rectangular rows of braided wire made from sheet gold, bordered by "pearled" wire.

The back of the cross is engraved in a decorative palmette motif with a four-petalled design at the crossing.

The Dumbarton cross is quite similar, in almost all details, to one in the Frühchristlich-Byzantinische Sammlung of the Staatlichen Museen Preussischer Kulturbesitz Berlin[2]. The three hollow crosses suspended from a sixth century earring in the Walters Art Gallery are less closely related[3]. The front of these crosses have incised lines somewhat similar to the back of the cross in Washington. Their central setting also was originally filled with green glass paste.

Ross concludes from the wide dispersal of the techniques involved in the manufacture of this cross, especially the wire braiding, that a central location is indicated for objects employing these methods. He suggests Constantinople, which seems likely, due to the declining importance of Antioch and Alexandria in the fifth century.

BTH

[1] HIGGINS, p. 16-17, fig. 3c-d.
[2] KRATZ, fig. 3, *passim*.
[3] Walters, 1979, p. 157, no. 446, illustrated in this cat. no. 43.

44

Necklace

Byzantine, provenance unknown, 6th c.
A.D.
L. 33.7 cm.
Field Museum of Natural History.
  Acc. no. 2262; cat. no. 239181.
Partial gift of H. N. Higinbotham; collector E. E. Ayer.

This necklace consists of gold wire and openwork discs, with pearls, green glass beads and amethyst drops.

The condition of the necklace is fairly good, although it is well-worn, especially the gemstones, and has obviously been altered since its original fabrication. For example, the leftmost pearl is strung on a link between the wire loop and its terminal wrap-around wire, the latter having broken loose (i.e., the pearl was added after the link's original completion). More obvious, the necklace has been awkwardly extended on the right. Further, many of its original elements are no longer in evidence.

The necklace is composed of gold wire links, looped at both ends, by which they are hooked to one another. Most of the loops on the left side wind back up around themselves two or three times. Between the loops six green glass beads are centrally strung, with a hollow-cylindrical green glass bead and two pearls to their left, and three pearls to their right. Soldered to the loops on the right side of ten central links are three additional gold wire loops, forming cross- or diamond-shaped configurations of four loops. In addition, the adjacent links flanking the ten central ones have an extra wire loop welded to their right side loops forming a figure-eight shape.

From the suspended loops hang ten v-shaped wire links that are secured by the loops at their tops. Nine amethyst drops hang from the loops at the bottom of the v-links. The wires pass down through the amethysts and have small loops at each end. With two exceptions, small gold bands are strung above the drops. They might have been used to protect the amethysts, as the two lacking them are fractured at their top openings.

Most of the "arms" of the v-links have these flat bands. Some of them also bear additional green glass beads.

Two more pearls and two encrusted blue glass beads with diamond-shaped facets are also suspended from the four-loop configurations. They hang on wire looped at both ends, with the small gold bands at top and bottom.

Finally, there are openwork discs at each end of the necklace. Both of them have thicker wire loops on one side, by which they are attached to the rest of the necklace. On their outer sides, one has a long wire hook and the other a wide band by which the discs fasten together. The discs themselves are carved into cross/rosette patterns. The designs are ringed with wire, shaped into a "beaded" motif.

This necklace was among a great quantity of ancient jewelry acquired for the Field Museum between 1895-1900 in Italy (especially Rome) and Egypt. The necklace was initially thought to date to the later Roman Empire, but the dating was revised to the sixth century Byzantine East.

The necklace is closely related to a gold necklace in the Museo Archeologico Nazionale, Syracuse (no. 53402)[1]. The latter was found in a woman's tomb in 1953 in Nissoria, Sicily. It is 37 cm in length and is composed of similar gold wire links looped at the ends, with an additional loop soldered to those on the right, forming a figure-eight. It likewise has openwork discs used as clasps[2], and is strung with pearls, prismatic emeralds and amethyst drops. It has been dated to the early Byzantine period.

The openwork discs of the necklace in Chicago are similar to a gold openwork medallion in the Virginia Museum of Fine Arts, Richmond[3], which Ross dates to the late sixth or early seventh century. It has a cross/rosette plant motif and is bordered by "beaded" wire.

The early Byzantine gemstone "palette" of pearls, emeralds and sapphires or amethysts was decreed by Justinian I (527-565) to be "solely reserved for the splendor and adornment of the sovereign ... (with the exception

45
Necklace

of ornaments usually worn by women)"[4]. This palette is in evidence in the court jewelry depicted in the contemporary mosaics of San Vitale in Ravenna[5].

The Field Museum gold necklace, thus, would seem to date to the sixth century. If not made in an imperial workshop, it certainly would have been fashioned for a woman of high social standing.

BTH

Byzantine, 11th century A.D. or later.
L. 42.7 cm.
Williams College Museum of Art, Rogers Collection.
Acc. no. E122.

The base of the necklace is a thick, finely braided loop-in-loop[1] chain with large hook and eye clasp. Upon the chain alternate ten complex fretted globules and nine filigree octagons with raised pearled-wire hemispheres. The globules, essentially cylindrical in form, support wide openwork diamond-shapes with centered gold studs. In the octagonal figures, a beaded or pearled wire rim borders on a narrow gold sheet inlay, which introduces slender-spun filigree work. From the center of the octagons rise the hemispheres, lavishly decorated with three-loop designs and pearled wire crossbars crowned with solid gold studs. The octagonal forms themselves are hollow on their reverse side.

Suspended from the octagons through looped wire are small openwork spheres of filigree loops, from which hang nine large globules. The hanging globules are essentially cubes. These are faced on all four sides with octagons of openwork and stud pattern similar to that of the supporting octagonal discs on the necklace itself. The bottom of each hanging globule is finished with a gold projection, which completes the line to the necklace proper through both sphere and cube suspensions.

The Williams College necklace is very similar in style to an eleventh century earring in the collection in the Benaki Museum, Athens[2]. The earring is a filigree cube with octagonal filigree facings. From these rise studded hemispheres decorated in a pearled wire three-loop pattern and crossbar strongly resembling the Williamstown piece. Another pair of earrings of this same type is found in the Stathatos collection[3]. In addition, a gold earring dating to the eleventh century in the Dumbarton Oaks collection[4] resembles the hanging globules of the Williamstown necklace. Though smaller, the main section of

[1] G. V. GENTILI, *Nissoria (Enna): Reperto di oreficerie bizantine*, in *Notizie degli scavi di antichità*, ser. 8, vol. 8, 1954, p. 403-405; C. CARDUCCI, *Gold and Silver Treasures of Ancient Italy*, exh. cat., Greenwich, Conn., p. 76, pl. 77a.

[2] The entire Syracuse necklace, including the spade-shaped openwork discs, is reproduced in GENTILI, fig. 1. The openwork discs are not illustrated in CARDUCCI, pl. 77a.

[3] M. ROSS, *Jewels of Byzantium*, in *Arts in Virginia*, 9, Fall, 1968, p. 21, no. 22.

[4] Justinian I, *Corpus Juris Civilis*, 11.11.1, 529-534, trans. in S. P. SCOTT, *The Civil Law*, New York, 1973 (orig. 1932), vol. 7 (orig. vol. 15, p. 178).

[5] See K. R. BROWN, *The Mosaics of San Vitale: Evidence for the Attribution of Some Early Byzantine Jewelry to Court Workshops*, in *Gesta*, 18, no. 1, 1979, p. 57-62.

the earring is a cube surmounted by five hemispheres of twisted wire with studded tops. The cube shape form decorated with hemispheres on all sides can be found in pieces from both earlier and later centuries. A fifth or sixth century earring from (Syria or Egypt) in the Walters Art Gallery collection shows the cube and hemisphere shapes with granulated surface, although there is no openwork or complex filigree [5].

Late Antique forms similar to the Walters piece are described in Segall [6], who indicates that tenth century or later forms — those which most resemble the Williamstown necklace — were an improvement on the Late Antique style, as filigree, granulation, and openwork were applied. In the eleventh century, the form was made even richer through the addition of studs, as seen in two Islamic earrings and a royal Byzantine armband [7]. A further eastern development of the cube and hemisphere form is seen in a fingerring found in south Russia, dated to the eleventh or twelfth century [8].

The octagonal forms on the Williamstown necklace most resemble rosette granulated and filigree discs on an Islamic necklace dated to the seventh through eleventh centuries [9].

BTH

[1] HIGGINS, 1980, p. 16-17, fig. 3c-d.

[2] SEGALL, 1938, p. 160-161, no. 252, pl. 50.

[3] AMANDRY, 1963, p. 287, nos. 218 and 220 bis, pl. 44 and fig. 178.

[4] ROSS, 1965, p. 93, no. 134, pl. 65.

[5] Walters, 1979, p. 157, no. 445.

[6] SEGALL, p. 180, nos. 286 and 287, pl. 56.

[7] E. VON BASSERMANN-JORDAN, *Der Schmuck*, Leipzig, 1909, fig. 58.

[8] GREIFENHAGEN, II, p. 113, pl. 77, nos. 8, 9.

[9] SEGALL, p. 280, no. 282, pl. 55.

46
Cross pendant

Provenance unknown, date uncertain.
H. 4 cm, width, 2.4 cm, depth, 0.5 cm.
Private collection.

This hollow cross is made of sheet-gold.
Its arms flare outward toward the ends,
which are highly concave. The points are
elongated into gold globules. At the crossing
of the arms there is a bezel set with a garnet
(?) cabochon. The bezel itself is not chased
around the setting. The motif of "braided
wire" that encircles it, the lack of discrete-
ness due not to wear but to flooding in its
manufacture, further confirms that the bezel
was cast. Atop the cross, rotated ninety
degrees, is a soldered wire loop for its
suspension.

The authenticity of this piece is in doubt.
While it is reminiscent of crosses of the fifth
and sixth centuries in its hollow box-like
construction and flaring arms with bezel
setting at their intersection [1], it lacks their
refinements of granulation, engraved pattern, braided-wire from sheet-gold, etc. In
the somewhat exaggerated flaring of the
arms into globules at the points, it also
seems to refer to a later period, the tenth
or eleventh centuries. For example, a tenth
century bronze cross from Nauplia in the
Corinth Museum [2] has similar arms flaring
asymmetrically into globules. Likewise, a
silver-gilt repousse panel in the Louvre, dating to the eleventh century from St. Denis,
has a jewelled cross whose flaring arms bear
discrete globules at their points [3].

Whether the cross pendant dates to the
tenth or eleventh centuries, with an inexpert
bezel setting referring back to the fifth or
sixth, or, indeed, is a more modern fabrication, remains uncertain.

BH

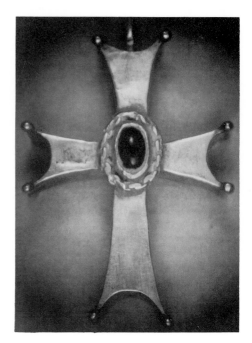

[1] Cf. AMANDRY, 1963, p. 289, no. 231, pl. 44;
WALTERS, 1979, p. 157, no. 446; ROSS, 1965,
p. 22, no. 16, pl. 23 and p. 136, no. 179H, pl. 97.
[2] *Byzantine Art: A European Art. Ninth Exhibition Held under the Auspices of the Council of
Europe*, Athens, 1964, p. 454, no. 555.
[3] DALTON, 1911, p. 560, fig. 343.

MATERIALS AND TECHNIQUES

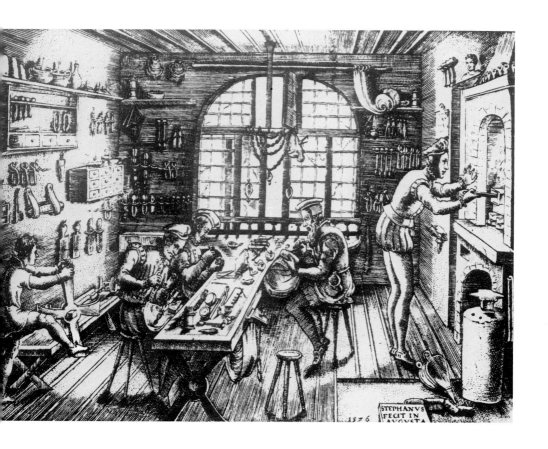

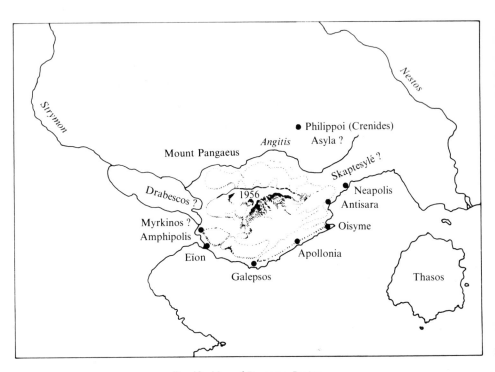

Fig. 19. Map of Pangaeus Region.

MOUNT PANGAEUS
STRUGGLES AROUND GOLD MINES IN ANTIQUITY

Mount Pangaeus (1956 meters high) is located in Thrace opposite Thasos between the river Strymon in the west, Mount Nestos in the east, Mount Angitis in the north and the Aegean Sea in the south [1].

Since ancient times, different travellers have written about the natural resources of the territory. With an abundance of waterways [2], the region is characterized by humid weather [3]. The flora and the fauna reflect these characteristics [4]. Warlike and very independent people, who worshipped Dionysos, were said to be living there [5]. From the Neolithic period on one finds traces of a dense population [6]. The Thracian tribes probably settled here during the Geometric period; however, this theory was disputed later on by the new Greek invaders who took over the mining resources, as documented by their archaic currency.

Geologically, Mount Pangaeus goes back to the Precambrian period; but, at the end of the Alpine fold, some continental movement allowed the engulfment and the expulsion of volcanic rocks that furthered mineralization. Thus is explained the presence of gold and silver in the body of the mountain. This is sometimes alluvial, mixed with a small percentage of silver and sometimes mixed with pyrites in quartz, silver and lead veins.

These metal deposits were quickly exploited and became an attractive resource through the Roman period. The different struggles that took place in the region are discussed here.

An old legend tells of the Phoenician Cadmos, πρῶτος εὑρέτης [7], who was the first to have dug gold mines at the Pangaeus. He seems to have invented gold smelting as well [8]. Moreover, Herodotus attested that he had seen, in Ainyra and

---

[1] J. WIESNER, *Die Thraker*, Stuttgart, 1963; D. LAZARIDIS, *Thasos and its Peraia*, Athens, 1971.

[2] THEOPHRASTUS, fragment 159 (Athenaeus, 2.16, p. 42b), fragment 161; PLUTARCH, *Moralia*, p. 914: *Quaestiones Naturales*, 7, *De Causis Plantarum*, 5.14.5-6; APPIAN, *Bella Civilia*, 4.105.

[3] THEOPHRASTUS, *Historia Plantarum*, 6.12.7; *idem*, *De Causis Plantarum*, 5.12.7.

[4] HERODOTUS, 7.126; 5.3; 7.11; PAUSANIAS, 6.5.3; XENOPHON, *Cynegeticus*, 2.1; THUCYDIDES, 4.108.

[5] HERODOTUS, 7.3; THUCYDIDES, 2.99.3-4; P. PERDRIZET, *Cultes et mythes du Pangée*, in *Annales de l'Est*, 1, 1910, p. 9-103.

[6] D. THEOCHARIS, *Prehistory of Eastern Macedonia and Thrace*, Athens, 1971.

[7] HYGINUS, *Fabulae*, 274; PLINY, *Natural History*, 7.195; CLEMENT OF ALEXANDRIA, *Stromateis*, 1.16; Ps. DICAEARCHUS, fragment 59.12 (K. MÜLLER, ed., *Fragmenta Historicorum Graecorum*, Paris, 1841-1870, 2, 258). NICOMACHUS OF GERASA, Exc., 1. p. 266, Jan; ARISTOTLE, fragment 501 Rose; R. B. EDWARDS, *Kadmos the Phoenician. A Study in Greek Legends and the Mycenaean Age*, Amsterdam, 1979, p. 32; A. KLEINGÜNTHER, Πρῶτος Εὑρέτης, in *Philologus*, suppl. 26, 1, 1933, p. 60-65.

[8] STRABO, 16.5.28. PLINY, *Natural History*, 7.197; CLEMENT OF ALEXANDRIA, *Stromateis*, 1.16.

Coinyra, the Phoenician mines on the island of Thasos[9]. Yet, not a single piece of archaeological evidence shows the Phoenician presence in this area, even though most of the literary sources attest to this and make it most probable. We will see how the Thasians took advantage of the legend. It was an historical claim used to justify the possession of both the mines of Thasos and the Peraea in the name of their eastern ancestors during the fifth century B.C.[10].

Peisistratus was the first to put Mount Pangaeus on the historical map. He probably stayed in the Pangaeus region during his second exile (556-546 B.C.)[11], not to colonize the region, but to accumulate riches quickly in order to return to Athens. Therefore, we may assume that the well-known *Wappenmünzen* were minted with silver from Pangaeus[12]. Moreover, his knowledge of the Thracian mines helped him to organize a methodical exploitation of Laurion mines[13]. In any case, he succeeded in bringing the Pangaeus to the attention of Athens until the end of the fourth century B.C.

Another adventurous tyrant, in alliance with the Persian king Darius I, settled at the Pangaeus[14]. He was Histiaeus of Miletus, who had received the territory of Mirkynos as a reward for his loyalty during the expedition against the Scythians. Realizing Histiaeus' potential great wealth, Darius demanded his return to Persia[15]. Some years later, Histiaeus' son-in-law and cousin escaped and tried to stay in Mirkynos, but he and his partisans were assassinated by the Thracians at Amphipolis[16]. A year later (495 B.C.), using Thasos as a base, Histiaeus tried again unsuccessfully to have the wealth he sought under his control[17]. Clearly, these two examples substantiate the attraction of the Pangaeus as well as the strong resistance of the local inhabitants. The Persians were never again to exploit the Pangaeus[18].

Did Miltiades try to prepare for an expedition against his colony of Thasos in order to take hold of the resources of the island and the bridgehead on the mainland when he laid siege to Paros? Some scholars have tried to prove this[19], suggesting a so-called incoherency of Herodotus' account of the siege which is mentioned just after Miltiades' victory at Marathon[20]. Even though this hypothesis

---

[9] HERODOTUS, 6.47.

[10] J. POUILLOUX, *Études thasiennes, 3, Recherches sur l'histoire et les cultes de Thasos, 1, De la fondation de la cité à 196 av. J.C.*, Paris, 1954, p. 18-22; P. COLLART, *Philippes, ville de Macédoine*, Paris, 1937, p. 93.

[11] HERODOTUS, 1.64; ARISTOTLE, *Athenaion Politeia*, 15.2; H. BERVE, *Die Tyrannis bei den Griechen*, Munich, 1967, 1, p. 47-63.

[12] C. M. KRAAY, *Gold and Copper Traces in Early Greek Silver*, in *Archaeometry*, 1, 1958, p. 1; 2, 1959, p. 1-6; W. P. WALLACE, *The Early Coinages of Athens and Euboia*, in *Numismatic Chronicle*, 1962, p. 26-28.

[13] E. ARDAILLON, *Les Mines du Laurion dans l'Antiquité*, Paris, 1897, p. 134-136.

[14] HERODOTUS, 5.11.

[15] HERODOTUS, 5.23.

[16] THUCYDIDES, 4.102; DIODORUS SICULUS, 12.38.1-2.

[17] HERODOTUS, 6.26-28; P. COLLART, *op. cit.*, p. 96.

[18] HERODOTUS, 7.112.

[19] P. PERDRIZET, *Skaptésylé*, in *Clio*, 10, 1910, p. 6.

[20] HERODOTUS, 6.132-136; EPHORUS 70F63J (STEPHANUS OF BYZANTIUM, s.v. Πάρος), CORNELIUS NEPOS, *Miltiades*, 7; SCHOLIA, *Aristide*, Ὑπὲρ τῶν τεττάρων 160.5; 177.2; 232.2; 244.3; K. H. KINZL, *Miltiades' Parosexpedition in der Geschichtsschreibung*, in *Hermes*, 104, 1976, p. 280-307.

places this event in the spotlight, it should receive a thorough re-evaluation, based on the following information. Herodotus first mentioned "Χρυσὸν ἄφθονον" as the point of the expedition, and then the family tie between Miltiades and the Thracians[21]. Actually, gold was obtained to blackmail the Parians (one hundred talents to halt the siege). Herodotus' text, therefore, is logical and clearly does not present external and possibly untrue elements. It now appears that Miltiades had nothing to do with the history of the Pangaeus.

A different situation occurs with his son, Cimon. In 476-475 B.C., two years after the foundation of the Delian League, Cimon freed Eion at the river Strymon from Persian rule[22]. The perceptive Thucydides understood that the history of the Athenian Empire began with this event in which Aeschylus also appears to have participated. Cimon, thus, taught the Athenians how to colonize a "very rich and beautiful" region, as we know from Plutarch[23]. The degree to which the winner was greater than that of Marathon and Salamis and shows clearly the importance of its value for the Athenians[24]: three herms were sculpted and commemorative epigrams were carved in the porch of Hermes on Thasos[25]. The Athenians were eager to control the mines of the Pangaeus and proceeded energetically with this new base of operations. It seems they tried immediately to dig deeper into the mountain. Other sources indicate this was stopped by the Thracians in Ennea-Odoi (later called Amphipolis); this constituted the beginning of a long series of defeats in that region[26].

Athens was not the only city interested in the Pangaeus at this time. The rich and prosperous island of Thasos was colonized by the Parians who took possession of the resources of the island and founded emporia in the neighboring regions (Neapolis, Antissara, Oisymé, Galepsos, Apollonia) from the seventh century B.C. on. A friendly alliance existed between the Thasians and the continental Thracians; the former were authorized to operate the well-known mine of Skaptesyle in the Pangaeus[27]. With an average income of eighty talents a year, the mine contributed largely to the growth of Thasian power in the fifth century[28]. In 465-464 B.C., there was a two-year siege by Athens at which time the Thasians surrendered and relinquished the emporia and mines[29]. During the siege the Athenians sent 10,000 colonists to Ennea-Odoi. In an attempt to penetrate deeper into the country, the invaders were massacred to the last man by the united Thracian forces[30].

---

[21] PLUTARCH, *Cimon*, 4; MARCELLINUS, *Life of Thucydides*, 10.
[22] HERODOTUS, 7.107; THUCYDIDES, 1.9; DIODORUS SICULUS, 11.60.2; PLUTARCH, *Cimon*, 7. CORNELIUS NEPOS, *Cimon*, 2.2; POLYAENUS, *Stratagems*, 7.24.
[23] PLUTARCH, *Cimon*, 7.
[24] PLUTARCH, *Cimon*, 8.
[25] AESCHINES, *Against Ctesiphon*, 183-185; PLUTARCH, *Cimon*, 7; TZETZES, *Ad Lycophron*, 5.417; H. T. WADE-GERY, *Classical Epigrams and Epitaphs*, in *JHS*, 53, 1933, p. 71-104.
[26] SCHOLIA AESCHINES, 2.34. PLUTARCH, *Cimon*, 8.
[27] J. POUILLOUX, *op. cit.*, p. 34.
[28] HERODOTUS, 6.46.
[29] THUCYDIDES, 1. 100-101; DIODORUS SICULUS, 11.70.5; PLUTARCH, *Cimon*, 14.2-4.
[30] HERODOTUS, 9.75; THUCYDIDES, 1.100; ISOCRATES, *De Pace*, 86; DIODORUS SICULUS, 11.70; 12.68.1-2; PAUSANIAS, 1.29.4; SCHOLIA AESCHINES, 2.34.

Even after this humiliating attempt, commemorated by a monument along the road leading to the Academy[31], the Athenians, nevertheless, remained the theoretical owners of the Thasian bridgehead. Whether or not they made a profit has never been answered definitely by literary sources. For example, Herodotus insisted on the continuous independence of the Satrians[32] at the same time the banished Thucydides found shelter in the Pangaeus region, a territory probably not under the control of Athens[33]. Numismatic evidence also fails to support this conclusion. An inscription (IG, I², 301) attests to the "skaptesitic golden money"[34]. The inscription can be read as a gift given by Thucydides[35] to Athens or as a Thasian tribute[36]. The text probably dates back to 410 B.C.[37] and relates to Thrasybulus' expedition into Thrace where he raided the mines of the Pangaeus[38]. It does not prove a continuous exploitation by the Athenians.

Isolated from its bridgehead in 463, Thasos reclaimed it in 446-445 as the sudden increase of its tribute seems to indicate; it rose from three to thirty talents. This new prosperity undoubtedly came from the restitution of its trading posts and from the mines on which it operated in 411[39]. Thucydides claimed he owned gold mines in Thrace[40]. It is not known whether he inherited them from his father, Oloros (the grandson of Miltiades the Younger, who married Hegesipyle, daughter of King Oloros[41] of Thrace) or from his wife. Marcellinus, the historian's biographer, writes that she was a rich heiress from Thrace[42]. Only family ties to the owner can explain such possessions. It is not realistic to assume that the Thracians would have offered mining concessions in the Pangaeus to foreigners[43]. This system is only attested to during the Macedonian period and was a considerable source of income for the State[44]. One should also remember that following the unfortunate events of 424 at Amphipolis, Thucydides lived now in exile at Skaptesyle, where he is said to have written his books and eventually died[45].

Pericles carefully avoided the Pangaeus problem. He founded the colony of Brea (to the west of the river Strymon) in 446-440 B.C.[46]. About ten years later, under the leadership of Nicias' son, Hagnon, the Athenians, facing Edonian

[31] PAUSANIAS, 1.29.4.
[32] HERODOTUS, 7.111.
[33] PLUTARCH, *Moralia*, 605; *De exilio*, 14. MARCELLINUS, *Life of Thucydides*, 40; 93.
[34] *Inscriptiones Graeca*, I², 301.1.114-120.
[35] P. PERDRIZET, *op. cit.*, p. 21.
[36] H. T. WADEGERY, *Numismatic Chronicle*, 10, 1930, p. 16-38; 333-334; *JHS*, 50, 1930, p. 293.
[37] W. S. FERGUSON, *The Treasurers of Athena*, Cambridge, 1932, p. 16-37.
[38] XENOPHON, *Hellenica*, 1.1.8-12.
[39] *Inscriptiones Graeca*, XII, suppl., 347, II, 1, 3, 4, 8.
[40] THUCYDIDES, 4.105.
[41] PLUTARCH, *Cimon*, 4.2.
[42] MARCELLINUS, *Life of Thucydides*, 30.
[43] P. PERDRIZET, *op. cit.*, p. 21-23. P. COLLART, *op. cit.*, p. 65, 2.
[44] LIVY, 45.18.
[45] MARCELLINUS, *Life of Thucydides*, 40.93.
[46] M. N. TOD, *Selection*, 1, 1946, p. 88.44; STEPHANUS OF BYZANTIUM, s.v. Βρέα; HESYCHIOS, s.v. Βρέα; PLUTARCH, *Pericles*, 2.5-6; J. A. VARTSOS, *The foundation of Brea*, in Ἀρχαία Μακεδονία, 2, Thessaloniki, 1977, p. 13-16.

resistance[47], founded Amphipolis. On the order of an oracle, Rhesos'[48] body was buried in Thrace; this fundamental step in Athenian expansion produced several legends: some refer to the advantages and others to the repeated defeats of the Athenians in the area[49]. Amphipolis, in addition to its strategic importance, was a great financial resource[50]; however, this status was short-lived as the citizens sided with Brasidas and the Spartans in 424 B.C. They probably wanted to take advantage of their strategic position[51]; therefore, the town remained a central point in the struggle. In spite of the Peace of Nicias in 421 B.C. and that of Callistratos in 371 B.C. and the expeditions in 414-368 B.C. and 364 B.C., the Athenians would never again have Amphipolis. When Sparta took Amphipolis[52], it was siding with Macedonia.

Earlier, the Thasians, led by Callistratos of Aphidnae established Crenides, also known as Daton and later Philippi[53], and exploited a new mine called Asyla. This improved the city's economy and is reflected in the famous coins with the legend: ΘΑΣΙΟΝ ΗΠΕΙΡΟ. Plato was probably asked to create a set of laws for Crenides, but this was attempted in vain[54]. The wealth of Crenides soon became legendary[55]. Threatened by the Thracian populations, the city called for Philip of Macedonia who had just settled in Amphipolis[56]. The more populous Crenides then became the city of Philippi. Intensively exploited, it gave Philip II, and later Alexander, the means for a policy of conquest. After approximately ten years, Philip II minted the famous "philippi" with the gold from the Pangaeus. Moreover, Diodorus tells us that this wealth allowed Philip II to create an infamous army of mercenaries and led many Greeks to betray their own country[57]. It is not necessary to be reminded of the luxury the Macedonian dynasty enjoyed and the finds of Vergina obviously prove this to be so[58].

Under Alexander and his successors, Philippi seems to have lost its prestige. Archaeological, epigraphical and literary evidence is silent; it leads us to suppose a

[47] THUCYDIDES, 4.102; DIODORUS SICULUS, 12.32.3; 12.68.1-2.

[48] POLYAENUS, *Strategems*, 6.53.

[49] AESCHINUS, 2.34; OVID, *Heroides*, 2; idem, *Remedia Amoris*, 55.519-606; idem, *Ars Amatoria*, 3.37; HYGINUS, 59; SCHOLIA LYCURGUS, 495.

[50] THUCYDIDES, 4.108.1.

[51] THUCYDIDES, 4.102.

[52] THUCYDIDES, 5.6-11, 18, 21, 26, 34-35; 7.9; DIODORUS SICULUS, 12.68. AESCHINUS, 2.32; ISOCRATES, 8; DEMOSTHENES, 33.130, 149, 151, 156.

[53] DIODORUS SICULUS, 16.3.7; SKYLAX, 67 (K. MÜLLER, *Geographici Graeci Minores*, Paris, 1855-1861), I, 54; ISOCRATES, *De Pace*, 24; ZENOBIUS, 4.34 (Leutsch-Schneidewin, 1.94); HIMERIUS, *Orations*, 6.2; P. COLLART, *op. cit.*, p. 131-137.

[54] F. SALVIAT, *La lettre XI de Platon, Léodamas de Thasos, Callistratos d'Athènes et la fondation de Krénides*, in *Annales de la Faculté des Lettres d'Aix*, 43, 1967, p. 43-56.

[55] STRABO, 7.331, fragments 33, 36; HARPOCRATION, s.v. Δάτος (Ephoros, 70F37J).

[56] STEPHANUS OF BYZANTIUM, s.v. Φίλιπποι.

[57] DIODORUS SICULUS, 16.8.6-7; 30.9.2; STRABO, 6.7-4; PLUTARCH, *Aemilius Paullus*, 12; G. LE RIDER, *Le monnayage d'argent et d'or de Philippe II, frappé de 359 à 294*, Paris, 1977, p. 438 ss.

[58] M. ANDRONIKOS, Οἱ Βασιιοί τάφοι τῶν Αἰγῶν (Βεργίνας), in Φίλιππος Βασιλεύς Μακεδόνων, Athens, 1980, p. 188-230.

reduction of mine production or even a complete halt to exploitation [59]. The latter is less likely, however, because by the second century regular and intensive work took place here. Philip V of Macedonia, in particular, assured this activity when he exploited abandoned mines [60]. His successor, Perseus, had accumulated fabulous riches which in the end, went to his enemies and conquerors, the Romans [61]. In 168 B.C., Macedonia became a Roman province and its treasures Roman property. Livy mentions the figure of twenty million gold and silver sesterces which would have been carried away to Rome by Aemilius Paullus, but he considers this figure much lower than it actually was [62].

In 167 B.C., the Romans decided to forbid the extraction of gold and silver [63] in order to put an end to the common practice which had made concessions available to the local people. From Cassiodorus we learn that the mines had been in use again as early as 158-157 B.C. [64]. Everything leads us to believe that all the mines of Macedonia and Thrace, including those of the Pangaeus, remained active throughout Roman times.

After a few centuries of relative obscurity, the Pangaeus reappears. In the sixteenth century, Pierre Belon, a doctor and naturalist from Le Mans visited the Pangaeus during his travels in northern Greece. He testified to the exploitation of lead, silver and some gold mines. Unfortunately, he did not stay there and cannot give us a description as detailed and picturesque as that of Siderocapsa.

Other scholars, travellers and engineers have shown interest in the riches of Mount Pangaeus, the mines of which are still called, by the local people, Alexander's mines. Since no serious archaeological expedition has yet been made, we find ourselves too often relying on hypotheses. In summary, we can say that exploitation spread all over the mountain but it seems that the eastern slope of the Pangaeus was of particular importance. One should search in this area for the site of Skaptesyle. An unknown building undoubtedly associated with the mines was found near Nikissiani [65]. We know for certain that Skaptesyle was not located at the foot of the mountain; this is clearly expressed with its toponym meaning "the carved woods". The other famous mine of Asyla has been more accurately located thanks to the writings of Appian [66]. It is approximately 1500 meters from the city of Philippi on the hill. L. Heuzey had located it in the pass of Raktcha to the west of the city, beyond the acropolis [67]; but this hypothesis is not unanimously accepted.

[59] P. COLLART, *op. cit.*, p. 190; V. MARTIN, *La durée d'exploitation des gisements aurifères de Philippes en Macédoine*, in *Études dédiées à la mémoire d'André Andréadès*, Athens, 1940, p. 17-22.

[60] LIVY, 39.24.2; ASCLEPIODOTUS in SENECA, *Quaestiones Naturales*, 5.15.1.

[61] LIVY, 42.12; DIODORUS SICULUS, 30.9.2; PLUTARCH, *Aemilius Paulus*, 12, 18, 23.

[62] LIVY, 45.40; DIODORUS SICULUS, 31.26.1; PLUTARCH, *Aemilius Paulus*, 28.

[63] LIVY, 45.18; 29.11; DIODORUS SICULUS, 31.8.6.

[64] CASSIODORUS, *Chronica*, 403. (J.P. MIGNE, *Patrologiae Cursus, Completus*, series Latina, Paris, p. 1223C).

[65] D. LAZARIDIS, *Fouilles dans la région du Pangée*, in *VIIIe Congrès International d'archéologie classique*, Paris, 1963.

[66] APPIAN, *Bella Civilia*, 4.106.

[67] L. HEUZEY and H. DAUMET, *Mission archéologique de Macédoine*, Paris, 1876, p. 55-60.

The toponym is again very important. Philip II appears to have declared this area a place of refuge for the slaves and criminals in order to have workers for his mines.

Even though doubtful, we must accept these hypotheses for the time being. A passage from Lucretius[68] gives us an idea of the working conditions in the mines of the Pangaeus.

> Again, when they follow veins of silver and gold,
> rummaging with their tools the innermost secret places
> of the earth, what smells Scaptesula exhales from
> below! Or what mischief do gold mines breathe out,
> what do they make men look like, what colours! Do you
> not see or hear in how short a time they are wont to
> perish, how their vital force fails, who are held fast
> in such work as this by the great constraint of
> necessity?

The Pangaeus mines have aroused much cupidity and have encountered many changes. Pisistratus began his expansion policy in this area. After two centuries and bitter defeats, Athens halted her mining operations. Thasos, more skillful in handling the people of Thrace, found here the means for a noteworthy rise. With Macedonia, the mining district for the first time saw a systematic exploitation which lasted through the Roman Empire.

Dimitri Tzavellas

---

[68] Lucretius, 6.808-817.

Fig. 20. Hellenistic Earring, Eros figurine executed in repoussé. 1st cent. B.C. Museum of RISD. Hackens no. 35.

REPOUSSÉ, STAMPING, CHASING
AND PUNCHING

In order to make jewels or metal vessels, many technical processes were used in antiquity. Four of them to be discussed here are repoussé, stamping, chasing and punching; all of these, in some way, formed or moulded metal sheets.

Repoussé, or embossing, is the more basic manufacturing process. Stamping, a more direct and stereotyped repoussé, was progressively used as objects or decorations needed to be produced in larger quantities. Chasing and punching enabled the execution of extended decoration in a sometimes systematized fashion; in addition, punching also means the repetition of details in design.

I. *Repoussé* [1]

The goldsmith produces thin sheets from gold or silver, or other metals such as copper or bronze, by hammering. The sheet must next be given the desired shape. The working of the sheet and of the decorative elements is called repoussé, in Greek σφυρήλατον. This term is appropriate because the work is executed from the back of the sheet. In antiquity, this process was used for various objects ranging from delicate earrings to wide plates with an *emblema*.

There are four types of repoussé: one done by hand on a cushion of soft material; another done on a positive mould; a third on a negative mould and a fourth, applied repoussé.

In working by hand on a cushion of soft material, the goldsmith used tools with rounded ends. Today, these are small steel rods about 12 cm high and filed to a point. If higher relief and more striking force were needed, a light hammer similar to an engraver's was used. The craftsman always worked on a cushion soft enough to prevent breaking the metal. The material most frequently used is bitumen, which becomes elastic with heating. It is possible that bitumen was used by ancient goldsmiths. The fusion point of wax is low; thus it could be softened very easily and quickly. Bitumen or wax was put on a board with framed edges. Nowadays, a hemispheric bowl of cast iron is preferred.

To begin with, the goldsmith takes a piece of metal which has been cut and which is a bit wider than the final product. Today, the edges of the metal sheet are not cut off so that they may serve to keep the object in its proper place on the bitumen. If the craftsman wishes to manufacture a decoration in high relief, he chooses a thicker sheet, since the metal will be drawn out.

---

[1] On Repoussé see P. AUGÉ, T. MCCREIGHT.

The bitumen is evenly heated until it is soft enough to receive the metal sheet. Today some craftsmen reverse the process by heating the metal which in turn softens the bitumen. Whatever the method, the metal presses into the bitumen creating a little roll of bitumen on the edge of the sheet, thus keeping it in position. When the bitumen is hard enough to keep the sheet from sliding when it is struck, the actual repoussé work may begin.

The first step consists of creating, with a scriber, a reversed outline of the design on the face side; this is the *au tracé* chasing which will be discussed in detail later. When the design is completed, the two materials are separated by heating them slightly. The metal is then heated to make it more malleable. Today, a goldsmith folds the edges of the sheet in grooves in order to attach it to the bitumen and fix the metal. Then the sheet of metal is turned face side down and once again placed on the hot bitumen. The metal is worked inside out by repoussé; i.e., the creation of form and design by the deformation of the metal. This stage, too, will be discussed in relation to chasing.

If further work is needed, the object may be heated again several times in order to anneal the metal and give it malleability again. The parts which are already worked by repoussé are protected from possible damage by the continuation of the work: the hollows are filled with bitumen, wax and lead.

Finally, the object must be cleaned to take away the marks of bitumen and a finishing touch is added by chasing the outlines.

In working with a positive mould, the goldsmith was able to create shapes on and around the moulds (cat. no. 13 and fig. 20). He put the golden sheet on the

Fig. 21. Disc with a Medusa head. Museum of RISD. Hackens no. 20.

plaster mould of the ornament in relief, and then hammered the sheet face out until the mould's design was perfectly reproduced. This method was frequently used in the ancient golden and silver vessels. Roman silverplate, such as the pieces of the Hildesheim treasure (Berlin, Staatliche Museen at Charlottenburg), are excellent examples for study. At the end of the Hellenistic period and at the beginning of the Roman empire, casting of decoration rather than embossing was preferred. By that time casting has been mastered by the goldsmiths. However, according to D. E. Strong (p. 11) sets of plaster moulds for the repoussé works seem to have been distributed and used as models or moulds for casted cups or other silverplate.

In working with a negative mould, the sheet of metal was laid on top of the wooden or stone mould (cat. no. 12 and fig. 20). Then, depending on the metal, either a metal or wooden hammer was used to work the sheet until it closely resembled the mould. One single or several partial moulds could be used. From the single mould, the entire object was created; a partial mould, on the other hand, enabled the craftsman to produce just one or several parts of the decoration (fig. 22). Therefore, he had to use the partial mould several times, moving the sheet of metal at each step (see catalogue, entries no. 3-4). There are different reasons for preferring a partial mould to a complete mould. For instance, it would be difficult to produce a very wide decorated object from one single mould. In addition, some craftsmen made several parts of an object separately and then joined or riveted them together (fig. 23).

The *applied repoussé* is a decoration whose components are worked indivi-dually, then united at the surface of the object. There are two easily distinguished

1 Oxford, Ashmolean Museum, inv. G 442b.
2 Boston, Museum of Fine Arts, inv. 99.383.
3 Paris, Louvre, inv. 51.218 (Bj. 2169).
4 Orléans, Musée historique et archéologique, inv. (1940) A 7064.

Fig. 22. Four rhodian repoussé plaques, VIIth cent. B.C., obtained by juxtaposition and combination of different partial moulds. After Laffineur, 1978.

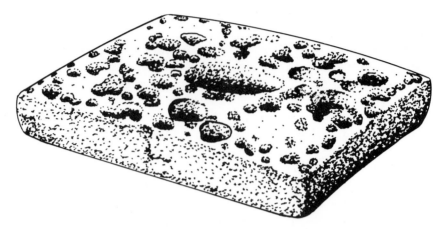

Fig. 23. Islamic jewelers tool with semicircular holes for repoussé. Drawn after Kalus, Studia Islamica, 1981. Original in Paris, Bibliothèque Nationale.

variants of this technique: the decoration attached to the base plate made in one piece and the decoration made of several individually fashioned elements.

II. *Stamping*

It means the reproduction on a piece of metal, in relief or in intaglio, of a design with the help of a matrix; that is, a mould carrying a raised or negative image, or dies (fig. 24) or stamps of either type. The metal is worked either cold or hot. Hot working is called *matriçage*. Stamping allows an unlimited repetition of the same design. A piece of stamped metal attains its shape and dimensions directly. This technique came to be employed frequently in place of handworked repoussé.

Stamping, also called *travail à la feuille*, is very simple: a shape carrying the design is laid down on a small thin gold or silver plate and on his is placed a lead weight to absorb the shock from a hammer or wooden mallet. If the sheet is thin enough and well annealed, a few blows will suffice to stamp the piece. Finishing can be done with a chisel (in modern times, with a file). The striking of coins with an upper and lower die is a development of this technique.

Matrices for stamping were made from hard wood, such as pear and box. For small and light work soft limestones (fig. 25) with very fine grain sufficed. Terracotta was less suitable. For larger scale work, preference was given to harder stones; for example, porphory moulds have been found. Sometimes the matrices were bronze or iron.

A die (intaglio) and a bronze matrix (relief), for the impression in series of decorative elements, are now preserved in the British Museum (fig. 26). The dies carry the image of a small amphora. The two pieces were soldered together along the edge. As provision for eyelets show, they were used as parts of necklaces or earrings. They are dated in the second and first centuries B.C. The stamp die may also be used by striking it on a semihard surface (see punching).

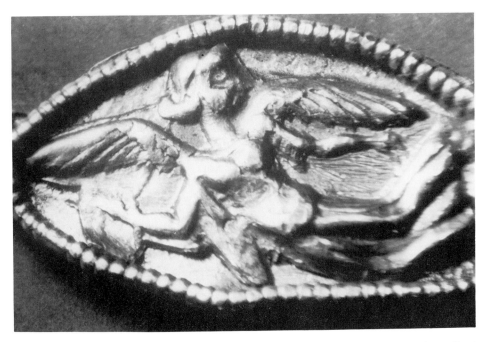

Fig. 24. Detail of the bezel of Greek Finger Ring, Vth cent. B.C., the Nike figure plaque fixed upon the bezel was produced by means of a die. Museum of RISD. Hackens no. 13.

III. *Chasing*

Chasing has been defined as the art of modeling the metal with a chaser and a hammer. This definition does not suffice. One should relate to it terms such as "to draw", "to carve" and "to model" the metal, because this covers all the varieties of chasing and all its effects. However, drawing a line on a metal may also be engraving in addition to chasing. Yet, these two processes differ. The tool used in engraving cuts the metal (cat. no. 20), whereas by chasing one drives into the metal and embosses the strip without taking anything away. Chasing is also different from engraving in that the chased lines have softer edges. Chasing produces a smooth and regular line without interruption. It is a technique suited for linear decoration (fig. 27, A-C).

The craftsman works on a hemispheric bowl filled with a shock-absorbing material. The bowl is laid down on a leather cushion, filled with sand. One may put it at any angle and it will still be securely placed. The craftsman's most important instruments are the chasers and the hammers. The hammer has a wide percussion surface, flat and rounded; at the opposite end, a thin handle.

Chasers are small square steel shafts, two centimeters long. The end can be rectangular, square, oval or triangular, half rounded or rounded, burnished or mat,

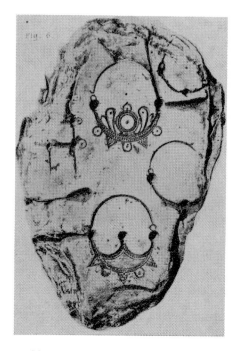

Fig. 25. Moulds in Limestone, after A. Lipinsky, 1975, p. 212.

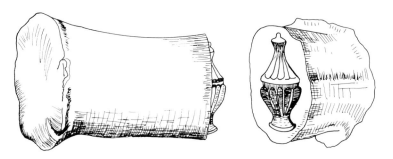

Fig. 26. Punches for stamping, after A. Lipinsky, 1975, p. 213.

all depending on what is needed. In antiquity the chasers were generally bronze. The most frequent shapes and types are illustrated here (fig. 28).

A sharp chislet, called nowadays a graver or a scriber, cuts, engraves or revives a relief; it is held obliquely and follows a previously traced line. It is also used to draw outlines meant to stand out clearly. The scriber, itself, is thin, full- or half-round.

The modern set of tools also includes *matoirs*, used to caulk the piece by combining lines or engraved points.

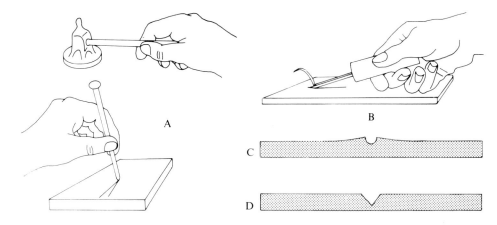

Fig. 27. A. Chasing   B. Engraving   C. Chased line (profile)   D. Engraved line (profile).

There are three types of chasing: *reparure, au tracé* and *repoussé. Reparure* chasing means finishing (by polishing, cutting and filing) the case (i.e., a gold or silver object cast with a mould) (cat. no. 44). When a piece leaves the mould, the depressions that were filled with metal and the points of the different parts of the mould, through which the metal was poured, produced ridges. These flaws are removed by the engraver, which obliterates the mark of the main pour (the main channel), of the other pours (cast branches) and of the scars (the ridges that mark the meeting of the parts of the mould). Moreover, melted gold and silver have rough surfaces. One must take away the crust in order to show the metal. This is done with scrapers and small files called *rifloirs*. Modern engravers often finish their work by creating various motifs along the edges of the metal surface using chasers, thus enlivening the surface.

In antiquity, the craftsman generally limited himself to smoothing and polishing the surfaces, as was done for the polishing of hard stones. For polish, he used the powder of these, or any other, stones, mixed with oil and water.

Au tracé chasing is the first step in repoussé work (fig. 29). The object to be decorated in first seated on a bitumen cushion. This provides support against accidental displacement by the tool. Second, the drawing is traced. Third, one administers repeated blows with a hammer and chaser. A deep or shallow furrow is created, depending upon the strength of the strokes of the instrument. If the bitumen supporting the metal is soft enough to absorb the shocks of the hammer, the decoration appears lightly modeled. If the bitumen is very hard, a harsher line will result.

For repoussé chasing, one begins, again, with the bitumen in order to execute the reverse image. This is done with a scriber. If the relief is poor, the image can be achieved by hammering, a less risky technique. When the first decoration is rendered, either with a scriber or with a bigger tool, called a *planoir*, one takes the object from the bitumen by heating it and clears the reverse side.

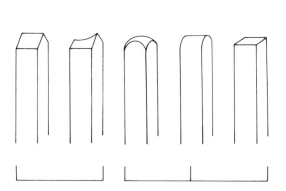

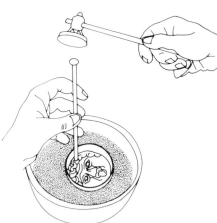

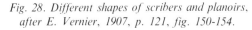

*Fig. 28. Different shapes of scribers and planoirs,
after E. Vernier, 1907, p. 121, fig. 150-154.*

Fig. 29. Chasing « au tracé ».

The following step gave this process its name: the relief model is attached to the bitumen and, guided by the pattern made during the first stage of work, the craftsman will now hammer out the place intended to appear as relief and, with the help of embossing, obtain the necessary fine details. Next the metal plate is removed from its cushion, cleaned and reversed on the bitumen to finish the work on the obverse side by chasing (fig. 30). The craftsman will now model the reliefs he has just created by moving and shaping the metal to give it the finishing.

This type of chasing is so named from the way it obtains relief — by embossing — and from the way they are used — in moving the metal.

IV. *Punching*

The technique of punching involves a metal tool, at the base of which there is an image in relief. This base may be cone-shaped, quadrangular, circular or the like (fig. 31). The tool is struck against the metal plate to imprint the image. With the metal plate now on a soft cushion, this technique is used either on the front or the back. Punching is especially useful in the continuous reproduction of a similar motif. Dies may have an image representing a figurative or isolated ornament. These are used as seals. The die's base may, for example, be carved in the shape of a palmette which is then repeated several times to create a row of the same motif.

During the nineteenth century, scholars were amazed by the thousands of stamped plaques that were (and still are) found on the Black Sea shores. Our present day information is based on sixteen dies coming from the northern and western shores of the Black Sea. Of special interest are those from Panticapaion (6),

Fig. 30. Chasing traces on an Hellenistic Earring, end IVth-early IIIrd cent. B.C. Museum of RISD. Hackens no. 26.

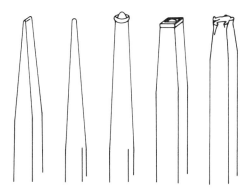

Fig. 31. Various types of punches.

Kamenskoe Gorodisce (2), Tirytake (1) and Pečica (1). Most are dated from the fourth century B.C. or in the Hellenistic period and have recently been commented on by St. Kołkòwna.

Myriam DESTRÉE

Selected Bibliography

AUGÉ, P., s.v. *Repoussé*, in *Larousse du XXᵉ siècle*, V, Paris, 1932, p. 65.
CHOATE, S., *Creative Gold and Silversmithing Jewelry — Decorative metalcraft*, New York, 1979.
HODGES, H., *Artefacts*, London, 1968, p. 79.
KALUS, L., *Un outil d'orfèvre musulman*, in *Studia Islamica*, 53, 1981, p. 51-60.
KOLKÒWNA, St., *Remarques sur les sources archéologiques antiques relatives à la production d'orfèvrerie sur les rivages septentrionaux et occidentaux de la Mer Noire*, in *Études sur l'orfèvrerie antique, Studies in Ancient Jewelry (Aurifex, 1)*, T. Hackens, ed., Louvain-la-Neuve, 1980, p. 106-154.
LIPINSKY, A., *Oro, argento, smalti e gemme*, Florence, 1975, p. 211-213.
MCCREIGHT, T., *Metalworking for Jewelry, Tools, Material, Techniques*, New York, 1979, p. 76-81.
STRONG, D.E., *Catalogue of the Carved Amber in the Department of Greek and Roman Antiquities*, London, 1966, Ch. 1.
STRONG, D.E., *Greek and Roman Gold and Silver Plate (Methuen's Handbook of Archaeology)*, London, 1966.
VERNIER, E., *Cairo*, 1907, p. 113-121.

CASTING

Casting was not used very often in ancient jewelry for an economic reason — gold and silver were not plentiful in ancient times; and a practical one — it is easier to work gold foils with the repoussé technique. In the Hellenistic period, more jewels were cast because of Alexander's conquests which caused a flow of precious metal from Macedonian mines and from the looting of oriental treasures [1]. As a country rich in gold resources, Pharaonic Egypt often used lost wax melting, especially in the new Kingdom [2]. Many other civilizations were familiar with cast objects in precious metal: some were found in e.g. the royal Tombs of Ur [3], and a large quantity of moulds from the surroundings of the Black Sea were used for casting earrings, pearls or pendants [4].

These notes deal exclusively with different techniques employed in the Egyptian, Hellenistic and Roman worlds and give examples of moulds and jewels in these civilizations.

Casting into a mould

    a) Flat casting: Here one side is modeled and the other flat.
— open mould: The metal is simply cast, the flat side kept in the open air (fig. 35).
— closed mould: Half the mould is hollowed, the other flat [5] (figs. 32).

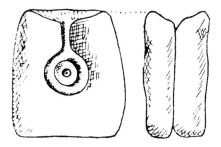

Fig. 32. Mould for casting earring s. Cluj, Historical Museum, Fond of Pecica. After St. Kolkowna,
Aurifex I, pl. XXIII.

[1] HIGGINS, *Classical Lands*, p. 16, 22; MARSHALL, p. LI; ALDRED, p. 114.
[2] ALDRED, p. 115; ZIEGLER, *Archeologia*, 40, p. 40.
[3] AITCHINSON, p. 172.
[4] *Aurifex*, I, p. 132-149.
[5] HOFFMANN, p. 32.

b) Casting in several parts (fig. 33).

The mould is composed of different adaptable elements, with adjusting marks on their rims[6].

Pieces of the mould were held together by plugs[7]. Various assumptions have been expressed concerning moulds still in existence:

— It has been believed that moulds only represented the remaining element from several moulds[8].

— Pernice made tests proving that melted metal destroyed moulds. He thought that moulds were used for wax models for the lost wax process[9].

— Many moulds could be used for glass casting. Some ornamental ware was sometimes covered by a gold foil[10].

— Moulds could have been used for direct casting of metal objects because of the strong resistance of steatite to high temperatures[11].

Some authors have asserted that gold and silver could be cast only in steatite moulds, and Higgins points out that the best moulds are made in this material[12].

— Hoffmann says that plaster, clay or other moulds were made from wood or cast bronze prototypes[13].

— Mixed moulds were used to cast an object or to work a gold foil[14].

Lost wax casting

a) A wax model is made.

b) The wax model is surrounded by a covering of clay (investment) with

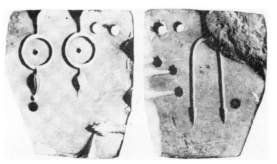

Fig. 33. Fragmentary three parts mould, for casting earrings and pendants. Bucarest, Historical Museum. After St. Kolkowna, Aurifex I, pl. XIX,3.

[6] HOFFMANN, p. 32. See part of steatite mould no. 609 in Marshall I, p. 210.
[7] HIGGINS, p. 16.
[8] HOFFMANN, p. 32.
[9] E. PERNICE, in *Ö.J.H.*, VII, 1904, p. 154-197; HIGGINS, p. 17; HOFFMANN, p. 32; MARSHALL, p. LII.
[10] See steatite moulds found in Mycenae, Knossos, etc., and EVANS, *Knossos*, I, fig. 349, p. 487.
[11] HIGGINS, p. 17.
[12] HIGGINS, p. 17.
[13] HOFFMANN, p. 32.
[14] MARSHALL, p. LII, no. 2112.

apertures on its inner part (for pouring the metal) and vent holes on its upper part (to allow air to escape when driven out by melted metal).

c) The whole object is heated so the wax melts and disappears and the clay dries and bakes to a certain point.

d) Molten metal is poured in place of the wax.

This process yields solid objects (fig. 34 and cat. no. 20). It is possible to make hollow jewels by placing a fire-proof clay core replica of the model in the center of the mould. This core is coated with wax and the process starts again from step b, remembering to fix "switches" to adjust the core to the investment for holding it in position when the wax flows out [15].

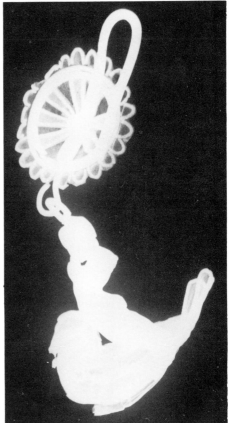

Fig. 34. Photograph and X-ray (due to the kindness of Prof. D. Avery, Brown Univ. Engineering Dept.) of Hellenistic Earring, showing that the Eros figurine is a lost wax casting. Museum of RISD, Hackens no. 30.

[15] Hoffmann, p. 33; Higgins, p. 17; Aitchinson, p. 172.

Hollow ornaments also have been modeled by casting metal into clay or stone moulds inside of which a core was secured with gold or copper nails [16].

Sabine CORNELIS

Selected Bibliography

AITCHINSON, L., *A History of Metals*, I, New-York, 1960.
ALDRED, C., *Jewels of the Pharaons. Egyptian Jewellery of the Dynastic Period*, London, 1971.
EVANS, A. J., *The Palace of Minos at Knossos*, I, London, 1921, reprint 1964.
HIGGINS, R. A., *Jewellery from Classical Lands*, London, 1965.
PERNICE, E., *Untersuchungen zur antiken Toreutik*, in *Jahreshefte des Österr. arch. Instituts*, VII, 1904, p. 154-197.
PETRIE, W. F., *Tanis II, Nesbeheh and Defenneh*, London, 1888.
ZIEGLER, C., *Les bijoux au temps des pharaons*, in *Les dossiers de l'archéologie*, 40, 1980.

[16] AITCHINSON, p. 172.

GRANULATION

Production of granules

There are simple methods of making granules that were known to premodern technology. Some are already described by authors of the sixteenth century. Others have been theorized over the last two centuries by scholars who, as Thouvenin notes [1], often seem "n'avoir jamais tenté de reconstituer ce qu'ils avançaient" (they seem to have proposed the existence of techniques and processes the efficiency and feasibility of which were never tried).

It is important to adopt a very critical stance before each of them and to test their practicality as to constant thicknesses and possibilities of mass production. These two criteria of production, conditions sine qua non of Etruscan granulation for example, in fact eliminate most of the hypotheses.

a) The easiest method is described by Diane Lee Carroll [2]: "Tiny spheres of the precious metals — gold, silver and certain of their alloys — are formed instantly when a small amount of the molten metal is dropped on a flat surface from a distance of several feet". In this way, we obtain grains of many dimensions (from 1 mm to very minute sizes) and it is necessary after that to sort them with different sieves.

b) Agricola [3] gives a variant of this process: to pour molten metal on a slab under flowing water in order to accelerate the cooling.

c) We also have granules produced in a similar way by dropping molten metal in a pot filled with water. In this case, it is necessary for the gold to pass through a sieve before being cooled in fresh water. This method is reminiscent of the lead bullets manufacture. Of course, in practice, this process encounters larger problems (dirt in the sieve, granules thickening). Moreover, the height seems to be important [4]: "On a même proposé de laisser tomber le métal en fusion depuis le haut d'une tour. À la condition de disposer d'une tour, de viser bien juste le bassin rempli d'eau et en évitant le souffle du vent"!

d) It has been proposed that granules were made by heating the tip of a gold wire until a drop fell by its own weight. In fact, spheres so obtained exceed the size of ancient granules. Moreover, granules are never exactly spheric unless remelted a second time. Therefore, this process requires at least three repetitions and the results

---

[1] A. THOUVENIN, *La soudure dans la construction des œuvres d'orfèvrerie antique et ancienne*, in *Revue Archéologique de l'Est et du Centre Est*, 24, 1973, p. 45.

[2] D. L. CARROLL, *A classification for Granulation in Ancient Metalwork*, in *AJA*, 78, 1974, p. 33-34.

[3] G. AGRICOLA, *De re metallica*, Basel, 1556, book 10.

[4] THOUVENIN, *op. cit.*, p. 46.

are still less than satisfactory. This process is in obvious contradiction with the criteria necessary for maximum reliability.

e) Cellini[5] obtained granules by pouring liquid metal into a vase full of charcoal powder. As Thouvenin observes, the granules obtained in this way are of all sizes and have nothing in common with ancient granulations[6].

f) V. Biringuccio claimed to produce granules by putting bits of gold wires into a crucible between layers of ash and heating the whole in a fire. According to D. L. Carroll[7], this is the only perfect method for obtaining granules all the same size. It is, however, very time and energy consuming since a high temperature (1093° C), hotter than the melting point of gold (1063° C) is needed.

The method of melting flakes advocated by Thouvenin is as follows: gold is beaten into thin leaves; these are cut out to make thin blades and thereafter thin and regular flakes. The flakes are put into the fire and shrinking takes place. By this metallic reaction, small errors in cutting disappear and granules have the same size. Thouvenin certifies[8] that he produced thousands of granules in this way. These look like the ancient granules and were made at an average of one hundred per hour. He adds that his attempts have demonstrated the uselessness of the charcoal as used by V. Biringuccio: anything combustible (ceramics, asbestos) is satisfactory.

g) Franz Chlebecek finally obtained granules after cutting gold wires into small cylinders which, placed in a closed crucible on a charcoal layer and brought to the correct temperature, are transformed into very small balls. However, the preparation of the cylinders is very involved and time consuming. It is probably incompatible with the huge number of granules produced in antiquity.

Positioning of the granules

The next stage of granulation work is to retain the granules on the unfinished piece of jewelry for a few moments before fixing them securely. This phase had never been difficult for goldsmiths. Since earliest antiquity, they had used a number of organic adhesives.

Theophilus[9] mentions a flour paste which served in granulation. Cellini[10] quotes tragacanth (gum). Zosimos talks about the "ox-glue" obtained from cattle hides. Biringuccio[11] specifies two other processes: quince paste and arabic gum. We know of this last adhesive from the Egyptians. We must also mention the use of fish glue (ἰχθυοκόλλα), which was so popular throughout antiquity[12]. this list is not

[5] B. CELLINI, *Due trattari: uno torno alle otto principali arti dell'oreficeria*, Florence, 1568, first part ch. II.

[6] THOUVENIN, *op. cit.*, p. 45.

[7] CARROLL, *op. cit.*, p. 34.

[8] THOUVENIN, *op. cit.*, p. 47.

[9] THEOPHILUS, *Schedula Diversarum Artum*, livre III, ch. 52.

[10] CELLINI, *op. cit.*, chap. 2.

[11] V. BIRINGUCCIO, *De la pirotechnia*, Venice, 1540, book 9, ch. IV.

[12] J. WOLTERS, *The Ancient Craft of Granulation*, in *Gold Bulletin*, 14, no. 3, 1981, p. 125.

all-inclusive [13]; the ancients possessed many more techniques. The main objective was always to obtain a temporary adhesion in order to make the actual soldering easy.

Joining process

This third and last part of the granulation process is by far the most difficult. All scholars have attempted to resolve it for two centuries. For this reason [14], granulation has long been called a "technological mystery". Nowadays, it is still difficult to single out one method from these doubtful solutions which have been treated in rather colored terms [15].

Nevertheless, one may rightly ask how the granules are gathered on the support without damaging it and without flooding the granules in too thick a flow.

1. One must eliminate an important category of granulated artifacts which may have been made by means of classical metal alloy. According to D. L. Carroll [16], when the number of granules does not exceed thirteen for each centimeter, it is possible to fix them by melting a narrow strip of alloy along which grains have been placed (cat. no. 11, fig. 2).

In the case of gold granulation, the alloy contains copper, silver and gold. In the case of silver granulation, only copper and silver are needed.

By this process, we have a rather flat and amorphous surface where each granule is covered to 25 and 50 percent. J. Wolters [17] mentions periods where the metal alloy was used: Egyptian Middle Kingdom, Iran since the end of Arsacides, Central Europe, Imperial Rome (second and third centuries A.D.). Some cultures knew only this process.

While this method is quite efficient, it does not solve all the problems. How did the ancients fix very small granules (sometimes more than 70 to each centimeter)? Even with a microscope, the eye cannot identify any trace of solder. This problem which concerns categories two and three of D. L. Carroll has long troubled scholars (see imitation by Castellani, cat. no. 27).

In spite of the large number (often several thousands) of granules, it has been seriously suggested that each and every granule was soldered one by one! Other ideas — ingenuous or naive — have been offered without resolving the problem.

2. The development of powder metallurgy led to the discovery of an important fact: there exist two different melting points for gold — the first, or lower, being the point at which the *surface* melts (a phasis called "sintering" or "fritting") [18].

---

[13] H. LITTLEDALE pretends to have used seccotine as provisionnal glue.

[14] In fact: only a part of this third aspect.

[15] For example: E. L. LEWIS: *The Rediscovery of the Lost Art of Granulation*; W. T. BLACKBAND: *My Rediscovery of the Etruscan Art of Granulation*.

[16] CARROLL, *op. cit.*, p. 35.

[17] WOLTERS, *op. cit.*, p. 122.

[18] Roughly speaking, this phenomenon is due to a less closely bound crystalline organization of the surface atoms which are therefore more "movable" when submitted to the action of fire.

This affects only very small granules (up to 75 per square cm) with highest purity (cat. nos. 25 and 27); but ancient peoples (especially the Etruscans, Greeks and Romans) have generally used gold containing a considerable percentage of silver and copper. Another inconvenience of this method is that it makes it difficult to apply multiple solderings (in order to add filigree, granules, etc.) onto an object without deforming it.

The process, however, does not require tools unknown to ancient technology: first, granules are fixed on the jewel with any type of glue. Second, the entire piece is put into the fire where the glue quickly burns and disappears. When the surface melting point is reached, the granules adhere to their support which remains perfectly solid.

This method concerns the second category of D. L. Carroll. It seems [19] that the first known instance of its use was a ring in Ur. It was later used by the Phoenicians, the Greeks and the Etruscans.

3. After the successive elimination of techniques, one type of granulation remains: the granulation called "medium" by D. L. Carroll (granules of medium size on a slightly rough surface, e.g. cat. nos. 26a and b).

This third category developed gradually and little by little replaced the thin granulation (category 1) to become the only type of granulation in use in the Hellenistic era.

Despite its obvious importance, the manufacturing process of this type of granulation has long remained a technological mystery.

As a result, scientists have had few clear ideas and have assumed [20] that: ancient granulation was an independent technique, unrelated to other jewelry techniques; it was based on only one joining process; knowledge of the process has been lost; no written record of granulation has survived; the details of the ancient technique could be established by experimentation only.

However, this takes into consideration only a part of the information and neglects the written sources.

Experimentations have been widely carried out, but it was only in 1933 that an English researcher, only remotely concerned with archaeology, rediscovered the ancient process [21].

The discovery of Littledale was patented [22] and called "colloidal (i.e., non-metallic) hard-soldering". He mixed coppersalts with some glue (this was part of the first method: solder alloy and flow). Yet, with the degree of temperature used for his work, he was close to the second method (surface melting point).

At $100°$ C, the compound coppersalt/glue becomes Copper II oxide (CuO). At $600°$ C, the glue burns and causes the reduction of the oxide to metallic copper. At $850°$ C, if gold contains a large percent of silver and at $900°$ C, it contains a large percent of copper, the liquid phase of this local alloy begins. At last gold and copper blend at $890°$ C.

[19] J. WOLTERS pretends however to have never clearly seen it.
[20] WOLTERS, *op. cit.*, p. 119.
[21] H. A. P. LITTLEDALE, *A New Process for Hard Soldering*, London, 1936.
[22] British Patent, no. 415181.

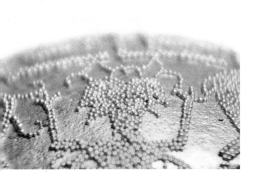

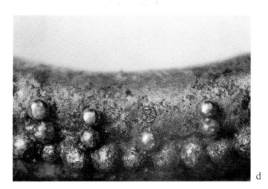

Fig. 35. a-b. Details of Etruscan Fibula, VIIth cent. B.C. Museum of RISD, Hackens no. 1, this cat. no. 22. b shows granules going astray when melting point is reached on the surface of the gold.
c. Detail of Hellenistic Fingerring, Museum of RISD, Hackens no. 38.
d. Detail of Roman Earring, I-II cent. A.D., Museum of RISD, Hackens no. 50.

By this process the joining is achieved at a melting point well below 1063°C, the melting point of gold.

Repetition of the process produces a greater diffusion of the copper in the gold and eventually no trace of copper remains at the surface.

Granules are then firmly fixed to their support without being flooded[23].

Unfortunately, the scientists neglected the written sources, even though over many centuries, ancient authors had written about several minerals containing copper[24].

We are concerned here with the five principal ones only.

The first is *chrysokolla* which, for obvious reasons, has always commanded attention. An in-depth study of ancient sources has allowed it to be identified as malachite ($CuCO_3 . CuOH_3$), a word of Egyptian origin (*Mafek*). *Chrysokolla* was used not only as a color pigment and a drug, but also in goldsmith work. It contains iron traces and zinc in proportions sometimes reaching 27 percent. In ancient times, certainly malachite was the most frequently used component for soldering the granules.

[23] See CARROLL, *op. cit.*, pl. 10, fig. 5.
[24] THEOPHRASTUS, *De lapidibus*, ch. 51.

a

b

Fig. 36. a. Etruscan Fingerring of Hellenistic Period, showing the use of granulation as a background (the opposite technique of fig. 35 a-b). Museum of RISD, Hackens no. 8.
b. Detail of granulation pyramid on Earring cat. no. 11. Granules of large diameter are soldered together.

In the next position of frequency, we find Azurite ($2CuCO_3.Cu(OH)_2$) quoted by Theophraste[24], verdigris ($Cu(OH_3Co_2.5H_2O)$)) obtained by action of vinegar on copper[25] and vitriol ($CuSO_4.5H_2O$) which is mentioned already by Dioscourides[26].

Finally, there is *santerna*, a compound of *chrysokolla*, verdigris, urine and nitra[27]. Probably this technique was developed by the Etruscans (*santerna* is a word of Etruscan origin).

In any case, the borax used by today's goldsmiths as a flux was unknown to the ancients. In the XVIth Century, Agricola[28] makes a clear distinction between "*chrysokolla* of the ancients and *chrysokolla* which is called borax".

In summary, it appears that the granules made by the flake melting method were provisionally attached on the surface by any type of organic glue. They were joined afterward by means of metallic alloy (for large granules), by surface melting (for very small granules of high purity) or, in most cases, by colloidal hard-soldering (utilizing a property of copper).

François DE CALLATAŸ

[25] PLINY, *Naturalis Historia*, book 33, 29; book 34, 26 and 28.
[26] DIOSCOURIDES, *Materia Medica*, book 5, p. 99-102.
[27] PLINY, *Naturalis Historia*, book 33, 29, 93.
[28] G. AGRICOLA, *De Re Metallica*, Basel, 1556, book VII.

Selected Bibliography

BLACKBAND, W. T., *My Rediscovery of the Etruscan Art of Granulation*, in *Illustrated London News*, 28, 1934, p. 658-659.

CARROLL, D. L., *A Classification for Granulation in Ancient Metalwork*, in *AJA*, 78, 1974, p. 33-39, pl. 10-11.

CHLEBECEK, F., *Beitrag zur Technik der Granulation*, in *StEtr*, 22, 1952/53, p. 203-205.

CURTIS, C. D., *Ancient Granulated Jewelry of the VIIth and Earlier*, in *MAAR*, I, 1917, p. 63-85.

FORBES, R. J., *Studies in Ancient Technology*, vol. 8, Leiden, 1954/55, p. 139 and 182.

HIGGINS, R. A., *Greek and Roman Jewellery*, London, 1961, p. 19-23.

PICCARDI, G. and BORDI, S., *Sull'oreficeria granulata etrusca*, in *StEtr*, 24, 1955/56, p. 353-363.

QUILLARD, B., *Bijoux Carthaginois. I: les Colliers (Aurifex, II)*, Louvain-la-Neuve, 1979, p. 39-43.

ROEDER, s.v. *Granulation*, in *Reallexikon der Vorgeschichte*, Berlin, 4, 1926, p. 497-498.

SINGER, C., et al., *Filigree and Granulation*, in *A History of Technology*, I, Oxford, 1967, 3rd ed., p. 654-658.

SMITH, C. S., *Metallurgical Footnotes to the History of Art*, in *Proceedings of the American Philosophical Society*, no. 116, 1972, p. 100-101, fig. 3-4.

STARK, J. and KULICKE, R., *Workshop Granulation*, in *Craft Horizons*, 32, no. 4, 1972, p. 32-35.

THOUVENIN, A., *La soudure dans la construction des œuvres d'orfèvrerie antique et ancienne*, in *Revue Archéologique de l'Est et du Centre Est*, no. 24, fasc. I, 1973, p. 45-61.

TRESKOW, E., *Über die Technik der Granulation*, in *Kunst und Leben der Etrusker*, Cologne, 1956, p. 46-50.

TROKAY, M., *Les origines du décor à granulations dans l'orfèvrerie égyptienne*, in *Chronique d'Égypte*, 43, 1968, p. 271-280.

VISSER, H. F. E., *Some Remarks on Old Granulation Work in China*, in *Artibus Asiae*, 15, 1952, p. 125-128.

WOLTERS, J., *The Ancient Craft of Granulation*, in *Gold Bulletin*, 14, 1981, p. 119-129.

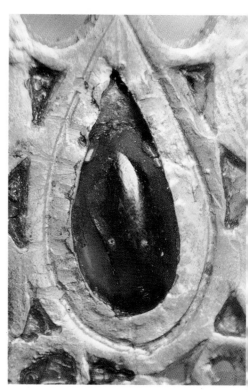

a

c

Fig. 37. a. Detail of a pair of Hellenistic Earrings, Museum of RISD, Hackens, no. 31
b. Detail of a Roman barrel earring, Museum of RISD, Hackens, no. 45.
c. Detail of a Syrian earring, denticulated collar surrounded by filigree and granulation, Private
Collection, Unpublished.
d. Detail of a pendant of a late Roman necklace, Museum of RISD, Hackens, no. 70.

STONE SETTING

Cutting of precious stones

The workman who cuts, polishes and engraves the stones creates three different types:

Chips: stones which were polished by an abrasive system on a lathe. Chips have no flat surfaces so it is difficult to set them.

Cabochons: polished stones with a slightly curved side. The opposite side may be slightly curved but is almost flat. Cabochons can be cut in several shapes (round, oval, square, etc.). They can be obtained in several thicknesses and heights and are easy to set.

Faceted stones are generally translucent or transparent. Their outside has been cut and polished in small flat surfaces called facets. The faceted stones can be shaped with different kinds of cuts and several compositions of the facets, for example the round stones that have fifty-six facets are called a brilliant cut. *Faceting was not used in Antiquity.*

The tools

The burins are gravers of different thicknesses and with a sharp point. They are used for overcutting. Claws are used for enlarging holes and fitting stones, while a corners' vice is like a nipper, which is used for holding rings where stones are to be set. The drills have different shapes and functions. The sledge is an iron shank in a wood stock used for pressing down metal over the precious stone.

Types of setting

A simple way to set a precious stone (or a similar object) in jewelry such as rings or pendants is by running a hole through the stone and then passing a metal wire in order to assemble the different parts of the object. For the protection of the sides of the stone a small band of the same metal is placed like a ring around the stone (fig. 37a).

Other methods for setting precious stones avoid doing damage to the stone. Each type of stone has its particular method for setting.

The round sides of the *chips* make firm setting difficult. One solution is the crown. The crown is just like a little flower made of thin metal and pushed over the pointed end of the stone and then stuck to it. Frequently a small ring is placed over the crown in order to suspend a little chain from it. Medium and large chips can also be embedded. Here a thin metal wire is used. It must be fine enough to be fitted closely along the sides of the stone. In the final stage, one brings the two ends of the wire together at the top of the stone creating a small ring. In a variation of this technique, a little groove is cut around the stone. A buckle larger than the circumference of the stone is made to fit the groove. At one end, the buckle is turned until set. There seem to be no examples of chips set either way in Antiquity.

Cabochons are generally set on a bezel which is a metal collar that overlaps the stone and is pressed on the stone to hold it in place. The bezel-box is the basis for a system which can be executed in various ways.

The metal element for the collar can be made of pure gold or copper; it can be shaped as a small band cut in a thin sheet of metal or as a flattened wire. For example, the band can be decorated by striations or other motives. But it can also be cut in an egg-and-dart pattern (fig. 37). If silver is present, a higher melting point is obtained so the bands do not melt during soldering; thus silver facilitates working. It is basically simple: the collar is shaped to the desired height and then is soldered to the sides. Then the stone is set and the bezel is drawn closer to the stone's side to hold it firmly.

When done is successive stages, the metal element is placed around the stone, measured and cut to fit. In modern times, the edges of the cuts are then filed. In the case of little stones, first the length is measured with an iron band around the stone to ascertain the correct shape and length of the stone; then this iron band is straightened and the future collar receives the same length. The collar is closed, soldered with a thin and hard solder. Then the inner surfaces of the collar are filed off, thus it can be made even thinner at the top to insure a better hold.

Afterwards the collar is soldered on a flat sheet that constitutes the back of the bezel-box. The thickness of this sheet changes with the length and weight of the stone. This back can be larger than the stone and can also be decorated like the

Fig. 38. Hellenistic. Finger ring, Museum of RISD, Hackens, n° 38.

collar. The joining between the collar and the back can be masked by a filigree that is either smooth, twisted or pearled. The stone is now set into the bezel to determine the necessary height of the collar. Either the collar is shortened or the stone is heightened by means of a little piece of copper placed under the stone. The bezel-box is then polished and filed off. Afterwards it is soldered to make the necessary bend and polished once again. When the bezel is curved to the inside, small pieces are held in a vice. The bezel is pushed into place with a sledge used with a turning movement kept high to protect the bezel from the stone. The metal must be compressed equally all around the gem. First, eight points are compressed, then the remaining metal is pushed in with the sledge so that the whole collar is leveled. The work is now polished and finishing touches are made (see this cat., fig. 5, p. 60).

The stone can also be set on a little box formed to elevate it; this piece can be decorated. This technique is usually used for fingerrings so that a small stone can create a better effect (fig. 38).

For cabochons and faceted stones the claws-bezel may be used. With this kind of setting the stone can achieve maximum brilliance. Claws are little elements of metal curved over the edges of the stone to hold it. When cabochons are square or rectangular, the collar can be taken off the sides and remain only at the corners. This is called "flap-setting". When cabochons are oval or round, the collar is shortened and claws are soldered and drawn closer to the stone to hold it. Later the bandlet is taken off.

For faceted stones, one uses three principal bezels:

In the *right bezel*, the circumference is the same at the top and back.
The *illusion bezel* is just like a section of a cone.
The *apparent bezel* is larger at the back than at the top.

For aesthetic and material reasons, the claws are put in a symmetrical manner for oval and round stones and at the corners for the square and rectangular stones.

Christiane LAROCK

Fig. 39. a. Detail of a pair of late Roman earrings, Museum of RISD, Hackens, no. 56.
b. Detail of a pair of Hellenistic earrings, Museum of RISD, Hackens, no. 28.
c. d. e. f. Details of two similar Hellenistic earrings, Museum of RISD, Hackens, no. 26.
g. h. Details of a Greek gold medallion, Museum of RISD, Hackens, no. 22.

FILIGREE

The word "filigree" is used in jewelry to designate ornaments made from metal wires which have been prepared by various techniques.

Wire manufactured by hammering is the simplest method. It consists of hammering out an ingot until a wire with a more or less round section is obtained. Generally, the wire has a faceted surface. This can be reduced by rolling it between two flat pieces of wood. The diameter of the wire is not constant along its length; the cross-section is solid. The wire presents short longitudinal "creases", usually a few millimeters in length (fig. 39a).

Block-twisting wire is made by hammering out an ingot to obtain a rod with a square section. This rod is then twisted as tightly as possible and rolled between two flat pieces of wood. This wire has a more or less round section, a solid cross-section and a regular diameter along the length (fig. 39b). This process was described in *Exodus* 39.3, "Beat the gold into thin plates and cut it into wires".

Strip-drawing wire is made by drawing a strip of metal foil through holes of decreasing diameter so that it curls in upon itself and forms a hollow tube (fig. 39c-d). It has a very even diameter along the length because it has been drawn through the draw-plate and is lengthened for the same reason. A longitudinal seam appears parallel with the axis of the wire. In some instances, there are scratches resulting from the use of the metal draw-plate.

Strip-twisting wire is made by twisting the strip of metal around a mandrel (or existing wire) which is then removed. For better results, the wire is then drawn through dies to finish it off and make it tighter. The twisted wire is a hollow tube with a round cross-section, a fairly even diameter and a single seam running in a helix around the wire (fig. 40.1). Of course, a hollow wire shows deformation more easily if it has been tightened or twisted too much.

In addition to the standard wires described previously, decorative filigrees may be obtained using the following methods. A wire with a rectangular cross-section or a strip becomes more decorative by employing different degrees of twisting (fig. 40.2). A wire with a round cross-section can produce various decorative results depending upon the thickness of the wire, the degree of twisting and/or the number of intertwined wires (frequently two or three) (fig. 40.3). Two intertwined wires can be set side to create a braided effect (fig. 40.4); or one can make some wires more complex by actually braiding them to obtain a chain (fig. 62b). Several combinations of wires of different metals (fig. 40.5), wires of different thicknesses (fig. 40.6) or both also produce a decorative filigree.

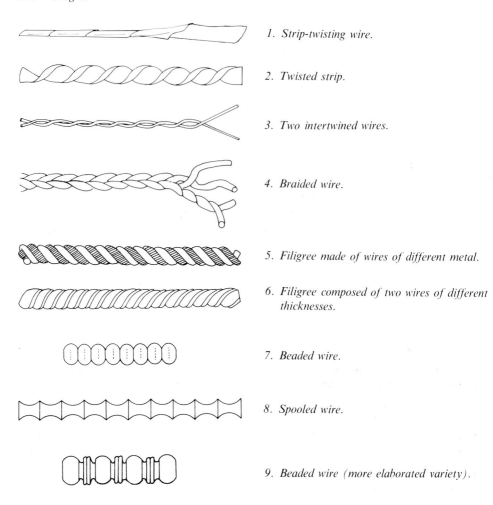

1. *Strip-twisting wire.*

2. *Twisted strip.*

3. *Two intertwined wires.*

4. *Braided wire.*

5. *Filigree made of wires of different metal.*

6. *Filigree composed of two wires of different thicknesses.*

7. *Beaded wire.*

8. *Spooled wire.*

9. *Beaded wire (more elaborated variety).*

Fig. 40. Different types of filigrees.

Finally, two special decorative variants should be mentioned: the *beaded* and the *spooled* wires. The *beaded* wire looks like a row of beads fastened together; however, they are not granulated (fig. 40.7). This result is obtained by stamping the metal into a mould. The monk Theophilus called it, in Book 3.9, *organarium* and also provided an illustration of it (fig. 41). Various sizes of beads can be seen from "bean" to "pea" to "lentil". Davidson considers this process too sophisticated for the Hellenistic period. She believes that the beaded wire is made by granules fastened together by rolling, because it is easier to solder granules into wire than to solder granule by granule on a sheet of gold. There are, of course, many imitations of beaded wire which are obtained by chiseling.

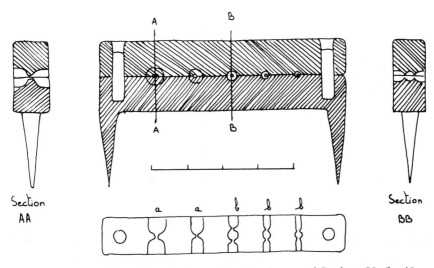

Fig. 41. Organarum of Theophilus. Redrawn after Hawthorne and Spith, p. 90, fig. 10.

The *spooled* wire looks like a series of spools fastened end to end (fig. 40.8) Parkhurst suggests that it is composed from separately made spools soldered together. This does not seem very defendable because if it is easy to produce fine granulation, it is extremely difficult to manufacture spools. It is also important to note that lines do appear on spooled wire sometimes at regular intervals and sometimes with a singular irregularity (cfr cat. no. 14). Davidson accepts a well known theory which states that spooled wire is, in fact, a transformation of beaded wire. One can imagine various types of wire between the beaded and the spooled types (fig. 40.9).

II. *The Draw-plate*

Compared with other metals which might be used to make filigree, gold is the most suitable due to its high ductility and malleability, allowing it to be drawn easily into very thin wires. For example, one gram of gold can be drawn into a wire a few kilometers long.

There is still some controversy among specialists concerning exactly where and when the gold wire-drawing technique was originally applied; however, this paper will not involve these questions.

The main tools for wire-drawing are the draw-plate, the tongs and the capstan.

According to the description given by the monk Theophilus, in his twelfth century treatise, *De Diversis Artibus*, 3.8 (eds. Hawthorne and Smith), the draw-plate consisted of "two iron implements, three fingers wide, with narrow top and

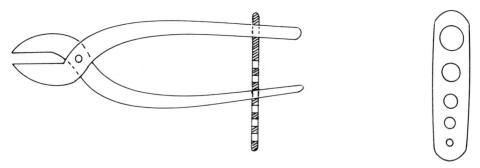

Fig. 42. Pincers of Theophilus. Redrawn after Hawthorne and Smith, p. 87, fig. 9.

bottom, having a constant thickness throughout and pierced with three or four rows of holes through which a wire may be drawn". Such a tool must have been quite common since Theophilus did not feel it was necessary to include a sketch of it and his description does not appear to be complete. He failed to mention that the diameters of the holes decreased gradually; nor did he explain why the plate had narrower tips (probably in order to fit it into a socle).

The tongs allow the craftsman to grip the wire and to pull it through the holes and the draw-plate. Although Theophilus described several types of pincers (fig. 42), he did not specify which ones were used for this kind of work (3.8). This method would have been used well before the twelfth century. Draw-plates dating from the La Tène period as well as from the Viking period in Sweden (fig. 43) have been found. Some particularities of these draw-plates should be mentioned. A groove connects the different holes of the draw-plate; probably for the purpose of supplying a lubricant which makes the wire-drawing process easier. The Swedish draw-plate is particularly interesting since the holes are fitted with replaceable inserts made of softer iron.

The capstan is a winch with upright shaft around which the wire can be twisted and drawn simultaneously. This process is more recent.

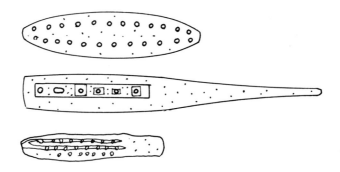

Fig. 43. Draw-plates of the Viking period. Redrawn after Foltz.

Fig. 44. The process of forging nails illustrated by the Mendel brothers. After Hawthorne and Smith, plate VI.

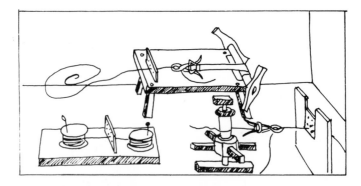

Fig. 45. a. Wire-drawing with capstan, windlass and drums.
b. Wire-drawing by means of water power.
Redrawn after Biringuccio, éd. 1966, p. 379-380.

It is interesting to note that the draw-plate illustrated here could also be used for forging nails (fig. 44). This process is explained in the 1389 A.D. *Hausbuch* by the Mendel brothers, now in Nuremberg. An illustration in the *Hausbuch* shows the draw-plate firmly fitted into the anvil. The artisan is sitting on a swinging seat holding a pair of pliers. He moves back and forth while drawing the wire. We can also imagine the artisan walking steadily backwards across his workshop to draw the wire.

Biringuccio published in 1540 A.D., *De La Pirotechnia*. In 3.8 are illustrations of three types of capstans and in 3.9 something which appears to be an innovation — the use of hydraulic power (fig. 45a-b).

In the British Museum there are two engravings by Stephanus showing two illustrations of a goldsmith's workshop, 1576 A.D. Note the capstan and the goldsmith at work (fig. 46 and p. 161). A 1698 A.D. illustration in Christoph Weigel's *Abbildung der gemein nützlichen Hauptstände*, shows the same type of capstan as in the Biringuccio engraving. The technique was well enough developed and did not require new improvements. The best reference dating from the eighteenth century is certainly the *Encyclopédie* by Diderot and d'Alembert (fig. 47). It contains illustrations of capstans and drawing mills. It is interesting

Fig. 46. Goldsmith's workshop. Engraving by Stephanus.

to note that these tools are still in use today. In India, for example, they are used particularly in the Orissa province. Other illustrations of such tools were presented at the exhibition *Bijoux moghols* in Brussels.

Frédérique DE CUYPER

Selected bibliography

CARROLL, D. L., *Drawn Wire and the Identification of Forgeries in Ancient Jewelry*, in *AJA*, 74, 1970, p. 401.

CARROLL, D. L., *Wire Drawing in Antiquity*, in *AJA*, 76, 1972, p. 321-323.

FOLTZ, E., *Antike Goldschmiedetechniken und ihre Erkennung*, in *Arbeitsblätter für Restauratoren*, 2, 1981.

GEOFFROY-DECHAUME, C., *Simple Craft Jewellery*, London, 1963, p. 34-35.

HAWTHORNE, J. G. and SMITH, C. S., *On Diverse Arts: The Treatise of Theophilus*, Chicago, 1963, p. 86-90.

HOFFMANN-DAVIDSON, *Greek Gold*, Mainz/Rhein, 1965, p. 18-48.

HOFFMANN-VON CLAER, *Antiker Gold und Silbersmuck*, Mainz/Rhein, 1968, p. 219-221.

JACOBI, G., *Drahtzieheisen der Latenezeit*, in *Germania*, 57, 1979, p. 111-115.

LATIF, M., *Bijoux Moghols: Bruxelles, Société Générale de Banque, 21 janvier-31 mars 1982*, Brussels, 1982.

MCCREIGHT, T., *Metalworking for Jewelry*, New York, 1979, p. 30.

ODDY, A., *The production of gold wire in Antiquity*, in *Gold Bulletin*, 10, no. 3, 1977, p. 79-87.

The Pirotechnia of Vannoccio Biringuccio, translation with introd. and notes by C. S. Smith and Martha Teach Gnudi, Cambridge, 1966.

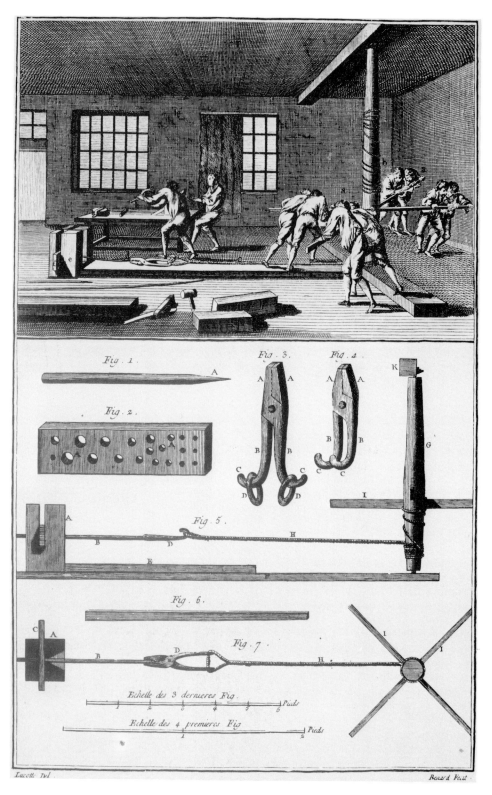

*Fig. 47. "Tireur d'or, Argue". After D. Diderot et M. d'Alembert, **Encyclopédie**, ou Dictionnaire raisonné…, Paris, 1751-1780, rééd. Paris, 1965 (Recueil de planches, sur les sciences, les arts libéraux et les arts mécaniques, avec leur explication, vol. X, pl. I).*

CHAINS AND NECKLACES

I. *Manufacturing Links*

These links are made as follows: once the wire has been produced, it is rolled onto a mandrel (or shaft of metal, stone or hardwood) of the desired shape and thickness (fig. 48).

The wire wound onto the end of the mandrel is then slid along and the rings are cut with a saw so as to separate them from one another. This is done one ring at a time, while continuing to slide the wire onto the end of the mandrel. In this way slightly open rings are obtained; at that point, it is necessary to squeeze them together and weld them at the same time as linking them together or before giving them their final shape.

Rings which are to be stretched are placed over the ends of a pair of round-nosed tongs. The desired ellipse is obtained by stretching them slowly while taking care of the weld. Finally, they are linked together according to the desired type of chain.

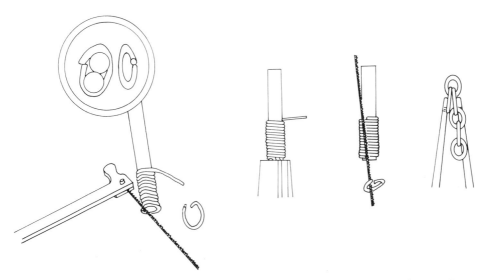

Fig. 48. Manufacturing links, drawn after T. Mac Creight, Metal Working for Jewellery, *1979, p. 31.*

II. *Types of Links and their Manufacture*

1) *Simple chain*[1]. The links consist of metal strips of wire folded so as to form circular, oval or even rectangular rings, each being inserted into the previous one and then welded together. Chains made of circular rings are also called *mail*[2] (fig. 49) and those of oval or rectangular rings are called *galley*[2].

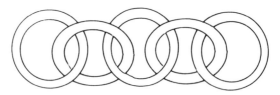

Fig. 49. Simple chain, Mail.

2) *Single loop-in-loop chain*[3]. This chain consists of hoops of wire which are given an elliptical shape, squeezed in the middle and straightened out so that the ends are parallel. The next ring is prepared in the same way and, after passing it through the parallel ends of the other ring, it is straightened out in the same way (figs. 50 and 51a).

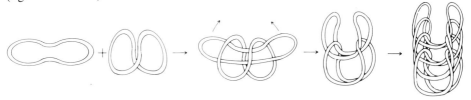

Fig. 50. Single loop-in-loop chain and double loop-in-loop chain.

3) *Single loop-in-loop chain*[4], but with links in the form of a twisted figure of eight. This is a variant of type 2. After being squeezed, each ring is bent so that the ends from two circles touching one another. The other part of the ring, formed by the link between the two circles, is then twisted at right angles (figs. 53 and 51b).

---

[1] W. and E. RUDOLPH, *Ancient Jewelry from the Collection of Burton Y. Berry*, Bloomington, Ind., 1973, p. 78-79 (Oval chain of the late Roman period); R. A. HIGGINS, *Greek and Roman Jewellery*, London, 1961, pl. 1 (a complex necklace with small circular type chain-links from Thyreatis. Helladic, ca. 2000 B.C.); necklace from the Field Museum of Natural History, this catalogue no. 38.

[2] A. BOITET, *Manuel pratique du bijoutier-joaillier*, Dunod, 1962, p. 158 ss.

[3] Examples for wire: Rudolph, *loc. cit.*, p. 89 (Late Roman); C. ANDREWS et allii, *Jewelry through 7000 Years*, 1976, p. 113, no. 157 (from Taormina, second century B.C.). This technique may also be used to cut pieces out of sheet metal. Such pieces consist of two hoops connected together by parallel strips which are bent in the middle after being passed through the parallel hoops of the previous link. An example for sheet metal: *Dossiers de l'Archéologie*, vol. 40, 1980, p. 87 (third century A.D.).

[4] RUDOLPH, *op. cit.*, p. 84-85 (the origin is unknown, first-third century A.D.); HIGGINS, *op. cit.*, pl. 51 (the origin is unknown, it belongs to the Hellenistic period); F. H. MARSHALL, *BMCJ*, pl. 61, no. 2727 (origin unknown, third century A.D.); MARSHALL, *op. cit.*, pl. 59, no. 2716 (from the site of the Roman wall near Newton, Carlisle, second century A.D.).

Fig. 51. a. Single loop-in-loop chain. Detail of a necklace of the IV cent. BC, Museum of RISD, Hackens, no. 21.
b. Single loop-in-loop, in eight twisted form chain and fixing link. Detail of late Roman necklace with pendant, IVth cent. AD, Museum of RISD, Hackens, n° 60.

Fig. 52. a. Column or snake chain, after R.A.Higgins, Greek and Roman Jewellery, 1961, fig. 4.d.
b. Column or snake chain. Detail of a pair of Hellenistic earrings, end of IInd cent. BC-IInd cent. AD, Museum of RISD, Hackens, n° 39.

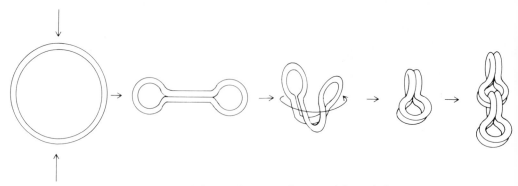

Fig. 53. Single loop-in-loop in eight twisted form chain.

4) *Double loop-in-loop chain*[5]. Each ring is passed through the ends of the two previous rings, which gives the chain a narrower and more compact structure (fig. 59, last drawing right; see also Hackens, cat. no. 55).

5) *Column or snake chain*[6], also known as "doubled quadruple (sextuple or octuple) loop-in-loop chain". These chains are most often made using the "double loop-in-loop" technique and less often the "single loop-in-loop" technique (fig. 52b).

It has sometimes been thought that these chains had been plaited but, one may observe that even if such chains existed, using this method would have eliminated the flexibility which the chains, in fact, do have. *Technique*: Two oval links are arranged to cross at right angles. Then, depending upon whether the single or double system is being used, each succeeding link is fitted so as to mesh either with the two preceding links or with the single preceding link. This is done alternately in one direction and then in the other (fig. 52a).

6) *Strap or Ribbon chain*[7]. These are composed of several chains of the "double loop-in-loop" or "single loop-in-loop" type, linked together along their sides to form a ribbon.

[5] Examples for wire: MARSHALL, *op. cit.*, no. 2725 (Roman, first-third century A.D.); Bull. Allen memorial Art Museum, vol. 18, p. 61 (from Caesarea in Cappadocia, first century A.D.). An example for sheet metal: Bull. Allen memorial Art Museum, vol. 18, p. 60 (from Southern Russia or the Fayum, Roman, second century A.D.).

[6] C. ANDREWS, et alii, *op. cit.*, p. 118, no. 172 (Saitic or Ptolemaic, 600-100 B.C.); C. ANDREWS, et alii, *op. cit.*, p. 125, no. 187 (origin in Calymnos in the Aegean. Early Christian, ca. 500 A.D.); MARSHALL, *op. cit.*, no. 2735 (Roman, first-third century A.D.), Field Museum of Natural History, this catalogue no. 36.

[7] Examples: MARSHALL, *op. cit.*, no. 1461, pl. 22 (origin la Maremma di Toscana. Etruscan, sixth century B.C.); MARSHALL, *op. cit.*, no. 1462, pl. 22 (origin is unknown, Etruscan, seventh century B.C.); MARSHALL, *op. cit.*, no. 1950 (from the Province of Valencia, Spain. Approximately third century B.C.); HIGGINS, *op. cit.*, pl. 55b (origin is unknown, Late-Roman ca. 300 A.D.).

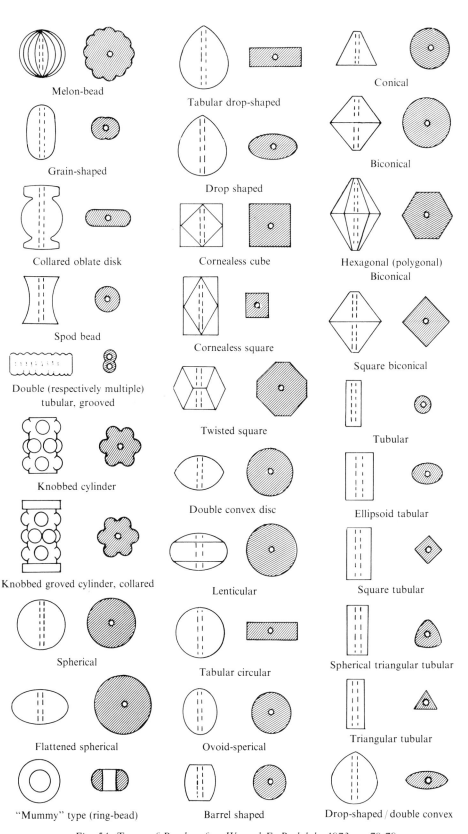

Melon-bead

Grain-shaped

Collared oblate disk

Spod bead

Double (respectively multiple)
tubular, grooved

Knobbed cylinder

Knobbed groved cylinder, collared

Spherical

Flattened spherical

"Mummy" type (ring-bead)

Tabular drop-shaped

Drop shaped

Cornealess cube

Cornealess square

Twisted square

Double convex disc

Lenticular

Tabular circular

Ovoid-sperical

Barrel shaped

Conical

Biconical

Hexagonal (polygonal)
Biconical

Square biconical

Tubular

Ellipsoid tabular

Square tubular

Spherical triangular tubular

Triangular tubular

Drop-shaped / double convex

Fig. 54. Types of Beads, after W. and E. Rudolph, 1973, p. 78-79.

III. *Mixed chains*

Mixed chains, which are also called necklaces, are made from links or lengths of chain of different types and beads of varying shapes, numbers and layouts.

1) *Types of beads* [8]. See fig. 54, p. 209.

2) *Fixing link*. In these mixed chains, there is a special link which I shall call a "fixing link". This link allows a bead or a segment comprising several elements forming a decorative unit to be attached to links, ornamental or otherwise, lengths of chain of various types or, again, metal segments with decoration fixed on tubes. This link is formed as follows: a wire is passed through the hole or holes of the bead or beads or segments and bent into a ring at each end (fig. 51b).

3) *Materials used in mixed chains*.

Stones: In the Bronze Age, the favorite stones were crystalline quartz, amethyst, cornelian, agate, chalcedony, jasper and lapis-lazuli. Sometimes, for poorer quality beads, steatite was used. During the Orientalizing period (800-600 B.C.), hard stones were again used; amber and crystalline quartz were popular at that time. During the Archaic and Classical periods (600-330 B.C.), stones were nearly always inlaid or set, but were nevertheless fairly rare, except in seals. During the Hellenistic period, garnet and cornelian were the most popular. Around 200 B.C. pearls and plasma, a green variety of chalcedony, became popular, and emeralds also began to be used. During the Roman period, the same stones were used as during the Hellenistic period, plus hard stones such as diamond, sapphire, aquamarine and topaz. Turquoise was also used in certain regions.

Glass: Glass beads appeared in Crete around 1600 B.C. and they were in continual use in the Aegean basin until the end of the Bronze Age. The colors are usually unidentifiable, but the favorites were blue, dark grey, white and yellow, in plain colors or combined. It is possible that this technique came from Egypt as corresponding shapes are found which could be a result of either importation of local imitations. After the bronze Age, all conceivable colors are found, and during the Roman period, all densities from total opacity to total transparency.

Pottery: This material was used essentially to make beads and amulets. They are obtained by moulding or modelling. They are found just about everywhere in the world, generally appearing soon after pottery and with developing techniques and decoration as time passes. They appeared around 1800 B.C. and around 1500 B.C. on the continent. In Egypt, they are found in the Badarian culture, at the end of the fifth millenium.

Metal: Metals were also used to make beads, generally by hammering a metal sheet, and then shaping as desired and welding together. The metals used were gold, silver and copper and bronze in more occasional use at later periods.

Anne Catherine LEMAIGRE

---

[8] The figures are based, with some alterations, on Rudolph, *op. cit.*, 22-23.

AMBER

Amber was a favorite material for jewelry throughout Antiquity (cat. no. 15). It is a fossilized resin of coniferous trees. The sources of amber are mostly situated on the coasts of the Baltic Sea, on the peninsula of Samland near Königsberg (now Kaliningrad, USSR, formerly Ostpreussen), in Poland (on the east coast facing Gdansk) or on the west coast of Jutland in the present-day Denmark.

There exist many kinds of amber differing from each other in chemical composition, color and origin. The following technical data are mainly derived from the study by D. E. Strong. Amber changes in color from pale yellow to brown, but sometimes, after a long time in the earth, red or red-brown discolorations appear. Amber may be transparent or cloudy.

There are Baltic, Sicilian, Rumanian and Burmese varieties of amber. *Baltic* amber has the chemical composition $C_{10}H_{16}O$ (79 % carbon; 10.5 % oxygen, 10.5 % hydrogen), some sulphur and a little inorganic material. The specific gravity is 1.05-1.10 and hardness, 2 to 2.5. This amber contains succinic acid which varies if amber is transparent (3 to 4 %) or cloudy (± 8 %). Amber is malleable in boiling linseed oil, dissolves in alcalis and melts between 600° and 615° Fahrenheit. It is entirely amorphous and non-crystalline. Its color varies from pale yellow to brown; altered amber is red or red-brown and is known as "succinite".

Sicilian amber is found mainly at the estuaries of rivers especially the Simeto near Catania (hence, the name "simetite"). Its chemical composition varies from Baltic amber in that it contains a higher proportion of sulphur (up to 2.46 %). It contains no succinic acid. It appears to be softer and has a greater range of colors, varying from reddish-yellow to wine red and, at time, is almost black.

Rumanian amber is found in Miocene strata especially on the river Buzau. Its structure, density and chemical composition are very similar to Baltic amber. It is yellow, red with different tones, as well as grey, blue and black, and generally transparent with an opaque crust darker in color than the inside.

Burmese amber is picked up in the clay beds of hills near Maingkwan on the Chindwin river. Its chemical composition is similar to Baltic amber, but it is harder and contains less succinic acid. It is light yellow to dark brown.

There are other beds of amber in the Italian Apennines, but this amber does not appear to be true succinite. A similar resin is found in the Lebanon near Sidon. It contains no succinite acid. It is very fragile and used only for making small beads.

The Greeks knew amber well. From the fourth century on, they called it ἤλεκτρον, while the Romans preferred the word *succinum* which is clearer than the Greek word *electrum*. In the *Odyssey* of Homer, *electrum* also means an alloy of gold and silver. The word *succinum*, derived from the Latin *succus* (sap) illustrates that the Romans interpreted amber as the sap of a tree.

Aristotle believed that amber originated from plants (*Meteor.*, IV, 10, 10). For Theophrastus, it was an ore or a stone because it came from the earth. Pliny, reviewing many writers, revives Aristotle's idea (*Natural History* 37, 2, 42-43). For others, it was a fossil, a marine concretion or even the urine of a lynx.

The ancients preferred red amber (*fulvum*). Yellow amber (*chryselectrum*) was used as ancient medicine. There is no clear statement as to the geographical origin of amber. For Herodotus (III.115) amber came from northern countries; Theophrastus believed that it came from Liguria (*De Lapidibus*, 16 and 29). Other cite Scythia, India or Egypt.

In the first century A.D., the Romans imported amber from Germany where it was called *glaesum*. Considering it of no value, the Germans burned it like wood (Tacitus, *Germania*, 45, 4-8). Pliny writes that it arrived at the Venetii and areas near the Adriatic coast, having crossed Pannonia via the estuary of the Vistula. He also believed that it came from the North Sea and arrived in Marseille via the river Rhône (Pliny, *Natural History* 37.1, 43).

Amber was frequently used and highly prized. Originally used for amulets or necklaces, during Roman times it was also carved into figurines, bases, little knives and used as part of furniture (Pliny, *Natural History*, 22.9, 99). It was desired for its fragrant aroma (like the odor of sulphur when it was rubbed) and because it felt pleasant to the touch. In ancient medicine, it was used to cure sore throat, which explains the use of amber necklaces. The ancients attributed magical powers to it. It was added to certain drinks or it was worn as an amulet to protect from madness or other illness (Pliny, *Natural History*, 37.2, 11, 44). Even in the nineteenth century it was still known for its medicinal virtues and nowadays it is used in homeopathy and in beauty creams.

The interest in amber goes back to earliest times. After a storm, it could be found on the shores of the Baltic, as it is still done today. In the paleolithic, amber was used as amulets and in the neolithic, it was used for the first time as decoration, such as the little horse of the third millenium — once in the Prähistorisches Museum, Berlin, but lost in 1945. In the Bronze Age, we find amber at Mycenae (LHI) and at Kakovatos (LHII), where it formed part of a necklace.

Imports of amber continued through the LHIII and in the Mycenean period. In Crete, amber was found in the LMIII but is generally rare. It is known in Rhodes and Cyprus. Between the Submycenean period and eighth century amber is rare, while during the Geometric period and Orientalizing period, it is, again, more frequently used as part of gold and ivory jewelry.

In Italy and Sicily we find it mostly during the seventh century. Etruscan tombs such as the Regolini-Galassi tomb in Caere contain amber. The center for amber trade was at this time Picenum. Later, in the VIIth century, many amber artifacts are found in southern Italy (Apulia and Lucania) as shown by the holdings of the Museum of Taranto.

Amber in very beautiful settings was worn during the Roman empire in Italy, especially during the Flavian to the Antonine periods. The success of this long distance trade is part of the explanation of the many Roman coin finds from these periods in the Baltic region. Aquileia was the principal center for working with amber. The production was abundant because of the demand that came from the Roman provinces. This flourishing trade appears to have found an end in the third century A.D. when the Goths arrived and interrupted relations between the North and the South. We know however that Theodoric received an amber present from envoys from the Baltic lands.

Many trade routes for amber existed already during the Bronze Age (fig. 55). The boats left the estuaries of the Weser and the Elbe rivers and entered the river Rhine, sailed up the Moselle to the Rhône and came finally to Marseille. Others followed the river Rhine to a place where Basel grew up and, then, by road, they traveled to the point where the Rhône and Lake Geneva join. Marseille was reached over the Rhône. Having traveled by different rivers in Germany, the Brenner pass was also open. This lead to the Mediterranean markets via Este and Adria.

At the end of the Iron Age, amber from the Vistule reached Jesenik and was brought with the caravans to Brno. From there, using the Morava, the merchants arrived at the site where the Romans were later to build Carnuntum, the capital of Pannonia. By caravan, they reached, in prehistoric times, the site that was to become Aquileia, also significant for amber during the Roman empire. Another road took a different direction at Jesenik toward the river Dnieper in Russia. over

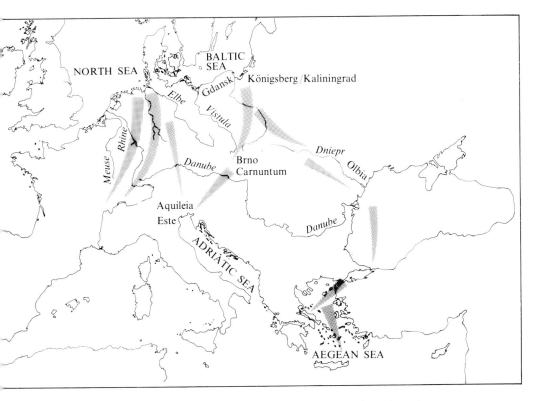

Fig. 55. Map showing the main directions of amber trade in Antiquity.

the Dnieper, one could reach the Greek colonies such as Olbia, at the Black Sea. From here amber was traded in the Aegean.

The existence of this east road is subject to controversy, because one knows of amber-producing deposits in south Russia. The amber found in Greece may, in fact, come from here since the contracts between Greece and the Black Sea were frequent. Yet, the rapid trade routes established in Italy during the Iron Age put an end to this eastern network.

Attention should be devoted to the transformation of the resin in amber. The liquid resin from the trees loses a part of its volatile components and becomes hard in contact with air. The resinous acid, quite plentiful in the resin, undergoes an oxidation process and an isometisation. With dehydration, those acids will be modified and stay in the amber. During hardening on the three, insects, twigs or leaves are trapped in the resin, and are sometimes found in amber. The reason some amber is green is that the chlorophyl of the leaf has dyed the resin during the drying process.

Amber is easy to carve and for this simple, mainly abrading, tools like a file or stylet were used. During the Iron Age, it was the shape of the amber that was important. During the Roman period, sculptors created pieces of art with greater refinement. They carved deeper and executed the details with greater precision. Sometimes, amber was colored to imitate precious stones (Pliny, *Natural History* 37.2, 48-51).

Francine LECOMTE

Selected Bibliography

Ambra, oro del Nord, exh. cat., Venice, 1980.
BOITET, A., *Manuel pratique du bijoutier joaillier*, Paris, 1962.
DE LA GENIÈRE, J. *À propos du catalogue des ambres sculptés du British Museum*, in *RA*, 1967, p. 297-304.
EBERT, M., *s.v. Bernstein*, in *Reallexikon der Vorgeschichte*, I, 1924.
FLON, C. and LUBIN, J.C., *Ambre*, in *Encyclopedia Universalis*, I, p. 838-839.
JACOB, A., *Electrum*, in *Daremberg and Saglio*, II/I, p. 531-536.
LIPINSKY, A., *Oro, argento, smalti e gemme*, Florence, 1975, p. 329-340 and 379-384.
MARIËN, M.E., *L'empreinte de Rome*, Antwerp, 1980.
MASSARO, D., *Le ambre di Vetulonia*, in *StEtr*, 17, 1943, p. 31-46. *Ambre etrusche nel R. Museo archeologico di Firenze*, in *StEtr*, 17, 1943, p. 455-458.
STRONG, D.E., *Catalogue of the Carved Amber in the Department of Greek and Roman Antiquities*, London, 1966.

TOPOGRAPHICAL NON-DESTRUCTIVE ANALYSIS OF GOLD JEWELRY

If magnifiers and optical microscopes are indispensable and powerful instruments for the examination of gold jewelry, non-destructive physical methods of analysis of the chemical elements are also useful to supply information about the actual composition of the objects. Both methods give valuable complementary information if they concern the same area of the sample under investigation. Topographical analyses using particle irradiation of narrow surfaces on artifacts are now possible on areas down to several thousandths of a square millimeter, on objects whose size may be up to 30 cm in each direction [1]. In most cases, numerous analyses of several surfaces of about one square millimeter on a single object may give enough information on the materials used to compose the jewel. Proton Induced X-ray Emission (now called by physicists the PIXE method) working with the sample to be analyzed in the air has been successfully applied to many pieces of jewelry. A complete description (in French) has been given in the previous edition

Fig. 56. Experimental set up for the PIXE technique.

of Aurifex where we have compared the performances of the PIXE technique with several others which have been used for many years in laboratories of archeometry: mainly, X-ray fluorescence and electron microprobe or microscope systems.

The PIXE technique

We will give here just a short description of the technique used for the topographical analysis of several objects described in this catalogue with special emphasis on the areas of the jewel where some soldering is expected and sometimes visible.

In the non-vacuum milliprobe arrangement, the incident proton beam crosses a thin foil of Al before reaching the sample situated at a distance of 1 cm in the air. The diameter of the proton beam is about 0.7 mm at the target position. Fig. 56 illustrates the target region of the experimental set up. The X-ray analysis is performed using a foil of zinc (5 mg/cm² thick), which is a selective absorber of gold X-rays, inserted between the target and the detector in order to reduce the mean counting rate by reducing the contribution of the dominant response due to the gold. Consequently, zinc X-rays produced by fluorescence also appear in the spectra, and Zn contained in the sample cannot be simultaneously analyzed. However, this element is expected to be, if present, in very low concentrations (‰ or at most %) and its K_α (8.631 keV) line interferes with L_1 of Au (8.493 keV) and its K_β (9.572 keV) with the L_α of Au (9.670 keV).

When zinc is to be determined, the Zn foil is removed and concentration of zinc down to 0.5 % may be quantitatively determined.

The thickness of the analyzed surface layer is less then 5 μm. For gold items this thickness is representative of the bulk material as demonstrated on several items where scratchings have been made [2] and measurement has been repeated.

A set of eighteen samples of known alloys is used as reference material for quantitative determination by PIXE: five alloys from DEGUSSA, six alloys (with low gold content) from private origins and seven Cu-Au and Au-Ag alloys prepared in our laboratory in a high-frequency induction furnace using high purity Cu, Ag and Au wires. The certified composition of the alloys with high concentrations of gold has been checked by an independent technique (PIGE) using pure Au, Cd, Ag, Cu metals as reference materials. Comparison of measured and certified values are in agreement.

The full X-ray spectra containing the information on all the elements of interest in the material are recorded on floppy discs and are processed by computer in order to subtract the actual background and to resolve peaks from neighboring elements.

As the peak intensities are not simply related to the actual concentrations of the elements in the sample, the results obtained by this first treatment of the spectra

[1] G. DEMORTIER, T. HACKENS, *Milliprobe and Microprobe Analysis of Gold Items of Ancient Jewelry*, in *Nuclear Instruments and Methods*, 197, 1982, p. 223-236.

[2] *Aurifex IV.*

X-ray intensity ⟶

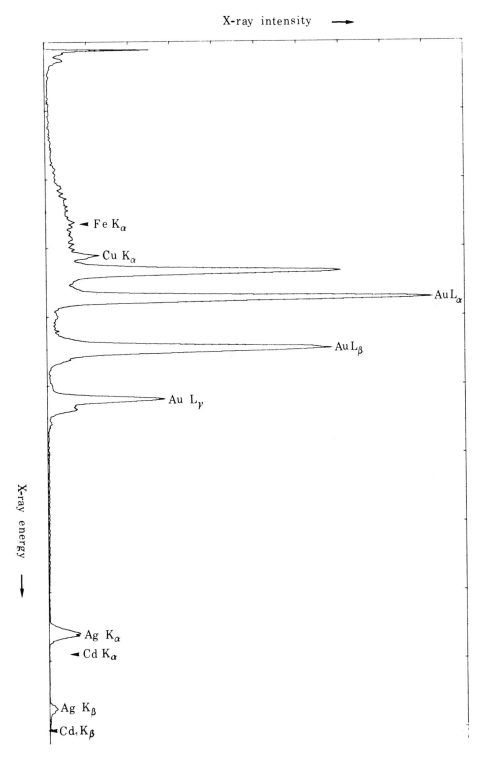

Fig. 57. Typical X-ray spectrum showing the presence of Cu, Au and Ag.

are then computerized for the physical parameters governing the emission, the absorption in the sample itself and the detection of X-rays[3]. A typical spectrum showing the presence of Cu, Au and Ag is given in fig. 57. Calibration curves have been obtained from reference materials and checked by calculation using known physical data. K_α lines are used for the analysis of Cu, Ag, Cd; L_β for the analysis of Au.

Accuracy of the results

The statistical errors on the measured values are always less than 1 % for Au, less than 5 % (relative) for Cu, Ag and Cd if they are present at concentrations higher than 3 %, but always better than 10 % in less favorable cases.

As each chemical element gives rise to more than one isolated peak in the X-ray spectrum, and as one single peak is sufficient to give the useful information for the analysis, we use the extra information to test the quality of our measurements. The ratio of the peak intensities for one single chemical element is indeed a constant physical parameter, and the ratio of the intensities of these X-ray lines of gold recorded in each experiment is used to check the accuracy of the technique.

For each measurement we give a "confidence factor" defined as follows: the ratio of the intensities of Au L_α and Au L_β lines is calcualted for each spectrum, its mean value for each run of experiments in the same geometrical arrangement (50 impacts or more) is then calculated. The confidence factor is defined as the actual ratio in one single spectrum divided by this mean value. Under these conditions, a confidence factor of less than 1 indicates a possible relative loss of counts for X-rays of lower energies (Cu K and Au L) due to shadow effects in the outgoing X-ray flux.

Thus, if we take as reference the confidence factor (equal to 1) given in Table 1 for the impact no. 6, we may conclude for the measurement of concentration at impact no. 1 (where the confidence factor is 0.92) that the concentration of Cu determined to be 2.05 % may be underestimated, but cannot be higher than $(2.05/0.92) = 2.21$ % and conversely at impact no. 14 (where the confidence factor is 1.05) that this Cu content may be overestimated but not lower than $(2.65/1.05) = 2.51$ %. For these reasons, copper concentrations at impacts 1, 2, 3, 6, 8, 9, 10, 12, 13 and 14 may be considered as identical as far as the statistical and geometrical parameters of the experiments are concerned. Results of copper concentrations at impacts 4, 5 and 7 are certainly different from the ones obtained for the impacts listed above but they may be considered as identical for this set of three impacts. The silver concentration at each impact is less dependent from the variation of this confidence factor.

Analysis of characteristic objects

Four Roman earrings, one Hellenistic piece of jewelry (all five described in Hackens)[4], one pendant and one ornament showing a vine leaf with grapes

[3] B. VAN OYSTAEYEN, G. DEMORTIER, *Matrix effects in PIXE Analysis* (in press).
[4] HACKENS, nos. 52a, 50, 53, 42, 39a.

(described elsewhere for this exhibition) have been analyzed with special emphasis on areas where some soldering is expected. The results are given in Tables 1 through 7. The corresponding impacts are reported in figs. 58 through 64. All the concentrations are given so that the total amount of material gives 100 %. Iron at trace level has been observed at several impacts on several objects, but the presence of iron is often not relevant for the purpose of the bulk initial composition of the jewelry; it is mainly for external and later corrosion. A more important concentration of iron may sometimes be observed, and then comments on the correlation of the Cu and Fe contents will be given in the discussion below.

Discussion

One Roman earring (Hackens, no. 52) (fig. 58) has been studied at 14 different impacts. Regions of apparent or suspected solders (4, 5, 7 and 10) contain a bit more copper than other regions such as flat gold, wires and loop. This situation may be partially explained by the argument that *chrysokolla* (copper mineral) has been used for soldering the elements, the conditions of "argenteous gold" being fulfilled [5] as reported in the *Natural History* of Pliny (Book 33). This explanation may be only partial because the amount of copper appears certainly insufficient, but it is not improbable that the region of solder is shadowed by the elements which have been soldered together. The soldering with *chrysokolla* seems to be more evident at impact 11 where the region of soldering is less shadowed by the worn granulation; a situation not observed in region 14 where the granulation seems to be well-preserved or at least less covered by some fluid solder. The classification of gold alloys used in the parts of the jewelry seems to be of three types with respect to the amount of silver: rich silver regions (20 to 24 %) in flat regions and the loop (1, 6, 8, 9 and 20); medium rich regions (15 to 17 %) in granulation; and lower rich regions (11 %) in several ornaments (wires) as in regions 1 and 2.

The content of silver in soldering regions (about 15 %) seems to indicate that *chrysokolla* may have been used with a gold and silver mixture also reported by Pliny [5].

The use of a gold-copper alloy to solder elements together is more evident in the earring no. 50 (fig. 59) at impacts 15 and 24 where the amount of copper and the decrease of gold concentrations may indicate that a low melting point ternary alloy (Cu-Ag-Au) has been used to bind together parts of the jewel.

No apparent trace of different composition of the basic alloy appears in the results on two different items of earrings of the same Roman times (figs. 60 and 61). The results given in Tables 3 and 4 reveal a good homogeneity of all the material. The elements of each piece of jewelry seem to have been bonded together by some kind of "forging", rather than the use of an additional alloy.

These four elements of jewelry from Roman times are made in different kinds of electrum, as observed when looking to the large amount of silver (always more than 10 %).

One piece of Hellenistic jewelry (fig. 62 and table 5) is made in alloy of higher

[5] PLINY, *Natural History*, 33.1.4; 33.26.86; 33.29.

gold concentration (about 95 %). Variations of the composition at different impact regions are not significant, except perhaps at impacts 29 and 30 where the composition of the alloy indicates a more important amount of Cu for impact 29 and of silver for impact 30.

Looking for the results on the pendant with "Victory" the different parts may be classified in several groups: the basic gold alloy (impacts 108 and 109), the alloy of the wire used for the loop (impact 110) and the soldering alloy (impacts 104, 105, 106, 107, 110, 112 and 113) where the content of copper is sufficient to be interpreted in the following manner. The basic gold alloy, with the composition measured at impacts 108 and 109, may have been worked with some copper mineral (i.e., malachite) to obtain a new alloy with a melting point lowered by about 50° C below the melting point of the basic alloy.

The composition of the "vine leaf" with grapes (Fig. 9, Table 7) is more surprising. The alloy is of very high fineness (about 0.25 % copper, 1 % silver and more than 98 % gold). Even more surprising is the amount of cadmium with a concentration unevenly distributed from zero to 0.4 %. The presence of cadmium in jewelry is often interpreted as being of modern origin: cadmium has been indeed identified as a new element only since approximately 1815. Nevertheless, we have demonstrated that cadmium has been found in many pieces of gold jewelry presented as antique and the composition of the alloys where cadmium has been found was often very different from modern alloys as far as the ratios of Cu/Cd and Ag/Cd contents were concerned [6].

A sufficient number of tests have been made which demonstrate that the criterion "Cadmium = Modern" is not absolute. Measurements on monetary medallions recently discovered in France [7] have shown cadmium at trace level. Cadmium has also been observed sometimes at concentrations of about several percent, but often lower at sites where soldering is necessary to bind elements together in a piece of jewelry. The presence of cadmium in the "vine leaf" object may be interpreted in the following manner: it has been made by using as basic alloy the product of melting an older piece of jewelry containing cadmium as a soldering component, this cadmium content being diluted and unevenly distributed in the metal when it was melted.

A complete discussion on the cadmium content in several necklaces from Iran and Syria has been published in Aurifex IV. New arguments taking into account new results on soldering alloys obtained in our laboratory by simply mixing natural minerals in a crucible will be published in the near future.

A simultaneous increase of copper and iron is sometimes observed. The fact may be explained if we keep in mind that natural copper minerals often contain some amount of iron as in the "yellow" chalcopyrite.

Guy DEMORTIER,
Facultés universitaires Notre-Dame de la Paix,
Namur, Belgium.

[6] Cfr. notes 1 and 2.
[7] J. FLOURET, G. NICOLINI and C. METZGER, *Les bijoux d'or gallo-romains de l'Houmeau*, in *Gallia*, 39, 1981, p. 85-101.

ANNEX: ANALYTICAL RESULTS

TABLE 1. ROMAN EARRING (HACKENS, no. 52a)

Impacts no.	Concentration in %				Confidence factor	Remarks
	Cu	Ag	Cd	Au		
1	2.05	21.40		76.55	0.92	flat region
2	2.50	11.65		85.85	0.98	ornament
3	2.95	10.40		86.65	0.97	ornament
4	3.90	14.70		81.40	0.84	solder ?
5	3.45	16.50		80.05	1.04	solder ?
6	2.35	24.20		73.45	1.00	flat region
7	3.25	15.35		81.40	0.98	solder ?
8	2.85	23.65		73.50	1.03	loop (twisted elements)
9	2.25	19.15		78.60	1.10	loop
10	2.80	15.80		81.40	1.09	soldering ?
11	4.80	17.15		78.05	0.99	soldering in granulations
12	1.95	20.80		77.25	0.89	flat region
13	2.30	14.05		83.65	1.03	soldering ?
14	2.65	15.25		82.10	1.05	granulations

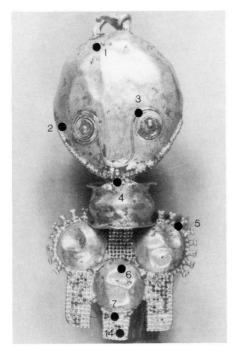 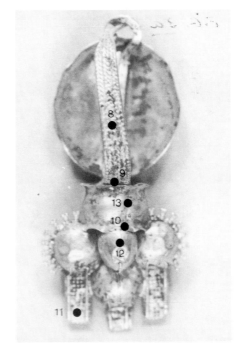

Fig. 58. Roman Earring, Museum of RISD, cat. no. 34.

TABLE 2. ROMAN EARRING (HACKENS, no. 50)

Impacts no.	Concentration in %				Confidence factor	Remarks
	Cu	Ag	Cd	Au		
15	6.25	27.90		65.85	1.03	soldering on a sphere
16	3.35	25.00		71.65	1.00	granulations
17	5.35	22.65		72.00	0.99	granulations
18	5.95	21.25		72.80	0.98	soldering on a sphere
19	2.80	30.45		66.75	0.96	sphere (out of soldering)
20	5.50	20.85		73.65	1.04	soldering on a sphere
21	3.30	24.55		72.15	1.05	wire
22	2.70	30.25		67.05	1.10	sphere
23	2.45	29.00		68.55	0.92	sphere
24	8.25	33.30		58.45	0.96	soldering on a sphere
25	3.35	21.30		75.35	0.99	granulations

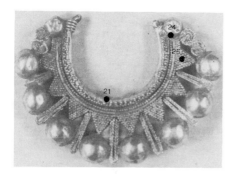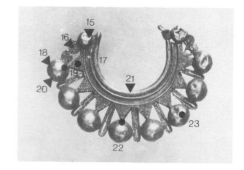

Fig. 59. Roman Earring, Museum of RISD, Hackens cat. no. 50.

TABLE 3. ROMAN EARRING (HACKENS, no. 53)

Impacts no.	Concentration in %				Confidence factor	Remarks
	Cu	Ag	Cd	Au		
38	1.20	16.30		82.50	0.97	
39	1.35	17.45		81.20	0.95	
40	1.55	17.85		80.60	0.99	
41	1.50	13.00		85.50	1.05	
42	1.70	14.95		83.35	1.01	
43	1.55	13.50		84.95	1.04	
44	1.15	17.35		81.50	1.00	
45	0.20	15.45		84.35	0.99	"ends" of the circular wire
46	1.00	15.75		83.25	1.03	
47	1.00	15.80		83.20	1.03	

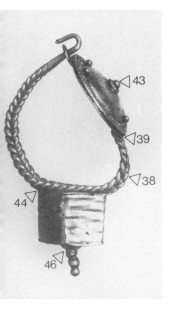

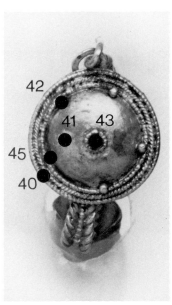

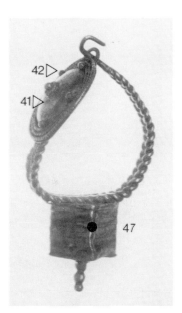

Fig. 60. *Roman Earring, Museum of RISD, this cat. no. 35.*

TABLE 4. ROMAN EARRING (HACKENS, no. 42)

Impacts no.	Concentration in %				Confidence factor	Remarks
	Cu	Ag	Cd	Au		
48	1.65	21.85		76.50	0.99	
49	1.65	21.95		76.40	0.97	
50	1.50	19.15		79.35	1.06	
51	1.40	21.75		76.85	0.93	

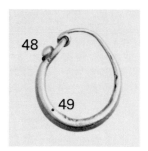 

Fig. 61. Roman Earring, Museum of RISD, Hackens cat. no. 42.

TABLE 5. HELLENISTIC EARRING (HACKENS, no. 39a)

Impacts no.	Concentration in %				Confidence factor	Remarks
	Cu	Ag	Cd	Au		
26	0.35	4.45		95.20	1.05	loop
27	0.40	4.55		95.05	1.00	loop
28	1.05	3.50		95.45	0.97	end of the chain
29	2.45	2.85		94.70	1.04	closing of the chain
30	0.95	5.65		93.40	1.03	chain
31	1.20	2.80		96.00	0.96	rear impact 28
32	0.95	2.45		96.60	0.97	
33	2.20	2.55		95.25	0.93	soldering ?
34	0.45	1.25		98.30	1.03	ornament
35	0.85	2.45		96.70	1.00	basic alloy (rear)
36	1.50	2.20		96.30	0.99	soldering ?
37	1.70	2.20		96.10	1.04	soldering ?

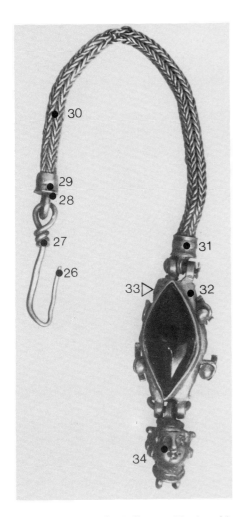 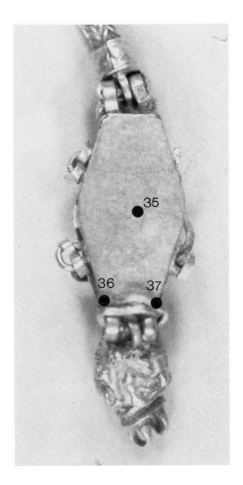

Fig. 62. Hellenistic Earring, Museum of RISD, Hackens, cat. no. 39a.

TABLE 6. PENDANT WITH A "VICTORY". Cat. no. 18.

Impacts no.	Concentration in %				Confidence factor	Remarks
	Cu	Ag	Cd	Au		
104	3.70	7.05		89.25	1.00	soldering
105	3.50	8.15		88.35	0.99	soldering
106	3.45	9.30		87.25	0.99	soldering
107	4.25	6.45		89.30	1.04	soldering
108	1.25	7.30		91.45	0.97	main alloy
109	1.25	7.75		91.00	0.99	main alloy
110	1.35	2.25		96.40	0.93	loop
111	6.00	4.15		89.85	0.93	soldering of the ring
112	3.45	7.65		88.90	1.03	soldering (rear)
113	2.25	7.95		89.80	1.03	soldering (rear)

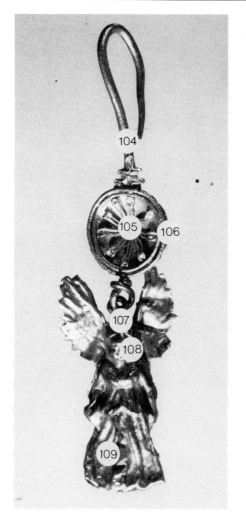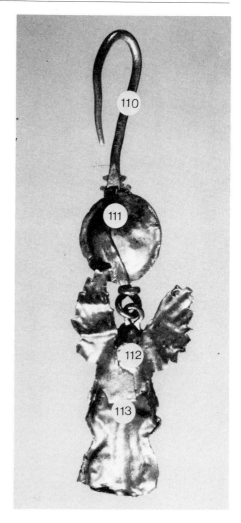

Fig. 63. Hellenistic Earring, this cat. no. 18. Private coll.

TABLE 7. VINE LEAF WITH GRAPES (Private collection)

Impacts no.	Concentration in %			Au	Confidence factor	Remarks
	Cu	Ag	Cd			
127	0.20	1.15	—	98.65	1.00	
128	0.25	1.00	0.40	98.35	1.02	
131	0.20	1.00	—	98.80	0.97	
132	0.20	1.10	0.25	98.45	0.95	
133	0.20	1.05	—	98.75	0.97	
134	0.35	1.00	0.15	98.60	1.02	
135	1.55	1.10	0.15	97.20	1.05	

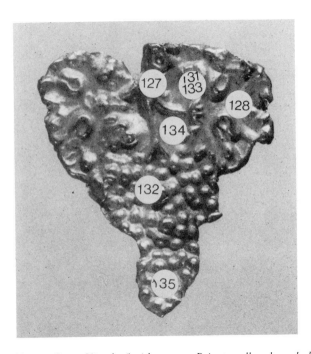

Fig. 64. Golden applique, Vine leaf with grapes, Private coll. enlarged about twice.